CRITICAL
INSIGHTS

I Know Why the
Caged Bird Sings

CRITICAL INSIGHTS

I Know Why the Caged Bird Sings

by Maya Angelou

Editor
Mildred R. Mickle
Penn State Greater Allegheny

Salem Press
Pasadena, California   Hackensack, New Jersey

Cover photo: ©Dreamstime.com/Seesea

Published by Salem Press

© 2010 by EBSCO Publishing
Editor's text © 2010 by Mildred R. Mickle
"The *Paris Review* Perspective" © 2010 by Christopher Cox for *The Paris Review*

∞ The paper used in these volumes conforms to the American National
Standard for Permanence of Paper for Printed Library Materials, Z39.48-1992
(R1997).

Library of Congress Cataloging-in-Publication Data
I know why the caged bird sings, by Maya Angelou / editor, Mildred R.
Mickle.
   p. cm. — (Critical insights)
Includes bibliographical references and index.
ISBN 978-1-58765-624-8 (alk. paper)
   1. Angelou, Maya. I know why the caged bird sings. 2. African Americans
in literature. 3. Racism in literature. 4. Southern States—In literature. I.
Mickle, Mildred R.
   PS3551.N464Z695 2009
   818'.5409—dc22

                                                          2009026306

                 PRINTED IN CANADA

Contents

The Book and Author

Critical Contexts

Critical Readings

Resources_____

About This Volume _____

Mildred R. Mickle

The essays in this volume pay tribute to Maya Angelou's first autobiography, *I Know Why the Caged Bird Sings* (1970). They explore Angelou's record of her early life dealing with racism in the segregated American South, her reaction to being sexually molested, and the solace she finds in literature. They also examine how she treats growing up, traveling west to California to escape segregation, discovering her sexuality, becoming an adult and a single mother, and adopting the calls of the Black Arts movement and the Black Power movement to promote images of a positive black aesthetic. Angelou uses the autobiographical form to present major American historical events, such as life under Jim Crow segregation and the employment opportunities made available to women and minorities during World War II, through the lens of a young black girl's experiences, continuing the work begun by other black artists in incorporating a neglected black experience and artistic contribution into American history and letters. The essays show what a brave first step Angelou took in revealing her life and her insecurities about her sexuality and her own appearance. Her honest and unflinching examination of her life and her major influences continues to speak to audiences today.

In addition to biographical information on Maya Angelou provided by Judith Barton Williamson, this volume contains essays that critique Angelou's first autobiography from historical, sociopolitical, and cultural perspectives; that provide close readings of the text; and that compare and contrast this autobiography with other authors' works. In "The *Paris Review* Perspective," Christopher Cox provides valuable insight into Angelou's perspective on her writing and how she overcame the experience of sexual abuse. Amy Sickels discusses the historical and cultural factors that give Angelou and her first autobiography their multidimensional appeal. She describes how Angelou's exposure to a variety of different literary periods, artists, and black nationalities, along with her knowledge of the tradition of the slave narrative, informs her first autobiography. Pamela Loos gives an overview of the different but predominantly positive scholarly reviews of Angelou's work. Neil Heims compares and contrasts Angelou's first autobiography with James Baldwin's fifth novel, *If Beale Street Could Talk* (1974), noting that the choice of genre informed the agendas of both authors. Whereas Baldwin focused on a universal message of understanding black identity, Heims writes, Angelou narrowed her focus to a single black woman's process of accepting herself. Robert C. Evans examines the appeal of using *I Know Why the Caged Bird Sings* as a way to teach readers survivals skills as well as the importance of learning to think and read critically.

In the "Critical Readings" section, Liliane K. Arensberg argues that the young Maya's physical and mental travels are important because they are representative of how she learns the value of flexibility. For Arensberg, Maya's metaphorical "deaths" represent her release of negative internal and external referents, allowing positive ways of thinking and acting to take their places. Martin A. Danahay argues for the necessity of learning to use autobiographies written by people from diverse cultures, such as Angelou's, as a first step in an extended exploration of the complexities of various cultures. Mary Vermillion investigates how Harriet Jacobs and Maya Angelou use their life stories to combat negative perceptions of the black female body and to assert positive examples of black beauty. Lyman B. Hagen maintains that a formalist reading of the work reveals Angelou's revolt against racism and calls for the audience to work toward equality. Pierre A. Walker explores how various scenes in the narrative demonstrate the young Maya's growing resistance to racism.

Yolanda M. Manora argues that in *I Know Why the Caged Bird Sings*, Angelou creates a parallel black female subjectivity that allows the author to operate both within and outside of the text that the young Maya inhabits. Further, Manora argues that this narrative control is ultimately empowering for Angelou and for the reader's understanding of the history of the formation of black female subjectivity. Myra K. McMurry discusses how "role-playing" in the work comments on the power of the imagination to either imprison or ensnare an individual. Cherron A. Barnwell discusses how Angelou uses blues music to infuse all of her autobiographies with messages of hope and how using the blues aesthetic in autobiographies offers a way to survive adversity. Clarence Nero discusses how Angelou combines her experiences with the black and white communities, with education, and with reading literature to craft a text that inspires readers to appreciate the lessons they can learn from their own communities. Suzette A. Henke discusses how Angelou's objective in her first autobiography is to raise public awareness about the impact that sexual abuse has on black girls and women and to encourage readers to act to prevent it.

The essays in this volume reflect a variety of interpretations of *I Know Why the Caged Bird Sings*. Understandably, these essays cannot capture all of the richness of Angelou's work, but they mark an excellent start; the authors' interpretations encourage debate, paving the way for further scholarly discussion of Angelou's extensive works and performances.

THE BOOK
AND
AUTHOR

On *I Know Why the Caged Bird Sings*_____
Mildred R. Mickle

Professor, actor, poet, autobiographer, and civil rights activist, Maya Angelou has demonstrated through her life and artistry what a remarkable black woman she is. Her words bring to life artistic and personal struggles that eighteenth-century authors such as Phillis Wheatley had to encode within the conventions of neoclassicism, that nineteenth-century authors such as Harriet Jacobs could only romanticize, and that authors such as Paul Laurence Dunbar had to encode in African American dialect. There is nothing understated or romantic about Angelou's graphic depictions of racism, sexual abuse, and the psychological struggle to reconcile black beauty with mainstream notions of white beauty. Angelou's first autobiography, *I Know Why the Caged Bird Sings* (1970), leaves the reader with a profound sense of ambivalence that combines a bittersweet nostalgia for lost innocence with pride in Angelou's hard-earned autonomy—and oh what autonomy Angelou has. She writes in "Still I Rise":

> Out of the huts of history's shame
> I rise
> Up from a past that's rooted in pain
> I rise
> I'm a black ocean, leaping and wide,
> Welling and swelling I bear the tide.
>
> Leaving behind nights of terror and fear
> I rise
> Into a daybreak that's wondrously clear
> I rise
> Bringing the gifts that my ancestors gave,
> I am the dream and the hope of the slave.
> I rise
> I rise
> I rise
>
> (29-43)

These lines are the final two stanzas of the poem, and they exemplify the indomitable spirit of a beautiful individual whose poetry and prose have touched millions of readers. They reflect a woman exulting in just being alive, and they allude to the horrors Angelou survived that help her appreciate each moment she has.

Arguably, these lines allude also to the African folktales that describe some enslaved Africans who, not liking what they experienced of slavery, escaped by ascending into the sky and flying back to the safe haven of Africa (Hill 64-65). These folktales of escape and entry into a place of love and acceptance were a coping mechanism much like the spirituals; both were implicit critiques of the atrocities of slavery and revolts against the systematic brainwashing that slaveholders and their representatives tried to inculcate in the enslaved. Many enslaved Africans in America refused to believe the lie that they were inferior and meant to be held within the limitations of slavery. In these two stanzas of "Still I Rise," Angelou praises the perseverance of the enslaved Africans of the nineteenth century and those blacks who, like her grandmother, Annie Henderson, defied racism and discrimination in the segregated South of the twentieth century.

To understand the significance of Maya Angelou's works in general and *I Know Why the Caged Bird Sings* in particular, it is necessary to examine some of Angelou's historical influences and to place the autobiography within the context of the work of key writers in the African American literary tradition. One of the historical influences on Angelou was Phillis Wheatley, the first African American to publish a volume of poems. Patricia Liggins Hill writes in "Phillis Wheatley (1753?-1784)":

Critical revaluation of Wheatley and her poetry began during the early years of the contemporary women's movement when eighteen African American women poets held the Phillis Wheatley Poetry Festival at Jackson State College, Mississippi, in 1973. Such writers as Margaret Walker, Sonia Sanchez, June Jordan, Audre Lorde, Lucille Clifton, Maya Angelou, and Alice Walker paid tribute to the poet and commemorated the two-hundredth anniversary of the publication of *Poems* [*on Various Subjects, Religious and Moral* (1773)]. Since then, Wheatley has been regarded as the foremother of the African American and women's literary traditions. (97)

Angelou has been an activist not only in the Civil Rights movement for social and political change in the United States but also in advocating for change within the curricula of American public schools. If not for the efforts of Angelou and the other prestigious black women writers listed above, Phillis Wheatley's poetry might have remained largely ignored by scholars and students.

Phillis Wheatley is an inspiration for Angelou and for those who study her because she was a revolutionary woman. When America was still a British colony and the Declaration of Independence had not been written, Wheatley, at great personal risk, took the initiative to write and publish her own truth—that all people are free and are entitled to an education that allows them freedom of expression. Wheatley was an advocate for equal opportunity and for the freedom of all Americans to live and express themselves, and she worked tirelessly, writing to such elite Americans as George Washington and Benjamin Franklin to encourage them to abolish slavery. Angelou, more than one hundred years later, used her own education to argue for another kind of liberation: She wrote to exorcise society's reticence to face the ugly truth of the victimization of individuals not only through racism but also through sexual abuse.

Although Angelou was not aware of it when she published *I Know Why the Caged Bird Sings*, she was not the first woman to chronicle her experiences of sexual abuse. That distinction goes to Harriet Jacobs, whose slave narrative, *Incidents in the Life of a Slave Girl* (1861),[1] details the psychological trauma of being a desirable and enslaved black girl. As a young girl, the light-skinned Jacobs had to use her wits and the respect the community held for her grandmother in a true-life chess match to outsmart her master, who tried to rape her. This game culminated in her voluntarily caging herself; she hid in her grandmother's attic crawl space for almost a decade to escape her licentious master.

Jacobs was constrained by the conventions of her day, so in writing her story she had to understate and romanticize the horrors she experienced in order to appeal to white readers. Jacobs had two primary objectives: to educate people about the realities faced by enslaved black women, in an effort to gain support for the abolition of slavery; and to take control over recording her own experiences as a slave. Jacobs's narrative counters the common misconception that permeated much of the nineteenth and twentieth centuries, the notion that black women are promiscuous and enjoy being raped. As an enslaved person, Jacobs was legally considered property; she had no redress under the law and could not defend herself, while her owner could rape her at liberty if he chose.

Some similarities and some differences can be discerned between Jacobs's work and Angelou's. While Jacobs was enslaved under the law, Angelou was not. Jacobs did escape being raped by choosing a white man to be her lover; Angelou was sexually molested by a black relative. Jacobs was unable to publish graphic depictions of the experiences of other enslaved black women whom she knew were repeatedly raped by her master; Angelou was freer to describe her experiences. Both works are autobiographical, however; both describe the writers' relationships with their grandmothers, strong and respected black matriarchs; and both chronicle the loss of innocence at an early age. Both authors were to a degree "caged" by racial discrimination, and both works reflect their authors' agenda to educate readers about the taboo topic of sexual abuse. Even though Angelou was not directly influenced by Jacobs's narrative, it is helpful to see how her autobiography fits within the larger context of African American nonfiction.

Perhaps Angelou's greatest literary influence is Paul Laurence Dunbar's poem "Sympathy," from which she drew the title of her first autobiography. Dunbar's parents were emancipated slaves who taught him about life on the plantation. Like Phillis Wheatley, whose poetry inspired him and to whom he wrote the poem "Phillis,"[2] Dunbar also believed in the liberating power of education and the right of individuals to express themselves. Like Wheatley and Jacobs, Dunbar found himself limited to producing work that fit the American publishing trend of his lifetime At the end of the nineteenth century this trend was realism, which sought to create accurate representations of life and language in the different regions of the United States. Publishers favored works written in black dialect and that told about life on plantations in the American South. Dunbar preferred to write poems in Standard American English, but he had to compromise by writing in dialect as well as Standard American English.

"Sympathy" was published in Dunbar's 1896 collection of poems *Lyrics of Lowly Life*. The poem, written in Standard American English, is Dunbar's testimony to his frustration at being "caged" by the literary conventions of a realism that in some instances was not truly accurate. Ironically, Dunbar wanted to write his experiences as accurately as he could, and his depictions of plantation life and his attempts at Black English dialect were secondhand, because they were not what he actually experienced. In her autobiography Angelou indicates that she drew comfort from Dunbar's words, for she, too, felt frustrated as a traumatized black girl afraid to speak and as an artist unsure of what kind of art to produce. She did not easily find the language to convey her experiences.

It was not until the 1960s that Angelou began to write. She found support in the revolutionary rhetoric of the Black Arts and Black Power movements, both of which called for black artists to use art to promote sociopolitical change; to address more directly a black audience, rather than cater to white, mainstream literary conventions; and to counter negative images of blackness with positive ones. The Black Arts movement made writing workshops accessible to black writers, and black publishers gave black artists a forum in which to disseminate their art.

Angelou first published during the height of the Black Arts movement. Her story of the pains and joys of her life—her literal travels out west to California and her metaphorical journeys into the unknown realms of choosing to be sexually active, becoming a single mother, and overcoming her insecurity at not meeting the American standard of beauty that stresses blond hair, blue eyes, and a straight nose—was appropriate for the day. American youth were thinking and acting critically. They questioned women's traditional roles as primarily wives and mothers, protested the American tactics used in the Vietnam War, and witnessed the continuing black struggle for civil rights and equality. In *I Know Why the Caged Bird Sings*, Angelou makes no apologies for being free to live and make her own mistakes as well as to accept responsibility for her mistakes. The true strength of this work, and what marks it as a substantial contribution to African American letters, is that Angelou takes the initiative to exorcise her own demons and embrace her own personal frontier, and in doing so she encourages those who read it to do the same.

Notes

1. Harriet Jacobs's *Incidents in the Life of a Slave Girl* was rediscovered and reprinted in the 1980s.
2. "Phillis" was published in Dunbar's *Lyrics of Lowly Life* (1896).

Works Cited

Angelou, Maya. "Still I Rise." *Maya Angelou: Poems*. New York: Bantam Books, 1993. 154-55.
Dunbar, Paul Laurence. "Sympathy." *Trouble the Water: 250 Years of African American Poetry*. Ed. Jerry W. Ward, Jr. New York: Mentor, 1997. 68-9.
Hill, Patricia Liggins, ed. "Phillis Wheatley (1753?-1784)." *Call and Response: The Riverside Anthology of the African American Literary Tradition*. Boston: Houghton Mifflin, 1998. 92-7.
_____. "Tales of Flying Africans: Two Tales." *Call and Response: The Riverside Anthology of the African American Literary Tradition*. Boston: Houghton Mifflin, 1998. 64-5.

Biography of Maya Angelou_____

Judith Barton Williamson

Born Marguerite Annie Johnson on April 4, 1928, Maya Angelou is the daughter of Vivian Baxter and Bailey Johnson. When her parents' marriage ended in divorce, she was sent to Stamps, Arkansas, to live with her paternal grandmother, Annie Henderson. Maya was three years old, and she was joined by her brother Bailey, who gave her the name Maya.

Angelou graduated with top honors from the Lafayette County Training School in 1940 and was sent to the San Francisco Bay Area, where her mother had moved. Continuing her education at George Washington High School, she also attended evening classes at the California Labor School, where she had a scholarship to study drama and dance. Shortly after receiving her high school diploma, she had a son, Guy Bailey Johnson. She began a career as a professional entertainer in the 1950s as a singer-dancer at the Purple Onion, a cabaret in California. She was invited to audition for a production of George Gershwin's *Porgy and Bess* (first produced in 1935) and did, in fact, receive a part in the musical, giving her the opportunity to travel widely with the cast in 1954 and 1955. In 1957, she appeared in the Off-Broadway play *Calypso Heatwave* and recorded "Miss Calypso" for Liberty Records.

Three years later, Angelou and her son moved to New York, where she joined the Harlem Writers Guild and collaborated to produce, direct, and star in *Cabaret for Freedom*, which raised funds for the Southern Christian Leadership Conference (SCLC). Upon the close of that show, she became northern coordinator for the SCLC at the invitation of Martin Luther King, Jr., with whom she worked.

Inspired by King and other civil rights leaders, Angelou decided to move to Africa, ostensibly so that her son could be educated in Ghana. While living there, she served as assistant administrator of the University of Ghana's School of Music and Drama and also worked for the

Ghanaian Broadcasting Corporation and as a freelance writer for the *Ghanaian Times*.

In subsequent years, Angelou performed in various theater productions, adapted plays for the stage, and contributed to the performing arts in multiple ways. She performed in Jean Genet's *The Blacks* in 1960 (joining a cast of stars that included James Earl Jones and Cicely Tyson) and adapted Sophocles' *Ajax* for its 1974 premiere performance at the Mark Taper Forum in Los Angeles. She also wrote the screenplays *Georgia, Georgia* (1972) and *All Day Long* (1974). Her television appearances have included the role of Kunta Kinte's grandmother in the 1977 miniseries *Roots*, serving as a guest interviewer on *Assignment America*, and appearing in a special series on creativity hosted by Bill Moyers.

Her most important contributions, however, are her writings. In 1970, she began a series of autobiographies with her book *I Know Why the Caged Bird Sings*, which was followed by subsequent autobiographies and several volumes of poetry. In 1993, she became only the second poet to read her work at a presidential inauguration when she read her poem "On the Pulse of Morning" at President Bill Clinton's inauguration ceremony. Since then, she has written more poems and books, including several works of nonfiction, children's books, and a cookbook. She has appeared in numerous television programs and movies. She is a coveted speaker and gives numerous interviews in which she promotes her activism.

Angelou has been the recipient of more than four dozen honorary degrees and numerous literary awards, among them the North Carolina Award in Literature and a lifetime appointment as the Reynolds Professor of American Studies at Wake Forest University in Winston-Salem, North Carolina. Her other honors include an appointment by Present Jimmy Carter to the commission of the International Women's Year and her recognition by *Ladies' Home Journal* as Woman of the Year in communications in 1975. In 1983, she received the Matrix Award in the field of books from the Association for Women in Communications. In addition, she has been honored with the Medal of Distinction from the University of Hawaii Board of Regents in 1994, a Gold Plaque Choice Award from the Chicago International Film Festival in 1998 for *Down in the Delta*, the Alston/Jones International Civil and Human Rights Award in 1998, a Sheila Award from the Tubman African American Museum in 1999, recognition as one of the one hundred best writers of the twentieth century from *Writer's Digest* in 1999, a National Medal of the Arts in 2000, and a Grammy Award in 2002 for her recording of *A Song Flung Up to Heaven*. Various buildings have been named after her, including the Maya Angelou Public Charter School Agency in Washington, D.C., and the Maya Angelou Southeast Library in Stockton, California.

From *Dictionary of World Biography: The 20th Century.* Pasadena, CA: Salem Press, 1999. Copyright © 1999 by Salem Press, Inc.

Bibliography

Bloom, Harold, ed. *Maya Angelou*. Philadelphia: Chelsea House, 1999. This selection of essays dealing with Angelou's poetry and prose broaches, among other subjects, the singular relationship of Angelou to her audience and her distinctively African American mode of literary expression.

Braxton, Joanne M. *Black Women Writing Autobiography: A Tradition Within a Tradition*. Philadelphia: Temple UP, 1989. Discusses how Angelou employs the image of the protecting mother as a primary archetype within her work. Traces Angelou's development of themes common to black female autobiography: the centrality of the family, the challenges of child rearing and single parenthood, and the burden of overcoming negative stereotypes of African American women.

Cudjoe, Selwyn. "Maya Angelou and the Autobiographical Statement." *Black Women Writers (1950-1980)*. Ed. Mari Evans. Garden City, NY: Anchor Press, 1983. Cudjoe discusses the importance of Angelou's biographical work, arguing that she represents "the condition of Afro-American womanhood in her quest for understanding and love rather than for bitterness and despair." Cudjoe stresses that by telling the story of her own life in *I Know Why the Caged Bird Sings*, Angelou shows the reader what it means to be a black female in America.

Elliot, Jeffrey M., ed. *Conversations with Maya Angelou*. Jackson: UP of Mississippi, 1989. Collection of more than thirty interviews with Angelou that originally appeared in various magazines and newspapers, accompanied by a chronology of her life. Provides a multifaceted perspective on the creative issues that have informed Angelou's work as an autobiographer and a poet.

Hagen, Lyman B. *Heart of a Woman, Mind of a Writer, and Soul of a Poet: A Critical Analysis of the Writings of Maya Angelou*. Lanham, MD: UP of America, 1997. While a number of scholarly works address the different literary forms Angelou has undertaken (most devoted to autobiography), few critical volumes survey her entire opus, and Hagen's is one of the best. Chapters include "Wit and Wisdom/Mirth and Mischief," "Abstracts in Ethics," and "Overview."

King, Sarah E. *Maya Angelou: Greeting the Morning*. Brookfield, CT: Millbrook Press, 1994. Examines Angelou's life, from her childhood in the segregated South to her rise to prominence as a writer. Includes biographical references and an index.

Lisandrelli, Elaine Slivinski. *Maya Angelou: More than a Poet*. Springfield, NJ: Enslow, 1996. Lisandrelli discusses the flamboyance of Angelou, comparing her to the earlier African American author Zora Neale Hurston. Both authors' hard work, optimism, perseverance, and belief in themselves are extolled.

Lupton, Mary Jane. *Maya Angelou: A Critical Companion*. Westport, CT: Greenwood Press, 1998. While focusing mainly on the autobiographies, Lupton's study is still useful as a balanced assessment of Angelou's writings. The volume also contains an excellent bibliography, particularly of Angelou's autobiographical works.

McPherson, Dolly A. *Order Out of Chaos: The Autobiographical Works of Maya Angelou*. New York: Peter Lang, 1990. Scholarly discussion focuses on Angelou's work in autobiography.

O'Neale, Sondra. "Reconstruction of the Composite Self: New Images of Black Women in Maya Angelou's Continuing Autobiography." *Black Women Writers (1950-1980)*. Ed. Mari Evans. Garden City, NY: Anchor Press, 1983. O'Neale argues that Angelou's primary contribution to the canon of African American literature lies in her realistic portrayal of the lives of black people, especially black women. O'Neale goes on to demonstrate the ways in which Angelou successfully destroys many of the stereotypes of black women.

Pettit, Jayne. *Maya Angelou: Journey of the Heart*. New York: Lodestar Books, 1996. Traces Angelou's journey from childhood through her life as entertainer, activist, writer, and university professor. Includes bibliographical references and an index.

Shapiro, Miles. *Maya Angelou*. New York: Chelsea House, 1994. Biography describes the life and work of the celebrated writer.

Tate, Claudia, ed. *Black Women Writers at Work*. New York: Continuum, 1983. Collection of interviews explores the personal lives and works of such African American writers as Gwendolyn Brooks, Alice Walker, and Toni Morrison. In her interview, Angelou discusses the importance of black role models.

Williams, Mary E., ed. *Readings on Maya Angelou*. San Diego: Greenhaven Press, 1997. Collection of essays by literary scholars and noted critics offers diverse approaches to Angelou's literary canon.

the PARIS
REVIEW

The *Paris Review* Perspective

Christopher Cox for *The Paris Review*

When she's writing, Maya Angelou gets up every morning at six, leaves her home, travels across town, and checks into a hotel room with several books, a pad of paper, a pen, and a bottle of sherry. "I lie across the bed," she told George Plimpton in an interview with *The Paris Review*, "so that this elbow is absolutely encrusted at the end, just so rough with calluses. I never allow the hotel people to change the bed, because I never sleep there." Writers' work routines are often marked by such eccentricities, but readers of *I Know Why the Caged Bird Sings* might recognize in Angelou's hotel suite something more than just a room of one's own: it's a safe haven in a life that rarely knew a home free from danger.

It's easy to forget how brave and how new Maya Angelou's book was when it first appeared. Today it's steeped in classroom piety, a member of that body of literature known as assigned reading. But when the book first appeared in 1970, it was a far more exotic creature: an autobiography, yes, though not of anyone famous or powerful—a politician, a head of state, a leader of men. Instead, it was the story of a poor black girl growing up in rural Arkansas. Angelou knew what she was getting into: she later said that she started writing her own life story after James Baldwin told her that making literature out of autobiography was almost impossible. She saw herself as an heir to Frederick Douglass, "speaking in the first-person singular talking about the first-person plural, always saying *I* meaning *we*. And what a responsibility!"

I Know Why the Caged Bird Sings and the five volumes of memoir that followed it leave no doubt as to Angelou's attitude toward ambition and difficulty. All of life is hard fought, she tells us, and the rewards barely make up for the pain of getting through it. Her Marguerite suffers through weeks of futile attempts to get a job on a streetcar—a job hitherto given only to whites—and her effort, when finally successful, gains her nothing more than a menial position. The very act of remembering is fraught with pain toward an uncertain end; the book begins with Marguerite saying that "I couldn't bring myself to remember." But at the same time, Angelou told Plimpton, the past never leaves you, no matter how painful:

> I never agreed with the Thomas Wolfe title *You Can't Go Home Again*. Instinctively I didn't. But the truth is, you can never *leave* home. You take it with you; it's under your fingernails; it's in the hair follicles; it's in the way you smile; it's in the ride of your hips, in the passage of your breasts; it's all there, no matter where you go.

By making this claim to autobiography, Angelou was carving a space for herself that wasn't usually granted to blacks in America. The slave, she wrote in an essay in *The New York Times*, "has no past, or certainly none worth mentioning."

In the face of these odds, Angelou's narrative voice can seem both hopeless and powerful, resigned and yet authoritative; stubbornness in the face of a fearsome and hostile world is its steadiest feature. (If you've heard Angelou speak in person, it's hard to get the vigorous tenor of her speaking voice out of your mind, even when reading the passages describing Marguerite at her most vulnerable.) Late in the book, Angelou admits that "the dread of futility has been my lifelong plague." Although she's never so self-pitying as to say it directly, the implication is that a life as hard as hers has to be worth something.

The stakes, Angelou never lets us forget, are high. Like most writers, she's carefully attuned to the way the people around her speak, from the slow cadences of Momma to her father's urbane stammering *ers* and *errers*, to her Uncle Tommy's roughneck patter: "He strung ordinary sentences together and they came out sounding either like the most pro-fane curses or like comical poetry." But Angelou takes things a step fur-ther: her mother, unknown to her as a young child, is in her imagination literally made of language, her face "like a big O, and since I couldn't fill in the features I printed M O T H E R across the O." After she is raped and the testimony she gives in court leads to the lynching of the rapist, she resolves to stay mute: "If I talked to anyone else that person might die too. Just my breath, carrying my words out, might poison people and they'd curl up and die like the black fat slugs that only pretended." Angelou eventually started to speak again, but the sense of the power of language never left her. "We survive," she claims in the book, "in exact relationship to the dedication of our poets." Critics regularly praise her for the fluidity of her prose, but as she said in her *Paris Review* interview, "those are the ones I want to grab by the throat and wrestle to the floor because it takes me forever to get it to sing. I *work* at the language." The difficult and the worthwhile, overlapping again.

Angelou's memoir thus never loses a sense of dramatic irony, as the assuredness of the language bumps up against Marguerite's inability to comprehend the traumas that beset her young life. Most of the story is told at child's-eye level, and the adult world remains hopelessly opaque: "There was an army of adults, whose motives and movements I just couldn't understand and who made no effort to understand mine." *Caged Bird*, which ends when Marguerite becomes a mother (child-birth being an extreme example of pain leading to reward), is in part the story of Marguerite shaking off her youthful ignorance, trading "the bright hours when the young rebelled against the descending sun" for "twenty-four-hour periods called 'days' that were named as well as numbered." Growing up, Angelou told Plimpton, is the most important of the hard-but-necessary tasks that make up a life:

Most people don't grow up. It's too damn difficult. What happens is most people get older. That's the truth of it. They honor their credit cards, they find parking spaces, they marry, they have the nerve to have children, but they don't grow up. Not really. They get older. But to grow up . . . means you take responsibility for the time you take up, for the space you occupy. It's serious business.

Works Cited

Angelou, Maya. "The Art of Fiction No. 119." Interview with George Plimpton. *The Paris Review* 116 (Fall 1990).
_____. "For Years, We Hated Ourselves." *The New York Times* 16 Apr. 1972.
_____. *I Know Why the Caged Bird Sings*. New York: Random House, 1970.
Goodman, George, Jr. "Maya Angelou's Lonely, Black Outlook." *The New York Times* 24 Mar. 1972.

CRITICAL
CONTEXTS

I Know Why the Caged Bird Sings:
African American Literary Tradition and the Civil Rights Era_____

Amy Sickels

Maya Angelou wrote *I Know Why the Caged Bird Sings* at the end of the civil rights struggles of the 1960s, one of the most turbulent times in modern American history. After the U.S. Supreme Court's ruling in *Brown v. Board of Education* outlawed school segregation in 1954, the Civil Rights movement gained power as increasing numbers of people rose up against bigotry and racism. As the movement gained momentum with sit-ins and marches, African Americans were also viciously attacked. Across the South, there were beatings, church bombings, and lynchings. The violence continued when President John F. Kennedy was assassinated on November 22, 1963, sending the nation into a state of grief and anxiety about the future; two years later, on February 21, black nationalist Malcolm X, whose fiery views had transformed to be more accepting of whites, was assassinated.

Despite these tremendous losses and the terror many African Americans faced, the hope for change and equality prevailed. The momentous March on Washington in 1963 helped lead to the passage of the most important pieces of legislation in the 1960s: the Civil Rights Act of 1964 and the Voting Rights Act of 1965. In addition, the success and energy of the Civil Rights movement inspired other movements, including the women's movement and the gay and lesbian movement. Tragically, with hope for the future in the air, on April 4, 1968 (coincidentally Maya Angelou's fortieth birthday), civil rights leader Martin Luther King, Jr., was assassinated. The nation was stunned and saddened, and his death set off a series of riots across the country.

Maya Angelou, active in the Civil Rights movement and friends with both Malcolm X and King, was, like so many others around the world, devastated by their deaths, yet she did not give up her hope for a better, more just world or her belief in the power of art to create change. Throughout the era, the Black Arts movement, the cultural wing of the Black Power movement that was started by the poet Amiri Baraka in 1965, was extremely influential in the work and development of many writers, including Angelou. Activist, poet, and performer, Angelou did not start writing until she was in her thirties, and *I Know Why the Caged Bird Sings* was not published until she was forty-one.

Angelou did not set out to write her autobiography, but some of her friends—the famous writer James Baldwin, cartoonist Jules Feiffer, and Feiffer's wife Judy—were convinced that Angelou should write about her childhood after they heard her stories about growing up in Stamps, Arkansas. When Judy Feiffer connected Angelou with Robert Loomis, an editor at Random House, Angelou at first refused Loomis's request that she write her autobiography:

> Loomis called me two or three times, but I continued to say that I was not interested. Then, I am sure, he talked to Baldwin because he used a ploy which I am not proud to say I haven't gained control of yet. He called and said, "Miss Angelou, it's been nice talking to you. But I'm rather glad that you decided not to write an autobiography because to write an autobiography as literature is a most difficult task." I said, "Then I'll do it." (quoted in McPherson 22)

By the time *Caged Bird* was published, the Black Arts movement was essentially over, but the work appeared at the beginning of a prolific period for African American authors, especially women—it is often referred to as the "renaissance" of black women writers. Toni Morrison, Nikki Giovanni, Angela Davis, Alice Walker, June Jordan, Toni Cade Bambara, Sonia Sanchez, and Lucille Clifton all began their careers around the same time. When *Caged Bird* appeared, many saw it as a turning point in African American and women's literature. Popular with both white and black audiences, the book received glowing reviews in *The New York Times*, *Newsweek*, and the *Wall Street Journal* and was nominated for the National Book Award. Further, "before the end of the year, other critics were heralding *Caged Bird* as marking the beginning of a new era in the consciousness of black men and women and creating a distinctive place in black autobiographical tradition" (Mcpherson 22). Scholar Sondra O'Neale notes:

> With the wide public and critical reception of *I Know Why the Caged Bird Sings* in the early seventies, Angelou bridged the gap between life and art, a step that is essential if Black women are to be deservedly credited with the mammoth and creative feat of noneffacing survival. Critics could not dismiss her work as so much "folksy" propaganda because her narrative was held together by controlled techniques of artistic fiction as well as by a historic-sociological study of Black feminine images seldom if ever viewed in American literature. (42)

What made *Caged Bird* distinct from the many other contemporary autobiographies by African American writers? What propelled its success, with critics such as Harold Bloom commenting, "Angelou's autobiographical tone is one of profound intimacy and radiates good will, even a serenity astonishingly at variance with the terrors and degradations she suffered as a child and as a very young woman" (7)? Critics have examined the work from a number of different perspectives—as a traditional African American autobiography, as a female coming-of-age story, as a rape-survivor's story, as a literary biography—and while *Caged Bird* is all of these, it also is a documentation of African American history and heritage. Though it incorporates many themes common in autobiographies by African American women—which critic Joanne M. Braxton describes as "the importance of the family and the nurturing and rearing of one's children, as well as the quest for self-sufficiency, self-reliance, personal dignity, and self-definition"—with her "unified point of view," Angelou focuses on "inner spaces of her emotional and personal life," making her work unlike many of the earlier biographies (*Black Women* 184). Braxton continues: "Angelou feels compelled to explore aspects of her coming of age that Ida B. Wells (and Zora Neale Hurston) chose to omit" (*Black Women* 184). Angelou's focus on the intimate details of her life, along with her documentation of the larger story of African American heritage and racism in the South, draws on traditional black autobiographical form while also, according to critic George E. Kent, creating

> a unique place within black autobiographical tradition, not by being "better" than the formidable autobiographical landmarks described [such as Richard Wright's *Black Boy* or Anne Moody's *Coming of Age in Mississippi*], but by its special stance toward the self, the community, and the universe, and by a form exploiting the full measure of imagination necessary to acknowledge both beauty and absurdity. (20)

I Know Why the Caged Bird Sings tells the story of the first seventeen years of Angelou's life. She matures as she moves from Stamps, Arkansas, to St. Louis, Missouri, and, eventually, to San Francisco, California. For much of her early life, she feels displaced and isolated in a world that equates beauty with whiteness: "If growing up is painful for the Southern Black girl, being aware of her displacement is the rust on the razor that threatens the throat," she writes as an adult (*Caged Bird* 6). But the book is also very much about the time period itself—a document of the oppression of black rural life in the South during the 1930s. According to Angelou:

> When I wrote *I Know Why the Caged Bird Sings*, I wasn't thinking so much about my own life or identity. I was thinking about a particular time in which I lived and the influences of that time on a number of people. I kept thinking, what about that time? What were the people around young Maya doing? I used the central figure—myself—as a focus to show how one person can make it through those times. (quoted in Tate 153)

The predominant setting for the book—the oppressive Jim Crow South—represents the very bigotry that Angelou was fighting against during the Civil Rights movement when she wrote it. Thus Angelou's southern roots and civil rights activism contributed to the writing of this book. While *Caged Bird* is deeply connected to the long history of African American autobiography, it grew out of the Civil Rights movement and then carved out a space for itself in the African American woman writers' renaissance as well as within the larger literary canon; this essay situates *Caged Bird* within the specific time period in which it was written, as well as within the time period in which it is set, in order to underscore these connections and to show why its legacy continues today.

Traditional African American Autobiography Meets the 1960s

To grasp the significance of the African American autobiographical tradition as well as the influence of sociopolitical issues on much African American literature, one need only glance at the history of African American writing. From its beginning, politics, social conditions, and culture have been entwined with such writing. Furthermore, the autobiographical form reflects a long history within the African American community, beginning with the slave narrative, a popular form of protest literature throughout the eighteenth and nineteenth centuries. As Selwyn R. Cudjoe observes, "The practice of the autobiographical statement, up until the contemporary era, remains the quintessential literary genre for capturing the cadences of the Afro-American being, revealing its deepest aspirations and tracing the evolution of the Afro-American psyche under the impact of slavery and modern U.S. imperialism" (55). Former slaves, including Harriet Jacobs, Frederick Douglass, and thousands of others, wrote narratives about their personal experiences as a way to articulate their individual stories while addressing the larger social issue of slavery and attempting to have an impact on the conscience of a nation. Scholar Harold Bloom is one of several critics who link these early autobiographies to the structure of *Caged Bird*, calling Maya Angelou "a natural autobiographer who works with considerable skill and with narrative cunning. Her voice interweaves other strands in the African-American oral tradition, but the implicit forms of sermon and slave narrative are ghostly presences in her rhetoric" (7).

After the Civil War ended, several well-known black writers and activists, including W. E. B. Du Bois, Booker T. Washington, and Marcus Garvey, wrote about the conditions of black lives in the United States, and their work made long-lasting impressions on social and cultural understandings of race. Slowly, African American literature, music, and art began to gain a wider appeal. Langston Hughes, Zora Neale Hurston, Jean Toomer, and Countée Cullen were all important writers of the Harlem Renaissance. Richard Wright's novel *Native Son* (1940), which protested the social conditions that white society imposed on African Americans, became an immediate best seller and was also a Book-of-the-Month Club selection. For the first time, African American authors were winning awards and honors that had previously been presented only to white writers. In 1950, poet Gwendolyn Brooks became the first African American to win the Pulitzer Prize for poetry, and Ralph Ellison won the National Book Award for his 1952 novel *Invisible Man*.

The 1950s also saw a rise in autobiographies by African Americans, as Braxton points out, with many penned by black women, including Marian Anderson, Leila Mae Barlow, Ella Earls Cotton, Helen Day Caldwell, and Katherine Dunham (*Black Women* 141). In George Kent's view, when Richard Wright's autobiography, *Black Boy*, was published in 1945, it "began the questioning which shook the fabric of the American Dream" (18). Several scholars have drawn strong links between *Black Boy* and *Caged Bird*. Braxton asserts, "Thematic and structural similarities between the autobiographies of Wright and Angelou result from the slave narratives and from the influence of

Russian writers, which both read" (*Black Women* 192), while Susan Gilbert takes a different view: "Much in *I Know Why the Caged Bird Sings* and in what Angelou has said about her writing shows her in opposition to Wright's dogma. Though the girl is lonely and hurt, she finds her way to survival in terms of the traditions of her family, her mother and her grandmother, not in opposition to them" (107).

Autobiography continued to be an important form for African American writers throughout the 1950s and 1960s: such works as Baldwin's *Notes of a Native Son* (1955), Anne Moody's *Coming of Age in Mississippi* (1968), *The Autobiography of Malcolm X* (1965), and Claude Brown's *Manchild in the Promised Land* (1965) combined individual story, social protest, and historical record. Yet, as Braxton explains in *Black Women Writing Autobiography*, "the pace of development of critical literature for autobiography as a genre did not begin to quicken until the 1960s, and there was little adequate treatment of black literature as a tradition until the 1970s," whereas women's autobiography was not examined by academic literary critics until the 1980s or later (6). Although these contemporary autobiographies differed in style and content from the early slave narratives, Sidonie Ann Smith points out similar themes:

> In Black American autobiography the opening almost invariably recreates the environment of enslavement from which the black self seeks escape. Such an environment was literal in the earliest form of black autobiography, the slave narrative, which traced the flight of the slave northward from slavery into full humanity. In later autobiography, however, the literal enslavement is replaced by more subtle forms of economic, historical, psychological, and spiritual imprisonment from which the black self still seeks an escape route to a "North." (5)

In *Caged Bird*, the young isolated Maya at first wants to wake from the "black ugly dream," but over the course of her literal and figurative journey toward freedom, she discovers a sense of self, black pride, and community (2). Even in the imprisonment of racism, Angelou still finds her voice and, like the caged bird, makes herself heard in the midst of struggle. That the title of *I Know Why the Caged Bird Sings* is from the poem "Sympathy" by late-nineteenth-century African American poet Paul Laurence Dunbar speaks to Angelou's awareness of the continuum of African American literature and the echoes of tradition.

Similarly, the desire for social change that fueled the slave narratives also influenced African American writing during the period of the Civil Rights movement. Thus, to understand the cultural context of *Caged Bird*, it is crucial not only to examine the African American autobiographical tradition but also to look at the political activism of this era. A strong connection between literary writing and activism existed throughout the 1950s and 1960s, as symbolized by Martin Luther King, Jr.'s famous *Letter from Birmingham City Jail* (1963) and the many writers, such as Baldwin, who advocated civil rights through their writing. Braxton writes that the autobiographical form and the Civil Rights movement were closely linked:

In the 1960s, the new social history and autobiography as a genre emerged as source material for the study of groups whose history had remained unwritten. The fact that the advent of this discovery coincides with the civil rights movement and the women's movement underscores the close relationship of the autobiographical genre to the political and historical moment; in fact, the political movements of the 1960s fostered an interest in and an attitude of receptivity toward the publications of autobiography by black Americans. (*Black Women* 142)

Many African American writers used fiction, poetry, and nonfiction to fuel social protest and call for change; for example, James Baldwin's collection of essays *Nobody Knows My Name: More Notes of a Native Son* (1961) shot straight to the best-seller lists, where it remained for six months, "marking . . . a period of reawakened consciousness in black autobiography" (Braxton, *Black Women* 142). Baldwin's writing illustrated the danger of a divided America and challenged both whites and blacks to reach out to each other. The Black Arts movement was also extremely influential in the work and development of many writers, including Angelou, and helped to form black publishing houses, theater troupes, and poetry readings. While much of the Black Power movement came from a male perspective, women writers such as June Jordan, Lucille Clifton, and Audre Lorde also made their voices heard.

Where did Maya Angelou fit into all of this, and how did this vibrant political atmosphere contribute to the writing of *I Know Why the Caged Bird Sings*? Angelou published *Caged Bird* during a critical decade for African American literature, as it began to gain a wider readership and, for the first time, to be defined as a genre and recognized as a crucial part of the larger category of American literature. Angelou wrote that the increased receptivity among publishers was linked "directly to the protest movements of the 1950s and 60s" (quoted in Braxton, *Black Women* 143).

Angelou was actively involved in the Civil Rights movement in several ways, including as a performer and as an organizer. When she was in her thirties, her circle of black intellectual and activist friends grew, and, inspired by writer and social activist John Killens, Angelou joined the Harlem Writers Guild, becoming a member of a group of writers that included Paule Marshall and James Baldwin. In 1959, at the request of Dr. Martin Luther King, Jr., she became the northern coordinator for the Southern Christian Leadership Conference (SCLC), a job she held for six months. In 1960 she produced, directed, and starred in *Cabaret for Freedom* to raise funds for the SCLC. Throughout the 1950s and 1960s, there was no distinct separation between art and activism—each inspired and challenged the other. Angelou recalls the spirited atmosphere:

The period was absolutely intoxicating. The streets were filled with people who were on their toes, figuratively, with alertness. There was a promise in the air, like a delicious aroma of a wonderful soup being cooked in the kitchen on a cold day when you are hungry. It really appeared as if we were going to overcome racism, sexism, violence, hate. (*Conversations* 196)

Angelou deepened her understanding of justice and race after she moved overseas and realized that the struggle for equality included black people across the world. In the period 1961-1962 she was associate editor of the *Arab Observer* in Cairo, Egypt, the only English-language newsweekly in the Middle East. When she and her son next moved to Ghana, freeing themselves from the racist bigotry in the United States, she was an assistant administrator at the University of Ghana's School of Music and Drama and a feature editor for the *African Review*. In Ghana, Angelou met Malcolm X; when she returned to the United States in 1964, she helped him build a new civil rights organization, the Organization of African American Unity, but shortly after her arrival, Malcolm X was assassinated. Engaged in political activism throughout the 1960s, Angelou soon turned to words. Her story of growing up in the oppressive, poverty-stricken Jim Crow South resonated deeply with the times.

What She Came From

To analyze the cultural context of *I Know Why the Caged Bird Sings*, it is helpful to understand the period in which the book is set and how Angelou's past connects to the activism in which she was engaged when she wrote the book. Angelou grew up in a place governed by intense racism, violence, and bigotry: "In Stamps the segregation was so complete that most Black children didn't really, absolutely know what whites looked like." Young Maya lives under the threats of terrifying lynch mobs and the daily realities of discrimination and humiliation. Each racist incident contributes to Maya's self-awareness and shapes her views about injustice. This is a place where her brother witnesses white men fishing the rotting corpse of a lynched black man out of the river and then making jokes, where her grandmother is humiliated by a group of poor white girls, and where her crippled uncle spends the night in a corn crib to avoid a lynch mob.

Part of what helps Maya survive the racism around her and feel more confident in herself is her connection to the black community and to the strong role models offered by her grandmother and Mrs. Bertha Flowers, "the aristocrat of Black Stamps," who takes Maya under her wing and coaxes her out of her shell—"another important turning point in the development of the autobiographer's consciousness" (Braxton, *Black Women* 195). Mrs. Flowers instills in Maya feelings of black pride and a love for literature, and also teaches her "lessons in living." Angelou recalls, "It would be safe to say that she made me proud to be Negro, just by being herself" (*Caged Bird* 79). Similarly, when the eighth-grade valedictorian leads the black audience in "Lift Ev'ry Voice and Sing," known as the Negro national anthem, he restores their confidence and Maya realizes, "I was no longer simply a member of the proud graduating class of 1940; I was a proud member of the wonderful, beautiful Negro race" (156). Maya's journey, then, is one of self-discovery, but it also leads her to embrace the African American community; the idea of black pride, as well as her creative journey, resonated strongly with the civil rights-era audience.

As *Caged Bird* follows Maya's transformation from an "unbeautiful, awkward, rather morose, dreamy, and 'too-big Negro girl'" (Arensberg 111) to a confident young woman who stands up to racist practices and asserts her independence, the book expresses themes that were timely to the 1960s and 1970s. The cultural idea of "Black Is Beautiful"—the reclamation of African American beauty—rises up from these pages as Angelou writes about growing up in a world that equates beauty with whiteness. She is reminded every day of her blackness, as when the white dentist in town refuses to treat her, claiming he would "rather stick my hand in a dog's mouth than a nigger's" (*Caged*

Bird 160). The same year that *Caged Bird* was published, Toni Morrison's *The Bluest Eye* appeared; in this novel, Morrison critiques how whiteness as the measure of beauty is deeply entrenched in American society by telling the story of one little African American girl's desire for love. Unlike the character of Pecola Breedlove in *The Bluest Eye*, however, Maya, who is loved, actively protests racism and develops into a strong, independent woman by the end of *Caged Bird*—this major theme of the work also speaks to the cultural context.

A Woman's Story

As Braxton notes, African American women were publishing autobiographies throughout the 1950s and 1960s: "The times had changed, and circumstances that encouraged the publication of these books by black men also made possible the publication of autobiographies and memoirs by black women" (*Black Women* 142). Most of these books, however, did not reach the wider public and eventually disappeared into obscurity. The 1970s, in contrast, were an especially vital and fruitful period for black women writers, helping to lay the foundation for literary scholarship on black women authors as well as developing the ideas of black feminist criticism. Maya Angelou's *I Know Why the Caged Bird Sings*, the anthology *The Black Woman*, edited by Toni Cade Bambara, and first novels by Alice Walker, June Jordan, and Toni Morrison were all published in 1970. "Critics of many races and nationalities began to speak simultaneously of 'the coming of age' of autobiography as a genre, as well as a 'renaissance' in black women's writing," attests Braxton (*Black Women* 143). She also emphasizes that *Caged Bird* "marks the coming of age, if not the full flowering, of a long continuum of black women's autobiography" (*Black Women* 208).

Angelou, in an interview with Devinia Sookia, is quick to point out that African American women have always been writing their stories, but the publishing climate and public had not always been receptive: "Well, Phillis Wheatley wrote 271 years ago when she was a slave.

Zora Neale and Nella Larsen wrote long ago. To be a woman writer and be accepted 40 years ago was not possible because of the social restrictions on black women, whereas it was not very difficult for black women writers in my time to be accepted" (*Conversations* 191). Critic Jill Ker Conway also notes: "The tradition of black women's narratives reaches beyond slavery, back to the role of women as storytellers and religious figures in African culture" (3), while Braxton links black women's autobiography with traditional stories that were passed down from generation to generation ("Interview" 4).

Critics have thoroughly analyzed the so-called differences between male and female autobiographies, tracing themes and delineating contrasts, an approach that can be illuminating but also risks being generalizing and stereotyping. However, as Selwyn Cudjoe argues, in the 1970s, an important decade for African American literature,

> there was a subtle distancing of the Afro-American women writers from their male counterparts, particularly in the manner in which they treated the subjectivity of their major protagonists; the manner in which these female protagonist were freed, not so much from the other, but from their own menfolk; the bold attempt to speak for the integrity of their selfhood and to define their being in their own terms. (60)

While *I Know Why the Caged Bird Sings* resonates on various levels—as a literary, creative autobiography; as a critique of racism and classism; as a depiction of an African American community in the South—and should not be pigeonholed, it is also important to see that it is first and foremost about the coming-of-age of a young black girl in the South. Similar to other work published during this time, *Caged Bird* focuses on themes of oppression, racism, and sexism and dismantles prevalent stereotypes of black women. Angelou shows how to be black and female is to be oppressed twice, and that for black women to survive, they must be strong: "The fact that the adult American Negro female emerges a formidable character is often met with amazement, distaste and even belligerence. It is seldom accepted as an inevitable outcome of the struggle won by survivors and deserves respect if not enthusiastic acceptance" (*Caged Bird* 265). Angelou begins the autobiography by highlighting young Maya's insecurity, how she feels she can never match up to the pretty white girls and only wants to wake from this "black ugly dream," symbolic of her disillusionment in American society; yet by the end, Maya feels proud of her black womanhood, passed down to her from the women in her family.

As much as this is a story about racism, it also unveils the truth about sexism: "The Black female is assaulted in her tender years by all those common forces of nature at the same time that she is caught in the tripartite crossfire of masculine prejudice, white illogical hate, and Black lack of power" (*Caged Bird* 265). During this period of African American women's writing and into the 1980s, books by black women authors often stirred up controversy by addressing sexism (in both the white and black communities), sexuality, and abuse. For example, Alice Walker's *The Color Purple* (1982) and Ntozake Shange's *for colored girls who have considered suicide/ when the rainbow is enuf* (1975) stirred up fierce debates within the African American community about sexism.

Similarly, *Caged Bird* has survived years of controversy and is a frequent target of censorship in high schools, usually for its frank depiction of rape. *Caged Bird* is read by many—both critics and popular audiences—as a rape victim's survival story, and it is both admired and targeted by censors because of this subject. Despite the controversy, Angelou stands by her decision to include the rape, and in an interview with Joanne Braxton she explains: "So I thought to myself, 'You write so that perhaps people who hadn't raped anybody yet might be discouraged, people who had might be informed, people who have not been raped might understand something, and people who have been raped might forgive themselves'" ("Interview" 12). Angelou's writing about being raped as a child was a momentous turning point in women's autobiography, as *Caged Bird* was published at a time when most rape victims and sexually abused children were encouraged to stay silent; Angelou's honesty opened the door for other women to share their stories. Despite the tragedy she endured, bitterness does not haunt the work, as Angelou writes about her family and community with love. Critic Sidonie Ann Smith points out the importance of Angelou telling this story in the form of autobiography: "That she chooses to create the past in its own sounds suggests to the reader that she accepts the past and recognizes its beauty and its ugliness, its assets and its liabilities, its strengths and its weakness" (13).

In *I Know Why the Caged Bird Sings*, Angelou depicts the isolation she felt as a young girl—enduring the racism of the South and surviving violent sexual trauma—and traces the journey of her development into a strong, independent woman. She also dispels stereotypes about black women and about African American people. For instance, by portraying her beautiful, absent, and kind mother, and her steadfast, strict, and loving grandmother, Angelou "effectively banishes several stereotypical myths about Black women which had remained unanswered in national literature" (O'Neale 52). *Caged Bird* marked a turning point in the visibility of African American and women's autobiography as "a conscious assertion of identity, as well as the presentation of an alternate version of reality seen from the point of view of the black female experience" (Braxton, *Black Women* 201).

When Angelou wrote *Caged Bird*, she was influenced by a rich tradition of African American literature—from slave narratives to women's autobiographies—during a period in the United States that rippled with tragedy, hope, and political fervor. The themes of the book connect deeply to the time in which it was constructed, making it a testament to the power of art, protest, and memory. *I Know Why the Caged Bird Sings* has endured not because it is a "black" autobiography or a "woman's" autobiography, but because it is a testament to the truth: "I speak to the black experience, but I am always talking about the human condition—about what we can endure, dream, fail at, and still survive" (Angelou quoted in Braxton, *Black Women* 182).

Works Cited

Angelou, Maya. *Conversations with Maya Angelou*. Ed. Jeffrey M. Elliot. Jackson: University Press of Mississippi, 1989.

_____. *I Know Why the Caged Bird Sings*. New York: Bantam Books, 1971.

Arensberg, Liliane K. "Death as Metaphor of Self." *Maya Angelou's "I Know Why the Caged Bird Sings": A Casebook*. Ed. Joanne M. Braxton. New York: Oxford University Press, 1999. 111-27.

Bloom, Harold. "Introduction." *Bloom's Guides: I Know Why the Caged Bird Sings*. Ed. Harold Bloom. Philadelphia: Chelsea House, 2004. 7-8.

Braxton, Joanne M. *Black Women Writing Autobiography: A Tradition Within a Tradition*. Philadelphia: Temple UP, 1989.

_____. "Interview with Maya Angelou." *Maya Angelou's "I Know Why the Caged Bird Sings": A Casebook*. Ed. Joanne M. Braxton. New York: Oxford University Press, 1999.

Conway, Jill Ker, ed. *Written by Herself*. New York: Vintage Books, 1992.

Cudjoe, Selwyn R. "Maya Angelou and the Autobiographical Statement." *Bloom's Modern Critical Views: Maya Angelou*. Ed. Harold Bloom. Philadelphia: Chelsea House, 2004. 55-74.

Gilbert, Susan. "Paths to Escape." *Maya Angelou's "I Know Why the Caged Bird Sings": A Casebook*. Ed. Joanne M. Braxton. New York: Oxford University Press, 1999. 99-110.

Kent, George E. "Maya Angelou's *I Know Why the Caged Bird Sings*." *Bloom's Modern Critical Views: Maya Angelou*. Ed. Harold Bloom. Philadelphia: Chelsea House, 2004. 15-24.

McPherson, Dolly A. "Initiation and Self-Discovery." *Maya Angelou's "I Know Why the Caged Bird Sings": A Casebook*. Ed. Joanne M. Braxton. New York: Oxford University Press, 1999. 21-48.

O'Neale, Sondra. "Reconstruction of the Composite Self: New Images of Black Women in Maya Angelou's Continuing Autobiography." *Bloom's Modern Critical Views: Maya Angelou*. Ed. Harold Bloom. Philadelphia: Chelsea House, 2004. 41-54.

Smith, Sidonie Ann. "The Song of a Caged Bird: Maya Angelou's Quest After Self-Acceptance." *Bloom's Modern Critical Views: Maya Angelou*. Ed. Harold Bloom. Philadelphia: Chelsea House, 2004. 3-14.

Tate, Claudia. "Maya Angelou: An Interview." *Maya Angelou's "I Know Why the Caged Bird Sings": A Casebook*. Ed. Joanne M. Braxton. New York: Oxford University Press, 1999. 149-58.

The Critical Reception of *I Know Why the Caged Bird Sings*

Pamela Loos

Although Maya Angelou has written several autobiographies, critics are in agreement that her first, *I Know Why the Caged Bird Sings*, is the best of them, partially because it is so finely crafted. In an early review of *I Know Why the Caged Bird Sings*, published in 1970, Ernece B. Kelly comments on Angelou's deftness at reaching back to her childhood and presenting it and all the pain it held for her as a young, sensitive girl (681). Years later, in an essay published in the early 1990s, Michael Craig Hillmann would remark on Angelou's gifts as a writer: "Angelou brings a rich and varied vocabulary, a feeling for the rhythms of speech, and a fertile imagination to bear on the slightest recollection from childhood. Her use of metaphor and simile . . . is especially engaging" (216). Hillmann notes that such skills are put to good use, adding to the intensity of the work. Kelly points out that there are some flaws in Angelou's poetic style but notes that the book still provides a powerful depiction of the life of a young black person growing up in the 1930s South. Referring to the book as "a novel," Kelly calls it a "miracle" that the young Angelou (Marguerite Johnson in the book) manages to become so self-assured in light of "the War" going on between blacks and whites at the time (682).

Few critics have disagreed with Kelly's assessment. For instance, in an article published in Auburn University's *Southern Humanities Review*, Sidonie Ann Smith agrees with Kelly in many respects and focuses on Angelou's description of the intense pain of entrapment for the young Marguerite. Smith discusses the opening of the autobiography at some length, describing how Marguerite is a prisoner in her own black body: "She is a black ugly reality, not a whitened dream. And the attendant self-consciousness and diminished self-image throb through her bodily prison until the bladder can do nothing but explode in a parody of release (freedom)" (368). Smith explains the significance of the work's opening to the totality of Angelou's quest for self-actualization, a quest, as Smith describes it, for self-confidence rather than self-consciousness. She comments, too, on Angelou's courage to face her past and write this work.

Whereas Smith spends only a bit of time in her commentary connecting Angelou's work to other black autobiography, other commentators have delved further into this aspect of *Caged Bird* and continue to do so. In a 1974 essay, Stephen Butterfield, for example, compares Angelou's *Caged Bird* to works by Ida Wells, Anne Moody, and Richard Wright. Butterfield makes clear, however, what makes Angelou's book different: "But her primary reasons for living, her happiness, sorrows, lessons, meanings, self-confidence, seem to come from within her private circle of light. Part of her is always untouched by the oppression, observing and commenting on it from a distance" (208). Butterfield supplies the reasons he believes Angelou grew as strong as she did, and he makes the key point that the most traumatic event of Angelou's young life actually had nothing to do with white oppression; it was a rape perpetrated by a black man, for which members of her own black circle inflicted the ultimate punishment of death. Butterfield comments as well on Angelou's humor, empathy, and "love for the sounds and sights of being alive" (205), part of what has added to the universality of the work and what has for years drawn readers to *Caged Bird*.

Similarly, in an essay on *Caged Bird* published in 1975, George E. Kent begins by providing an overview of key works of black autobiography. He views Angelou's work as creating a unique place in this history, "not by being 'better' than the formidable autobiographical landmarks described, but by its special stance toward the self, the community, and the universe, and by a form exploiting the full measure of imagination necessary to acknowledge both beauty and absurdity" (75). Like Butterfield, then, Kent sees Angelou's gift in how she responded to her circumstances as a young girl, how she used what the circumstances had to offer, and how she told her story. He, too, remarks on her community, describing the young Marguerite's reliance on two basic areas of adult black life—the traditional religious realm of her grandmother in Arkansas and the blues traditions of her mother in St. Louis and California. From Kent's perspective, while conflict exists between the world at large and the young girl, at the same time there is an understanding that that young girl must create her own path, order, and coherence. The ego can remain stable no matter the circumstance, and so, in the world Angelou creates, the text can utilize poetry and a mellow, confessional form, according to Kent.

In her 1976 essay on *Caged Bird*, Myra K. McMurry remarks on the book's "almost novelistic clarity" (106) and Angelou's description of how she transcended her circumstances. McMurry also brings up the idea of Angelou's recollected self and authorial self, again pointing out the issue of autobiography versus more highly crafted types of writing. This critic also sees Angelou's work as about transcending circumstance but describes the process of that transcendence as requiring people to take on various roles, with the young Marguerite seemingly suffering from the most repression by virtue of being a child and having to follow adults' rules but seeing that nearly everyone in her young world is also repressed. As the book progresses, Marguerite sees how other individuals, and even groups, handle repression. McMurry also points out that Angelou, like Ralph Ellison, sees art as part of the answer; she notes that "art protects the human values of compassion, love, and innocence, and makes the freedom for the self-realization necessary for real survival" (111).

For another critic writing in the 1970s, however, Angelou manages not only by assuming a role or roles but also by creating a self through a continuous and more drastic process of dying and rebirth. This critic, Liliane K. Arensberg, points out that *Caged Bird* starts on Easter Sunday, a day known for celebration of the rebirth of Jesus Christ, but a day when the young Angelou does not get her wish of being transformed into a white girl. Through the rest of the text, in Arensberg's view, Angelou faces the test of confronting annihilation and overcoming it, and it is significant that the book ends with Angelou giving life to her own son.

Another critic who has focused on *Caged Bird*'s death imagery is Karen Chandler. In a 1999 essay, Chandler points out that in *Caged Bird* Angelou feels surrounded by threats of death, both of the body and of the spirit, as the work's repeated death imagery shows. The young girl feels that her maturation is threatened by prejudiced whites as well as by her own family and community, most notably her parents, who send her and her brother away at very young ages without explanation. Chandler draws analogies between Angelou's writing and African and African American cultural traditions that involve symbolic death followed by a rebirth "to permit heightened awareness of self and other and to integrate the self into an adult world of responsibility" (242). This imagery is common in black songs and stories as well, Chandler points out.

In the 1980s, a number of commentators began to focus further on *Caged Bird* as part of the African American, and especially the African American female, autobiographical tradition. Regina Blackburn, for example, points out recurring themes in African American women's autobiography: coming to an understanding of the self, assigning value to the black self, and managing the difficulty of being both black and female. These writers take their experiences and respond in a variety of ways, Blackburn notes, from feeling helpless to being ready to put up an incredible fight to become the strongest, best self possible. As Blackburn observes, much of *Caged Bird* describes Angelou's self-loathing based on her appearance; her hatred of her appearance is intense in comparison to what is described in other works.

Selwyn R. Cudjoe, in her 1980s commentary on *Caged Bird* and other Angelou works, provides an explanation of the African American literary tradition. She points out, for example, that what is described in works of African American autobiography could be so horrific that the works' authenticity as nonfiction may be questioned. Additionally, she notes, whereas initially men were writing African

American autobiography and not clearly portraying African American women's lives, as these women started writing too, the extent of their unfortunate position was revealed. Cudjoe points out how *Caged Bird* shows these women's struggles not only against white oppression but also against black powerlessness and male prejudice. Angelou found it important not just to show the damage from external forces but also to examine the flaws of African Americans themselves within their own interpersonal relationships.

Sondra O'Neale, in an essay also written in the 1980s, describes the lack of understanding of the African American female. She argues that for African American women to achieve true liberation, they need realistic perspectives on who they are as well as role models to inspire them. O'Neale points out that *Caged Bird* fits these needs, stating that Angelou's "narrative was held together by controlled techniques of artistic fiction as well as by a historic-sociological study of Black feminine images seldom if ever viewed in American literature" (26). *Caged Bird*, then, in O'Neale's view, is not about Angelou but about the collective African American woman, who has powerful female ancestors, whose self can withstand what comes her way, who manages to create a new path for herself.

For Lucinda H. Mackethan, another critic writing on *Caged Bird* in the 1980s, what helps the young Marguerite become her true self are words. According to Mackethan, Marguerite's quest is for a name and words. Indeed, the book opens with Marguerite struggling to remember someone else's words at an Easter celebration. She succeeds in her quest as she gains greater exposure to words, through her brother, her mother, her teachers, and the slick men with whom her mother associates. As Mackethan explains, Marguerite's mother provides a strong example of how to prevail, not only because she appears fearless and forever resourceful but also because she has a storehouse of expressions that she puts to use as occasions arise, expressions that also proclaim her undaunted self. By the end of *Caged Bird*, Marguerite is a mother herself; she has withstood nearly her whole pregnancy on her own and now has an array of resources, some of which make it possible for her to use her own words to tell her story in *Caged Bird*.

Other critics have discussed the power of words in *Caged Bird* as well. Christine Froula discusses the history of women's missing voice, a voice that, in her view, has been purposefully suppressed by men. Froula draws on the story of *The Iliad*, in which the silencing of Helen is a crucial part of the epic. Froula also addresses Sigmund Freud's work with hysterics and how he cut off his own research on them, again silencing women's chance to be heard. In this case, the women whom Freud interviewed, Froula asserts, were not unlike the young Marguerite: they had been sexually abused by members of their families, usually their fathers. Froula describes how Angelou shows the silencing to which Marguerite subjected herself after she was raped and her assailant was killed. Froula also notes how when Angelou revealed the story years later, she upset the rules and showed an escape route from subjection.

The missing female African American voice is also the subject of Keneth Kinnamon's essay on *Caged Bird*, which compares Angelou's book to Richard Wright's *Black Boy* (1945). Kinnamon discusses Angelou's work as a response to Wright's, for, he points out, Angelou tells not just the story of blacks' subjection but also the methods blacks developed for managing in such an environment. Kinnamon remarks that Angelou and other female African American writers are more concerned than male African American authors about community, sexism, and interpersonal relationships, and he calls for a new criticism that acknowledges the concerns of both male and female African American writers.

Critic Susan Gilbert has stepped away from evaluating Angelou's work purely in an African American context. In a 1987 essay, she compares Angelou to other southern writers, particularly in regard to her ability to capture speech patterns. Additionally, Gilbert describes Angelou's work as fitting into the "long Western tradition of the *bildungsroman*" (104) and being somewhat of a combination of Western and

African American autobiographical traditions. Gilbert points out, however, that while Angelou insists on a positive vision of the black tradition, she does admit to having learned little about tenderness. Critics have remarked on the lack of notable men in Angelou's work, and while Angelou persists in her optimism about the power of the black female to transcend the most dire circumstances, in fact, most black women do not achieve this.

Joanne M. Braxton has also pointed out comparisons between *Caged Bird* and works that were not created by African Americans. She explains how, aside from fitting in with the slave narrative, *Caged Bird* was influenced by Russian works. Also, given that Angelou saw herself as part of the Great Migration (the black movement from the South to the urban North), Braxton compares the experience of those who were part of this movement to the experience of Europeans who emigrated to the United States and faced difficulties with their identities.

Françoise Lionnet has also compared *Caged Bird* with works that were not created by African Americans. More specifically, Lionnet states that Angelou owes part of her stylistic skill to her familiarity with such eighteenth- and nineteenth-century English narratives as those of Jonathan Swift, Daniel Defoe, and Charles Dickens. Lionnet also notes that Angelou took the religious tradition taught to her by her grandmother and turned it on its head. Further, Lionnet observes how Angelou's work deftly uses various elements of traditional oral narratives such as jokes, ghost stories, and fantasy. According to Lionnet, Angelou remains realistic in her depictions of people and their language, and she probably wrote *Caged Bird* with an educated white reader in mind.

The 1990s witnessed intensified scholarly and critical interest in Angelou's work, with critics continuing to examine how *Caged Bird* fits into literary traditions. In an essay published in 1990, for example, Dolly A. McPherson points out that black autobiographers usually protest against society for what they have had to endure yet manage to make their responses positive, partially by using humor and irony. McPherson praises in particular Angelou's use of comic irony when writing of interpersonal relationships. She notes that many other black authors, from Frederick Douglass to Toni Morrison, have used sympathetic irony in describing their relationships. She points out, however, that "Angelou's effective use of self-parody is something new in Black autobiography and, thus, creates a unique place in Black autobiographical tradition" (125). McPherson views Angelou's personality as one needing a "vital tension between stability and instability," and therefore her story is not the usual one of experience followed by a lesson and a moving forward (125).

Mary Vermillion has compared *Caged Bird* to *Incidents in the Life of a Slave Girl*, specifically analyzing how the author of each work handles the subject of rape. Because *Slave Girl* was published in 1861, its author, Harriet Jacobs, could not write as freely as Angelou could about her rape. Regardless of this fact, Vermillion notes, Angelou initially internalizes society's disdain of the female body and then grows to reject it, whereas Jacobs never accepts society's notions about the body, always seeing it as separate from her self. Vermillion observes that even though the two authors handle the topic of rape differently, there are similarities in how they fight racist body imagery. "In order to challenge racist stereotypes that associate black women with illicit sexuality," Vermillion states, "both writers obscure their corporeality in the early part of their texts by transforming the suffering connected with rape into a metaphor for the suffering of their race" (252).

Suzette A. Henke has compared *Caged Bird* with Maxine Hong Kingston's *The Woman Warrior* and Alice Walker's *The Color Purple*. Henke discusses "women's life-writing" rather than autobiography only, pointing out that there is an overlap between biography and the autobiographical or confessional novel, since biography has a narrative form that the author creates and the autobiographical or confessional novel contains individual and social history. These writings, Henke argues, are perfectly suited for bringing about revolution and liberation. Authors of such works "reinscribe the claims of feminine desire onto the text of a resistant patriarchal culture. In so doing, they begin to celebrate a maternal subculture that has long served as a fertile source for utopian visions of a feminized and egalitarian society" (211). In writing specifically about *Caged Bird*, Henke points out how African Americans traditionally are not overly distressed by out-of-wedlock births. The young, unmarried Angelou gets support when her family finds out about her pregnancy. As Henke observes, she "finally attains through her infant son much of the warmth and affection she desperately craved as an isolated young girl" (214).

Lyman B. Hagen has also written of how the birth of a son brought additional status to Marguerite, and Hagen points out how Marguerite's mother, Vivian, then gained status, too, by becoming a grandmother. While many critics have written about Angelou's feelings as a young girl toward her mother, Hagen goes a step further by pointing out that while Angelou suffers much as a result of being sent away from her mother and having no contact with her for a long time when she is very young, later in *Caged Bird* Angelou and her brother idolize their mother even when her mothering is lacking. This lack of condemnation, Hagen observes, seems to be a common element in all of Angelou's writing. *Caged Bird* is about overcoming and surviving, but, in Hagen's view, it is more about black American life. Angelou's "real purpose . . . is to illuminate and explain her race's condition by protesting against white misconceptions and legitimatizing the extremes sometimes required for survival" (72). Rather than chastising whites, Angelou presents the conditions black Americans endure and with which the reader can empathize.

Elizabeth Fox-Genovese reminds readers that in *Caged Bird*, Angelou the author is looking back on her life as a child and purposefully choosing certain events, ordering those events, and presenting a highly crafted perspective. Angelou relived her pain to present the story of a survivor. Fox-Genovese, like other critics, discusses the role of Mrs. Flowers in the young Angelou's life, and she makes a point of drawing attention to the fact that Mrs. Flowers not only helps the young girl learn about literature but also connects literature to young Angelou's black life in Stamps, Arkansas. Mrs. Flowers explains to the girl how a lack of a formal education does not mean a lack of wisdom and how the young Marguerite should not dismiss the oral culture of her black community.

Marion M. Tangum and Marjorie Smelstor point to how both Angelou and Zora Neale Hurston are concerned about memory and how both control the reader by using common visual techniques that provide immediacy but then use linguistic shifts to pull the reader away from that immediacy. According to Tangum and Smelstor, Angelou wants to ensure that the reader truly sees and is made uncomfortable by the painful situations she depicts. Likewise, Onita Estes-Hicks points out the similarities between Angelou's past and that of Hurston and comments on how Angelou writes of her years in the South as a time that created stability through community rituals. Angelou's grandmother's store gave the young Marguerite a key vantage point from which to observe African American life in the 1930s and to see "the mutual need, reciprocal respect, and shared compassion which oppression encouraged" (11).

Critics have also pointed out that Angelou is not content to work around prejudice but needs to confront it directly. Pierre A. Walker, for instance, discusses such confrontations in *Caged Bird*. He points out that the ultimate confrontation in the book occurs when Maya succeeds in becoming the first African American streetcar operator in San Francisco. Prior to this success, Angelou describes the more subtle rebellion that occurred during her graduation ceremony as well as a confrontation that occurred between her grandmother and a white dentist and the double-crossing that Daddy Clidell's friend inflicted on a white man. Walker notes that the young Marguerite imagined a different scenario at the dentist's office than the one that actually occurred and that this incident ties in with Angelou's overall views about resistance.

Fred Lee Hord has addressed how Marguerite's imagination brings her an escape from the subjection of the black experience. Hord describes how Marguerite embraces books and how Mrs. Flowers helps her to realize that fictional worlds create other places where she can be free from subjection. In these places, one can freely inhabit other lives; there are no restrictions. Although William Shakespeare is Marguerite's early love, she later sees how African American writers are "not only kindred souls in the free book world, but they enlarged the space in the real one by expanding the spirit until one felt the very power" (78).

Mrs. Flowers was one person outside Angelou's immediate family who had a profound effect on her, and Angelou attributes to such people her successful survival. Joanne Megna-Wallace explains how Angelou's grandmother, while strict and, in the young Marguerite's mind, overly religious, provided great security for the child and served as a surrogate mother. In fact, the young girl referred to her grandmother as "Momma." Others who helped Marguerite by providing security and affection were her brother, Bailey; her friend Louise; and her mother, Vivian Baxter; all of them, according to Megna-Wallace, combined with Marguerite's own strength and certain key events, contributed to her survival.

Some critics, however, have not seen Angelou's writing about her grandmother as so clearly positive. Mary Jane Lupton, for example, has noted that although Momma is the key adult in *Caged Bird*, the center of the black community because of her ownership of the general store and the "moral center" of the family, Marguerite has ambivalent feelings about her. Lupton points out that Momma has some money and therefore some possible leverage against the prejudiced whites, but she refuses to stand up to them—not because, in Momma's view, she is cowardly but because she is a realist.

Various critics have provided differing interpretations of the incident in which Momma brings her granddaughter to the dentist. For Lupton, Marguerite's fantastical description of what she wished would have happened is again indicative of her ambivalence and disappointment about her grandmother. "It would seem," Lupton states, "that

Maya is so shattered by her grandmother's reaction to Dentist Lincoln, so destroyed by her illusions of Annie Henderson's power in relationship to white people, that she compensates by reversing the true situation" (261).

The issue of security for the young Marguerite has also been explored by Daniel D. Challener. Whereas other critics have pointed to the strength and support Marguerite gains from people in her childhood, Challener notes that her experiences are also deeply unsettling. Marguerite and her brother are never told why they are being sent away from their divorcing parents, and they assume that they are being punished. Once they arrive in Arkansas, Angelou describes the pain of alienation and not fitting in. Challener points out that the townspeople leave her with the impression of being accepted but not deeply loved. He mentions some key elements in the opening scene of *Caged Bird*, in which Marguerite's lines at the Easter celebration reinforce her feelings of estrangement and the lack of permanence of her home in Stamps. Additionally, Challener comments on the fact that the lines she cannot remember are the ones that concern love. When Marguerite runs from the church in embarrassment, Challener points out, she does not run to her grandmother or to anyone else in the community. It is only later that the young girl gains a new perspective when she realizes that Mrs. Flowers has chosen her, sent for her even though she is not required to, and sent for her over Bailey.

Carol E. Neubauer compares Angelou to contemporary southern women writers. She explains that while the South holds nightmarish memories for African Americans, it also "represents a life-affirming force energized by a somewhat spiritual bond to the land itself. . . . it is here that ties to forebears whose very blood has nourished the soil are most vibrant and resilient" (116). Gina Wisker looks at *Caged Bird* from a larger, worldwide perspective, comparing the work to writings of Aboriginal women and Bessie Head, a South African writer. As Wisker and others have observed, *Caged Bird* is personal but also about the larger black experience. Whereas some critics have seen the book as written for a white audience, to let whites know what black life is like, Wisker argues that Angelou's purpose is to inspire others in similar predicaments toward self-empowerment. Wisker also quotes Angelou's own words about the struggles specific to the black artist:

> So the black writer, the black artist probably has to convince family and friends that what he or she is about is worthwhile. Now that is damned difficult when one comes from a family, an environment, a neighbourhood or a group of friends who have never met writers, who have only heard of writers, maybe read some poetry in school. (51)

Siphokazi Koyana and Rosemary Gray also examine *Caged Bird* in comparison to the work of a South African author, examining Angelou's life and autobiography alongside that of the South African Sindiwe Magona and her book *To My Children's Children*. Magona's work was published in 1990, much later than *Caged Bird*, and, as Koyana and Gray note, Magona and Angelou "have much in common, but ultimately bear an inverse relationship to each other" (85). More specifically, both live in a repressed place, but whereas Angelou struggles against the horrors of repression, Magona has nearly no contact with whites and lives a happy childhood. Angelou has no parents taking care of her when she is very young and suffers greatly as a result, whereas Magona has an extended family nearby and feels secure and loved. Koyana and Gray note that both young women become pregnant at a young age and that, for each, the experience is striking in nearly opposite respects: Angelou feels stronger and as if she has gained a new place in the mature world, whereas Magona, living in a culture that sees the pregnancy as taboo, feels that her world is falling apart and is married off to an unsuitable man.

Rather than comparing *Caged Bird* to other works, Yolanda M. Manora examines the interpretations of earlier writers on *Caged Bird* and finds some of them lacking. Most notably, Manora states that it is simplistic to see *Caged Bird*'s as the story of a girl's quest to find herself. Rather, Angelou rejects the roles that society sets out for black girls and women and instead "escapes stasis to become a subject in the perpetual process of forming and emerging" (374). Angelou does not arrive at a self in *Caged Bird* but will continue to change and grow, Manora argues. Similarly, Manora disagrees with some critics' comments on the strong women in *Caged Bird*. Rather than celebrating the women for their individual strengths, Manora observes, Angelou instead portrays them as flowing together. They, too, need not conform to certain images. As a result, Angelou "writes her way out of her own displacement and into a new narrative of black female subjectivity" (373).

Critics have commented on the various African American cultural elements that Angelou uses in *Caged Bird*, and Cherron A. Barnwell looks specifically at Angelou's use of the blues: "The blues shapes its form and content, and in using the blues aesthetic, Angelou meets the challenge of writing autobiography as literature" (48). Barnwell notes that the blues is about the black experience within America and is significant because its meaning is autobiographical. In the opening of *Caged Bird*, when Marguerite forgets her lines in church, Barnwell remarks on the immediacy of her words, "What you looking at me for?" and sees those as addressed not only to the other young black children in the church but also to the black readers of *Caged Bird*. These readers are called upon to remember what it was like to be a young black person sitting in church, and Angelou is encouraging them to sing their own blues. Barnwell also explains how the lines are actually like blues music in their structure and goes on to explain other similarities between the blues and *Caged Bird*.

Clarence Nero also points to the importance of music in *Caged Bird*. At Marguerite's graduation, the group singing together inspires hope in spite of the remarks of the prejudiced man who has spoken of the graduates' severely limited future. Nero notes how music also comes to Momma's aid when she is confronted by taunting white girls and must remain respectful. Song and music also get attention when Angelou describes a church revival. What is notable to the young girl is that, here, people of many different denominations have gathered together. Nero concludes that education, language, and community are what allow the black community to survive.

Angelou's work, African American writing in general, and American race relations may very well be heading into new territory with Barack Obama taking the helm as the first mixed-race president of the United States. There are still places in the United States where people of other races have no direct contact with African Americans, just as there are places where people have witnessed some of the most horrific treatment of African Americans. It is likely that writers like Angelou will continue to help enlighten generations to come, all the while inspiring readers with their insistence that something better awaits them and that, in the meantime, they can transcend present antagonisms.

Works Cited

Arensberg, Liliane K. "Death as Metaphor of Self in *I Know Why the Caged Bird Sings.*" *College Language Association Journal* 20.2 (1976): 273-91.

Barnwell, Cherron A. "Singin' de Blues, Writing Black Female Survival in *I Know Why the Caged Bird Sings.*" *Langston Hughes Review* 19 (Spring 2005): 48-60.

Blackburn, Regina. "In Search of the Black Female Self: African-American Women's Autobiographies and Ethnicity." *Women's Autobiography: Essays in Criticism.* Ed. Estelle C. Jelinek. Bloomington: Indiana University Press, 1980. 133-48.

Braxton, Joanne M. "A Song of Transcendence: Maya Angelou." *Black Women Writing Autobiography: A Tradition Within a Tradition.* Philadelphia: Temple University Press, 1989. 181-202.

Butterfield, Stephen. "Autobiographies of Black Women: Ida Wells, Maya Angelou, Anne Moody." *Black Autobiography in America.* Amherst: University of Massachusetts Press, 1974. 184-217.

Challener, Daniel D. "When a Whole Village Raises a Child: *I Know Why the Caged Bird Sings.*" *Stories of Resilience in Childhood.* New York: Garland, 1997. 21-51.

Chandler, Karen. "Funeral Imagery in Maya Angelou's *I Know Why the Caged Bird Sings,*" *Obsidian III* 1.1 (1999): 239-50.

Cudjoe, Selwyn R. "Maya Angelou and the Autobiographical Statement." *Black Women Writers (1950-1980): A Critical Evaluation*. Ed. Mari Evans. Garden City, NY: Anchor-Doubleday, 1984. 6-24.

Estes-Hicks, Onita. "The Way We Were: Precious Memories of the Black Segregated South." *African American Review* 27.1 (Spring 1993): 9-18.

Fox-Genovese, Elizabeth. "Myth and History: Discourse of Origins in Zora Neale Hurston and Maya Angelou." *Black American Literature Forum* 24.2 (Summer 1990): 221-36.

Froula, Christine. "The Daughter's Seduction: Sexual Violence and Literary History." *Signs: Journal of Women in Culture and Society* 11.4 (Summer 1986): 621-44.

Gilbert, Susan. "Maya Angelou's *I Know Why the Caged Bird Sings*: Paths to Escape." *Mount Olive Review* 1.1 (Spring 1987): 39-50.

Hagen, Lyman B. "The Autobiographies." *Heart of a Woman, Mind of a Writer, and Soul of a Poet: A Critical Analysis of the Writings of Maya Angelou*. Lanham, MD: University Press of America, 1997.

Henke, Suzette A. "Women's Life-Writing and the Minority Voice: Maya Angelou, Maxine Hong Kingston, and Alice Walker." *Traditions, Voices, and Dreams: The American Novel Since the 1960s*. Ed. Melvin J. Friedman and Ben Siegel. Newark: University of Delaware Press, 1995. 210-32.

Hillmann, Michael Craig. "*I Know Why the Caged Bird Sings*." *Masterpieces of African-American Literature*. Ed. Frank N. Magill. New York: HarperCollins, 1992. 214-17.

Hord, Fred Lee. "Someplace to Be a Black Girl." *Reconstructing Memory: Black Literary Criticism*. Chicago: Third World Press, 1991. 75-85.

Kelly, Ernece B. Review of *I Know Why the Caged Bird Sings*, by Maya Angelou. *Harvard Educational Review* 40.4 (1970): 681-82.

Kent, George E. "Maya Angelou's *I Know Why the Caged Bird Sings* and Black Autobiographical Tradition." *Kansas Quarterly* 7.3 (1975): 72-78.

Kinnamon, Keneth. "Call and Response: Intertextuality in Two Autobiographical Works by Richard Wright and Maya Angelou." *Belief Versus Theory in Black American Literary Criticism*. Ed. Joe Weixlmann and Chester J. Fontenot. Greenwood, FL: Penkevill, 1986. 121-34.

Koyana, Siphokazi, and Rosemary Gray. "Growing up with Maya Angelou and Sindiwe Magona: A Comparison." *English in Africa* 29.1 (May 2002): 85-98.

Lionnet, Françoise. "Con Artists and Storytellers: Maya Angelou's Problematic Sense of Audience." *Autobiographical Voices: Race, Gender, Self-Portraiture*. Ithaca, NY: Cornell University Press, 1989. 130-66.

Lupton, Mary Jane. "Singing the Black Mother: Maya Angelou and Autobiographical Continuity." *Black American Literature Forum* 24.2 (Summer 1990): 257-77.

Mackethan, Lucinda H. "Mother Wit: Humor in Afro-American Women's Autobiography." *Studies in American Humor* 4 (Spring/Summer 1985): 51-61.

Manora, Yolanda M. "'What You Looking at Me For? I Didn't Come to Stay': Displacement, Disruption, and Black Female Subjectivity in Maya Angelou's *I*

Know Why the Caged Bird Sings." *Women's Studies* 34.5 (July/Aug. 2005): 359-75.

McMurry, Myra K. "Role Playing as Art in Maya Angelou's *Caged Bird.*" *South Atlantic Bulletin* 41.2 (May 1976): 106-11.

McPherson, Dolly A. "The Significance of Maya Angelou in Black Autobiographical Tradition." *Order Out of Chaos: The Autobiographical Works of Maya Angelou.* New York: Peter Lang, 1990.

Megna-Wallace, Joanne. "The Journey to Maturity and Self-Esteem: A Literary Analysis of Maya Angelou's *I Know Why the Caged Bird Sings.*" *Understanding "I Know Why the Caged Bird Sings": A Student Casebook to Issues, Sources, and Historical Documents.* Westport, CT: Greenwood Press, 1998. 1-10.

Nero, Clarence. "A Discursive Trifecta: Community, Education, and Language in *I Know Why the Caged Bird Sings.*" *Langston Hughes Review* 19 (Spring 2005): 61-65.

Neubauer, Carol E. "Maya Angelou: Self and a Song of Freedom in the Southern Tradition." *Southern Women Writers: The New Generation.* Ed. Tonette Bond Inge. Tuscaloosa: University of Alabama Press, 1990. 114-42.

O'Neale, Sondra. "Reconstruction of the Composite Self: New Images of Black Women in Maya Angelou's Continuing Autobiography." *Black Women Writers (1950-1980): A Critical Evaluation.* Ed. Mari Evans. Garden City, NY: Anchor-Doubleday, 1984. 25-36.

Smith, Sidonie Ann. "The Song of a Caged Bird: Maya Angelou's Quest After Self-Acceptance." *Southern Humanities Review* 7.4 (Fall 1973): 365-75.

Tangum, Marion M., and Marjorie Smelstor. "Hurston's and Angelou's Visual Art: The Distancing Vision and the Beckoning Gaze." *Southern Literary Journal* 31.1 (Fall 1998): 80-96.

Vermillion, Mary. "Reembodying the Self: Representations of Rape in *Incidents in the Life of a Slave Girl* and *I Know Why the Caged Bird Sings.*" *Biography* 15.3 (Summer 1992): 243-60.

Walker, Pierre A. "Racial Protest, Identity, Words, and Form in Maya Angelou's *I Know Why the Caged Bird Sings.*" *College Literature* 22.3 (October 1995): 91-108.

Wisker, Gina. "Identity and Selfhood: The Fictionalised Autobiography—Maya Angelou." *Post-colonial and African American Women's Writing: A Critical Introduction.* Houndmills, Basingstoke, Hampshire: Palgrave Macmillan, 2000. 49-52.

The Matter of Identity in Maya Angelou's *I Know Why the Caged Bird Sings* and James Baldwin's *If Beale Street Could Talk*_____

Neil Heims

I

The problem of identity has been particularly knotty for African Americans and a recurrent theme for African American writers. Inside the context of the racism that has surrounded them since before the founding of the United States and that continues through the present, black Americans have been shaped by violent oppositions. From without, American society has historically been hostile to and denigrated black Americans; even the U.S. Constitution originally valued black slaves at three-fifths of a white person. From within, however, threatened yet vibrant black communities have formed and struggled to protect and assert themselves and allow their members to blossom in the face of a hostile larger society.

I Know Why the Caged Bird Sings tells what has become, by now, a familiar story of black life in the rural South and in urban ghettos during the 1930s. When the book was first published in 1970, this story was new. The 1960s were a decade of great social turbulence during which the black freedom movement recast both black and white racial identities. Oppressive institutions of segregation and discrimination were dismantled, but racial oppression was not entirely defeated; instead, it was frequently recast in new forms. *I Know Why the Caged Bird Sings* presents scenes from the lives of complex people whose identities are shaped inside an oppressive, terrifying, and absurd society that devalues their humanity. They are forced to conform within a society that defines them as inherently inferior. Still, at the same time, they are people who strive to transcend this conformity and live with some integrity. In her depictions of black communities of the 1930s, Maya Angelou presents people whose worlds exist inside a larger, racist world. They are always at its mercy, yet they are also a world apart from it within their own communities. Never free from the identity imposed on them by a racist world, they nevertheless have their own rich personal stories.

Despite how fresh the story told in *Caged Bird* was in 1970, the work's preoccupation with identity has a long history. Other African American writers, such as Nella Larsen (1891-1964), Richard Wright (1908-1960), Ralph Ellison (1914-1994), and James Baldwin (1924-1987), struggled with the problem of black identity before Angelou. Baldwin, in fact, brought the issue to the foreground in his 1961 collection of essays *Nobody Knows My Name*. In 1974, four years after *I Know Why the Caged Bird Sings* was published, Baldwin returned to it again in *If Beale Street Could Talk*. This novel has a special place as a complement to Angelou's memoir. Angelou wrote *I Know Why the Caged Bird Sings* with Baldwin's encouragement and drew on his insights into black namelessness. Like *Caged Bird*, *If Beale Street Could Talk* is also concerned with discovering and claiming one's identity under circumstances that challenge one's very right to have a self-defined identity. Its title comes from a street in Memphis that composers and musicians such as W. C. Handy, Louis Armstrong, Muddy Waters, and B. B. King made famous as the home of the blues during the early twentieth century. Baldwin's novel seeks to replicate the structure of blues music with a long first part that ecstatically evokes the characters' trials and a shorter second part that slowly and quietly leads the novel to an indefinite ending.

Baldwin's treatment of the problem of identity differs from Angelou's, however, in that his focus is not on the central characters of his book but on humankind as a whole. Unlike Angelou, who focuses on her characters' individuality, Baldwin writes about the fates of blacks and whites with regard to racism as a social institution. Further, in *If Beale Street Could Talk* racial oppression is socially embedded as well as a function of the legal system. While Angelou's memoir charts a world of possibilities discoverable in nature and in culture despite the oppressive conditions of racism, Baldwin's novel maps the topography of a world of obstacles. These obstacles created by racial hatred thwart Baldwin's characters' natures and test their identities.

II

In *I Know Why the Caged Bird Sings*, Angelou describes how the cotton pickers "would step out of the backs of trucks and fold down, dirt-disappointed, to the ground" when they came back from the cotton fields at the end of a long, debilitating day (10). They knew that "no matter how much they had picked it wasn't enough," and that they would never be able to pay off the debts they accumulated in the course of living their poor and difficult lives (10). Angelou recalls: "In later years I was to confront the stereotyped picture of gay song-singing cotton pickers with such inordinate rage that I was told even by fellow Blacks that my paranoia was embarrassing. But I had seen the fingers cut by the mean little cotton bolls, and I had witnessed the backs and shoulders and arms and legs resisting any further demands" (10).

It is not the singing Angelou repudiates—it is the distortion of the meaning of the singing, the misidentification of what the singing signifies. This singing is not happy-go-lucky. It is the kind of singing that Paul Laurence Dunbar described in his poem "Sympathy," from which Angelou took the title of her book:

> I know why the caged bird sings, ah me,
> When his wing is bruised and his bosom sore,—
> When he beats his bars and he would be free;
> It is not a carol of joy or glee,
> But a prayer that he sends from his heart's deep core,
> But a plea, that upward to Heaven he flings—
> I know why the caged bird sings! (15-21)

I Know Why the Caged Bird Sings is the story of Angelou's triumph over the inhumanity and oppression that she faced as a black girl in the rural South. It charts her intellectual, emotional, and social growth throughout her early years and the way in which she fashioned an identity that, although surrounded by racial oppression, managed to transcend it. Though the story concentrates on Angelou's younger self, it is told by an older, experienced narrator. The older Angelou commands the memories she recounts, even when the memories are of painful or shameful events that might have overwhelmed her. That they have not is a testament to her strength: she has achieved perspective and authority over them. Her art transforms the events and experiences of her life into a story of which she is in full command; she has made her story her own despite the fact that, in reality, an antipathetic, racist society was poised to dictate her story to her and, in consequence, to control her very identity.

I Know Why the Caged Bird Sings is a story about confronting violence, anger, and humiliation, and it is the story of a girl who could reasonably feel, "It was awful to be Negro and have no control over my life. It was brutal to be young and already trained to sit quietly and listen to charges brought [at her graduation by a white speaker] against my color" (176). It is no wonder she should feel, "We should all be dead" (176). The story opens in the cotton fields of the rural South in Stamps, Arkansas, where the narrator's grandmother owns and runs a general store. Life is poor, insecure, and communal. Angelou begins her memoir with a scene of herself, at around five or seven years old, standing in front of the congregation in church and nervously reciting, and forgetting, the words to an Easter rhyme that begins, "What you looking at me for?" That question appears as the first sentence of the book and, for the reader, its reference must initially be ambiguous. The words exist inside two separate contexts. The question is asked by the little girl to the church congregation as well as by the grown memoirist to her readers. A reader's answer must be, "Because you put yourself in front of me with this book, and I want to learn more about you." The reader's assumption is that Angelou's experiences have given her something to teach, that there is some wisdom to be gathered from her story. For the writer, the very fact of having a story indicates that, despite racist assumptions, she has a unique and valuable story and, thereby, an actual, valuable existence as a person.

From the congregation, however, the answer, as Marguerite felt it to be, is, "We are inspecting you, watching to see how you perform, how you present yourself, how you will falter." Both contexts reveal an essential insight into Angelou: she watches herself, she watches how people watch her, and she has a sense of herself as a performer who must satisfy a high level of expectation. It is not surprising that she became a dancer and an actor as well as a writer. Her sense of herself and the figure she presents are of real importance to her. One may guess that it underlies her power as a memoirist. She is confident and proud as she presents herself to her reader.

Standing in front of the congregation as a child, however, she is self-conscious and frightened. To the congregation, the question "What you looking at me for?" is posed with implicit self-loathing. Such loathing is a nearly inevitable response to the sense of inferiority that racism forced "Negroes" to internalize. When, as a child, Angelou looked at herself, she appeared to herself as a mistake. She lived with the torment of knowing that her "real" self was going unrecognized. One day, she imagines, everyone who assumed that she was a black girl would

> be surprised when . . . I woke out of my black ugly dream, and my real hair, which was long and blond, would take the place of the kinky mass that Momma wouldn't let me straighten. My light blue eyes were going to hypnotize them. . . . I was really white . . . a cruel fairy stepmother . . . understandably jealous of my beauty, had turned me into a too-big Negro girl, with nappy hair, broad feet and a space between her teeth that would hold a number-two pencil. (4)

This is a telling image. It conflates the gap-toothed girl who rejected herself with the writer who recovered herself, redeeming herself through writing. But, as a still self-conscious child, Angelou runs, escaping from the congregation's collective gaze by running to the toilet, trying unsuccessfully to hold her bladder until she reaches it. Still, this scene alludes to the independence Angelou will develop later in life despite her insecurity as a child. As Angelou writes, the pleasure of the evacuation trumps her anxiety about the punishment she knows is waiting for her—a whipping from her grandmother. In this way, the scene encapsulates how the story will trace Angelou's development from an unsure girl into a writer capable of shaping her own and her people's story, image, and history.

Aside from her independence, what also seems to save Angelou from the defeat inherent to resignation or despair is her anger. When she thinks, "We should all be dead," she includes whites as well as blacks. Her socially imposed self-hatred protectively expands to become anger at the entire species. "As a species," Angelou concludes at the graduation ceremony, "we were an abomination. All of us" (176). Still, her anger is tempered, informed, and given definition by a satirist's mockery. The species may well be an abomination, to her, but it is also a ridiculous abomination, a collection of fools acting out bizarre roles and conforming to lifeless stereotypes. In her disdain, there is a germ of strength, of a detachment that she can employ to free herself from the stereotyped identity imposed on her.

The first fact of someone's identity is his or her name, as James Baldwin notes in *Nobody Knows My Name*. When "powhitetrash"— what impoverished, undereducated, white dirt farmers were pejoratively called in the South—come into Angelou's grandmother's store, the writer notes that "they called my uncle by his first name and ordered him around the store." When she hears "the grimy, snotty-nosed girls" call her grandmother "Annie" rather than Mrs. Henderson, all Angelou can say in an aside to the reader is an aghast, "to Momma? Who owned the land they lived on? Who forgot more than they would ever learn?" (27-28). Further, this problem of identity is not limited to individuals' identities. The interdependence of Angelou's individual identity and the identity of her people is made explicit when Angelou describes the oppressive effect of the condescending white speaker at her eighth-grade graduation. "We were going to be made to look bad," she writes. "I distinctly remember being explicit in the choice of the pronoun. It was 'we' the graduating class, the unit that concerned me" (172). In finding her rightful name, then, Angelou contributes to asserting her community's rightful identity. The implicit and interwoven tasks Angelou sets about and accomplishes in *I Know Why the Caged Bird Sings* are to discover, reclaim, and proclaim her own identity and the communal, cultural identity of black people. She must teach herself to assert not only her own name but also that of the black community so that it can no longer be said that "nobody knows my name."

Angelou's first conscious encounter with the problem of her own identity comes when she is stripped of her own name. She is hired, at the age of ten or eleven, to help a black maid—the reader is told at first that her name is Glory—in the kitchen of a white woman, Mrs. Cullinan, in order to learn domestic service. Young Maya is impressed by the grandeur of the house and by its rigid orderliness, and she is sympathetic to her rather ugly and unpleasant mistress because she learns, from Glory, that Mrs. Cullinan is incapable of having children and, from her brother, Bailey, that Cullinan's husband is the father of a black woman's two children. Maya works diligently and cheerfully, but when she is serving Mrs. Cullinan and her ladies' circle one afternoon, one of her employer's friends declares that Maya's full name, Marguerite, is "too long. I'd never bother myself. I'd call her Mary if I was you" (104). These words, "I'd never bother myself," express the essence of racism: for this woman, Maya's name and identity are beneath consideration. She simply cannot be bothered to recognize a black person's humanity or individuality.

The young Maya soon learns that name loss is widespread. Glory, for instance, was born Hallelujah. She begins to wonder about the actual name of each maid she meets, and it infuriates her when Mrs. Cullinan starts calling her "Mary." Angelou ultimately attempts to take back her name through an act of sabotage. She deliberately drops a tray, letting Mrs. Cullinan's precious teacups shatter on the kitchen floor. When the woman who had advised her to substitute "Mary" for "Marguerite" hears Mrs. Cullinan's curses after the accident, she asks, "Was it Mary? Who did it?" In her fury, Mrs. Cullinan answers, "Her name's Margaret, goddamn it, her name's Margaret" (107-8). The outburst indicates that Mrs. Cullinan has realized that she has just paid for denying Maya's fundamental identity. Even so, she cannot get the name precisely right, saying "Margaret" instead of "Marguerite," indicating that she never bothered to hear the name rightly in the first place.

* * *

In the course of the remainder of the story, Angelou and her brother live with their mother and her mother's family in St. Louis. There Maya learns about urban degradation, family loyalty, violence, political power, and political corruption, and she is raped by her mother's male companion. She returns to Stamps for a few years, still bearing the injury of rape as guilt and near muteness, then she and Bailey are moved to San Francisco to live, again, with their mother. It is in California that Maya achieves the first real sense of herself as a person capable of expressing her own will, bearing her own responsibilities, and pursuing her own wishes. There, she frees herself from the identity imposed on her by racism. She comes to terms with her father, a vain, self-involved man, when she drives his car through the tortuous Mexico landscape back to California as he lies knocked out drunk in the back. She spends a month living in an automobile graveyard with a group of other stray kids around her age. And through unrelenting determination and unyielding persistence, she succeeds in getting a job as a cable car conductor—a job open to women but not to blacks—during World War II. Most significant, she undergoes a sexual identity crisis, becomes pregnant, and gives birth to a son.

Her liberation is the result of her struggle against racial restrictions. Living in a community with fewer racial restrictions than she faced in the South, she is able to assert her strong will to become self-determining and recover her identity. In the course of the memoir, Angelou leaves behind her identity as a helpless girl in a poor, rural setting to become a strong and rather self-sufficient young woman capable of asserting herself and negotiating the intricacies of the city. Her story transforms her from someone who is determined by circumstances into someone capable of playing a part in determining her own circumstances.

III

If Beale Street Could Talk displays a similar concern with identity. It begins, in fact, with naming and proclaiming names, indicating that the act of naming is one of establishing and securing an identity. Tish begins her narrative with the image of herself looking into a mirror and identifying herself to the reader. She then segues from her image to her name: "I know that I was christened Clementine, and so it would make sense if people called me Clem, or even . . . Clementine, since that's my name: but they don't. People call me Tish." When she begins, in the second paragraph, to talk about the young black man she is going to marry and who is the father of the child she is carrying, the instability and the importance of a name recur. "Today, I went to see Fonny. That's not *his* name either, he was christened Alonzo: and it might make sense if people called him Lonnie. But, no, we've always called him Fonny. Alonzo Hunt, that's his name. . . . But I only call him Alonzo when I have to break down some real heavy shit to him." When she goes on to say, "Today, I said, '—Alonzo—?'" the reader is forewarned that Tish has something important to tell him: that she is carrying his child (3).

As one who is going to give birth to the next generation and who is also confronting the obstacles faced by the people of her own generation, Tish represents the intersection of bitterness and joy, the place where the struggle between possibility and restriction is enacted. Like *I Know Why the Caged Bird Sings*, *If Beale Street Could Talk* is concerned with characters who must define themselves and establish their identities within a social system that denies their value and autonomy.

Whereas, as a memoir, *I Know Why the Caged Bird Sings* ought to be read as a true account of Maya Angelou's lived experience, *If Beale Street Could Talk* is a novel, an account of imaginary events narrated by an invented character. The novel's truth lies not in a set of particulars but in the authenticity of the world these particulars create.

Like *I Know Why the Caged Bird Sings*, *If Beale Street Could Talk* is a first-person narrative. The driving forces of the two narratives differ, however. Because *I Know Why the Caged Bird Sings* is a memoir, told by a narrator who has survived, the story is not propelled by suspense. After all, no matter how harrowing the events recounted, the reader knows the narrator has survived. The memoir thus concerns itself with how something was achieved rather than what ultimately happens. The narrative, in consequence, is linear and progressive. It is a story of growth, of a chronological sequence of events that grow out of qualities in the narrator and her environment. In Maya Angelou's case, the unyielding rectitude and strictness of her grandmother, the support of her brother, the mentoring of Bertha Flowers, the world-wisdom of her mother, the spirit of her people, and even the benign neglect of her vain father all congeal in her to become the rock on which her strength is founded. The very narrative trajectory makes hers a story of hopefulness. *If Beale Street Could Talk*, in contrast, is driven by suspense, the question of what will happen. Throughout the course of the novel, this suspense shifts from being focused on the central characters to being concentrated on humankind as a whole, for Baldwin is concerned with the consequences of racism for everyone, not just his characters.

IV

If Beale Street Could Talk begins in the middle of the events it recounts, much in the same way that classical epics like *The Odyssey* begin. The novel is thus the epic story, the odyssey, of a young black man and those close to him as they navigate the obstacles to adulthood that racism creates. The story unfolds as Tish reveals its various events, not in a strict chronological sequence but rather like disjointed pieces of a puzzle that, when put together, begin to form a complex picture. Tish brings the reader into a world composed of black families as well as into the world of a racist penal system. Although the story is set in New York City during an era of ostensible integration rather than the racially segregated rural South or wartime San Francisco, *If Beale Street Could Talk* shows the same landscape of rejection and humiliation that Angelou describes in *I Know Why the Caged Bird Sings*. Society is no more congenial to black people in Baldwin's New York City than it is in Angelou's memoir, and, moreover, it has grown more complicated and alienated. The novel's two principal characters, Tish and Fonny, are individuals as well as representatives of the black struggle for identity and life within a racist society. Like Angelou, Tish must negotiate the outer world to find and nurture hope, in this case in the form of her fiancé Fonny, an artist who relies on some inner prompting to achieve his and humankind's fuller identity.

The first time the reader sees Tish and Fonny together, she is visiting him in jail, where a plate of glass separates them. In *I Know Why the Caged Bird Sings*, oppression is part of the social fabric, but a strong, organic black community exists, even if the members of this community lead precarious lives. Marguerite is protected and disciplined by her grandmother and her uncle, and in her brother she has someone she deeply loves. Her mother turns out to be a decent woman and a caring, wise parent for her daughter. After Marguerite's ordeal in St. Louis, Bertha Flowers gives her cookies and lemonade and introduces her to books.

In *If Beale Street Could Talk*, the black community is fractured. Even after the height of the Civil Rights movement, Baldwin's New York, paradoxically, is less nurturing to his characters than Angelou's pre-civil rights South. Despite, or perhaps because of, the overt, institutional, and socially sanctioned racism of the South in the 1930s, the black community was strong, as Angelou shows in her descriptions of Christian revival meetings, the congregations of black people at her grandmother's store, the graduation exercise, and countless other times when members of the community came together and offered one another aid.

Baldwin's New York has much more in common with Angelou's St. Louis, a model of alienation where, despite its urban environment, the students are far less educated than the students in Stamps. Whereas the size of Stamps helped build a cohesive and coherent black community where teachers knew and cared about their students, the communities in St. Louis and New York are alienated and fragmented. Baldwin shows how the random contact between the races, even in an environment with no legally enforced segregation, is still fraught with danger for black people. In New York, racist attitudes are still psychically present, particularly among the police, and racism still operates systematically, even if not legally, inside the penal system.

Fonny is being held in the Tombs, a Manhattan jail, as he awaits trial for a rape he did not commit but of which he is accused simply because of a white police officer's resentment of him. The central concern of the plot is whether Fonny can be gotten out of jail. Whereas Angelou's memoir charts a world of possibilities that can be realized despite the oppression of racism, Baldwin's novel maps the topography of a world of obstacles. The obstacles created by racism oppose the identities and cultures of Baldwin's characters and test their love and their very sense of themselves. The black characters live in a society that brutalizes them and sabotages their attempts to assert outwardly the identities they know to be their own. It is, in the world of Baldwin's novel, the next thing to a miracle that Fonny has grown into the sweet-tempered artist he is. His identity is his own, although he can keep it only through psychic struggle, given that this identity is always under siege. Still, Fonny is an artisan; his art gives him the strength to retain his identity and resist the dehumanizing effects of racism. His identity is formed by and contingent on his own vocation and the support of

Tish, her family, and his father. Like Angelou, Fonny finds his actuality in his art.

Ultimately, *If Beale Street Could Talk* is a social novel that uses the lives of its characters to illuminate the nature of the world they are made to inhabit. The novel is not really about these characters as people but about the world in which they and the novel's readers live. Fonny is an ideal established to show how society limits life's possibilities as well as how these possibilities may still may be kept alive through stubborn integrity and community. Tish's heroic stamina makes her an ideal, too, as it shows how one can stand up to adversity. Many of the other characters represent ways of coping with being defined as people whose names do not matter. Even Fonny's mother and sisters are drawn in such a way as to show that their disdain of Fonny is, in large part, a response to their racial plight.

The suspense that propels the plot of *If Beale Street Could Talk* disappears in the novel's final paragraph, not because Fonny's fate is clearly revealed but because the narrative refuses to make any closure. Baldwin ends the novel with a kind of narrative ambiguity. The novelist and critic Joyce Carol Oates, in a review of *If Beale Street Could Talk* written for *The New York Times*, states that "at the novel's end, Fonny is out on bail, his trial postponed indefinitely, neither free nor imprisoned but at least returned to the world of the living." This may or may not be so. The last direct reference to Fonny's fate is indefinite. As Tish recounts, "Hayward arranges the possibility of bail for Fonny. But it is high" (236). It is left unknown whether this possibility becomes an actuality, and there is no word about Fonny's trial or its outcome.

Without any introduction or explanation, Fonny appears in the final paragraphs of the novel. There has been nothing in the paragraph preceding it to prepare for his *actual*, as opposed to his imaginary, presence. In the novel's penultimate paragraph, Tish begins to say something to her mother, but she is overwhelmed by the onset of labor. "When I opened my mouth, I couldn't catch my breath. Everything disappeared, except my mother's eyes. . . . Then, all I could see was

Fonny. And then I screamed, and my time had come" (241). Fonny is present to Tish as she falls into semiconsciousness.

In the final paragraph, "Fonny is working on the wood, on the stone, whistling, smiling. And from far away, but coming nearer, the baby cries and cries and cries and cries and cries and cries and cries and cries and cries, cries like it meant to wake the dead" (242). It is not clear whether Fonny's presence is actual or imagined. "Fonny . . . working on the wood, on the stone, whistling, smiling" may not actually be Fonny but a vision of Fonny that Tish sees in her postdelivery sleep as the cries of the newborn penetrate her consciousness. Despite the grim present that impinges on the possibilities of his characters, in *If Beale Street Could Talk* Baldwin offers a story that is as much a triumph as Angelou's. Angelou shows how she has made a place for herself in the world on her own terms. Fonny and Tish are characters whom Baldwin endows with the strength to know what their own terms are—dignity, equality, and liberty—and to remain steadfast in their dedication to them. Even inside a wider world that has yet to grant them a rightful place in it, Tish can give birth to a baby and Fonny can labor to be the artist and man he is as well as to recover the name that has been taken from him.

Works Cited

Angelou, Maya. *I Know Why the Caged Bird Sings*. 1970. London: Little, Brown, 1984.

Baldwin, James. *If Beale Street Could Talk*. New York: Signet, 1974.

_____. *Nobody Knows My Name: More Notes of a Native Son*. 1961. New York: Vintage, 1992.

Dunbar, Paul Laurence. *The Collected Poetry of Paul Laurence Dunbar*. Ed. Joanne M. Braxton. Charlottesville: University of Virginia Press, 1993.

Oates, Joyce Carol. Review of *If Beale Street Could Talk*, by James Baldwin. *The New York Times* 19 May 1974.

"The Only Teacher I Remembered":
Schools, Schooling, and Education in Maya Angelou's *I Know Why the Caged Bird Sings*_____
Robert C. Evans

Education is obviously an important theme in Maya Angelou's autobiography *I Know Why the Caged Bird Sings*. Indeed, the book has often been interpreted as a bildungsroman—a "'novel of education' or a 'coming-of-age' story" that traces the growth of a young protagonist (Lupton 30). The mere fact that the text traces the physical, psychological, and social growth of two main characters (Maya and her brother, Bailey) from early childhood to late adolescence almost guarantees that the book involve a wide variety of learning from many different kinds of sources, including parents, teachers, other adults, and even other children. Sometimes the instruction is deliberate and explicit; at other times it is inadvertent and merely implied. Adults often teach children lessons that are far more significant than they intend them to be, and sometimes these lessons (as in the rape of Maya by her mother's boyfriend, Mr. Freeman) are unpleasant or even ugly.[1] In any case, Maya learns a great deal as she moves through the book, and so do her readers.

Almost inevitably (given the ages of Maya and Bailey), schools are important sites of instruction in this story, and formal schooling is a recurring theme, though one that has been relatively neglected by critics.[2] Schools of various sorts are either mentioned briefly or described at length throughout the text, from its earliest pages to its very last. References to Sunday school and to other sorts of church instruction, for instance, appear throughout the book, as do many references to teachers and educational administrators. Yet the themes of schooling and of schools themselves—of secular instruction conducted in places deliberately set aside for formal learning—have not received much attention in discussions of *I Know Why the Caged Bird Sings*. This is surprising, given that schools provide key settings throughout the book and that the people and events encountered in schools are so significant to the development of both the protagonist and the plot. Indeed, education has long been valued in the African American community. As Clarence Nero has pointed out,

> Slave masters understood that "knowledge is power," and through communication access to the world is gained. They therefore denied slaves the right to available forms of education. The canon of black literature responded by making education an important symbol affirming the black identity and demonstrating black intelligence and ability to survive within American culture. (63)

For a variety of reasons, Angelou's emphasis on schools and on formal schooling helps contribute to the appeal and effectiveness of her story. In the first place, most readers are instantly able to relate to her descriptions of schools and schooling, since they themselves have been through a lengthy educational process. Nearly all readers of Angelou's book, then, are likely to find many points of contact between the experiences described in the book and experiences in their own lives. Readers are also likely to be interested in both the similarities and the differences between Maya's experiences at school and their own, and the fact that the book is set in an increasingly remote past only enhances the appeal of Angelou's descriptions of what schools and schooling were like for a young black person in the 1930s and 1940s. Many readers are likely to be as intrigued by the contrasts with their own, more recent experiences with education as they are by the obvious points of similarity.

Almost by definition, schools are among the most crucial influences in a child's development, and certainly this is true of the Maya depicted in Angelou's work. For practically everyone in American culture, school provides the first extended—and extensive—contact with persons beyond the immediate family; schools are among the places where individuals first encounter a larger world outside the home. That world is inevitably far more diverse and challenging than the literally familiar environment provided by parents, grandparents, and siblings, and experiences at school are often crucial in shaping the ways people interact with others for the rest of their lives. Teachers can often function (or fail to function) as substitute parents; whether for good or for ill, they are highly influential adult role models whose impacts on their students' later lives are often far more significant than either students or teachers are likely to realize at the time of their contact.

Schooling, meanwhile, is part of a common experience of initiation into expanding responsibilities at each stage of our development, and our relations with our classmates often become at least as important as (and sometimes even more important than) our relations with our immediate families. Schools are places where we make friends and make enemies; they are places where we both cooperate and compete. In them, we learn not only from adults but also from our peers, and they are places where some of the most enduring traits of our personalities are shaped and reinforced. Success or failure in school—whether defined in academic, athletic, or social terms—often crucially affects our success or failure later in life. For these reasons and many others, then, it seems worthwhile to examine the numerous ways in which schools and schooling help affect the structure, characterization, and meanings of Angelou's autobiography.

I

One of the very first references to a school in *I Know Why the Caged Bird Sings* occurs in the opening paragraphs of the second chapter. Here, Angelou describes how she and Bailey would do their math homework in the presence of Uncle Willie while all three sat inside the small country store owned by Maya's grandmother (known as Momma). Angelou reports that she and Bailey would speedily "rattle off the times tables" while their uncle would listen to them "testify to the Lafayette County Training School's abilities" (10). School and schooling, in this instance as so often elsewhere, is part of the bond that tightly ties together Maya and Bailey; it is part of a crucial shared experience that links them throughout their childhood and adolescence. Their experiences at school both bind them together (since both are genuinely devoted to learning) and set them apart—from the other students, who take school less seriously than they do, as well as from adults like Uncle Willie, whose own school days are far in the past.

In this very early reference to schooling, then, Angelou begins developing several important motifs that she will flesh out in the rest of the book. These motifs include the special relationship between Maya and Bailey, the unusual commitment each child has to learning, and the real learning that takes place even in the most rural, remote, disadvantaged, and segregated schools. Maya and Bailey take genuine pride in their school, and that pride is key to the self-respect both of them develop and display, both in themselves and in their racial community, not only early in the text but also throughout the book.

Maya learns more from school, however, than merely the rules of multiplication or other forms of book knowledge. She quickly begins to realize that educators—even black educators—live relatively privileged lives. They often think of themselves, and are often thought of by others, as superior to most other African Americans, especially the working poor. Thus at one point Maya returns from school to find Uncle Willie engaged in conversation with two black schoolteachers, who have pulled off the road to buy soft drinks at the country store, and sees that he is pretending he is not disabled (11-13). The fact that the visitors are teachers gives them a superior social status and thus helps explain Uncle Willie's desire to appear physically "normal" in their presence.

This connection between formal education and superior social status is reiterated frequently throughout the book. A little later, Angelou describes a black neighbor, Mr. McElroy, as "the only Negro I knew, except for the school principal and the visiting teachers, who wore matching pants and jackets" (20). Even at this early age, however, Maya is as often inclined to challenge any kind of superficial or presumed superiority as to respect it, as she shows when she immediately remarks, "When I learned that men's clothes were sold like that and called suits, I remember thinking that somebody had been very bright, for it made men look less manly, less threatening and a little more like women" (20-21). As this comment shows, teachers, like most adults in the story, do not instantly win Maya's respect, no matter how much they may try to compel it through dress, talk, or behavior. Like everyone else in the book, teachers must *earn* Maya's respect, and (as will be seen) the teachers who often impress her most are the ones who least obviously try to be impressive.

One passage that most clearly implies the connection between formal education and elevated social status occurs in chapter 10, in which Angelou describes the pretentious teachers she encounters when she and Bailey temporarily relocate from rural Stamps, Arkansas, to the big city of St. Louis, Missouri. Ironically, the schools, students, and teachers in the city quickly prove disappointing and even academically inferior to the ones Maya knew in Stamps. The teachers in particular teach vivid lessons—ones that they probably do not intend to impart:

St. Louis teachers . . . tended to act very siditty, and talked down to their students from the lofty heights of education and whitefolks' enunciation. They, women as well as men, all sounded like my father with their *ers* and *errers*. They walked with their knees together and talked through tight lips as if they were as afraid to let the sound out as they were to inhale the dirty air that the listener gave off. (64)

These are not the sort of educators, black or white, whom Maya values, as later passages also show. They are people who take themselves too seriously—people who use their knowledge and social status to intimidate others. Instead of exhibiting or inspiring the kind of genuine love of learning that both Maya and Bailey display independently throughout the book, these teachers give formal education a bad name and discourage their best students from wanting to emulate them. Instead of acting as admirable role models, they appear as representatives of a distant, uncaring, and condescending power structure. Ironically, their very pretentiousness implies their own fundamental insecurity; their need to mimic "whitefolks' enunciation" suggests that they are literally uncomfortable in their own skins. They move and speak so awkwardly because they lack the kind of easy self-confidence that Bailey, for instance, has in abundance. Maya learns from teachers like these, but she learns, mainly, not to want to follow in their inhibited, inhibiting footsteps.

Part of the further irony of Maya's educational experiences in St. Louis involves the inferiority of the students she encounters there as well as the quality of education these students are receiving from their pretentious teachers. When she and Bailey arrive from rural Stamps, it quickly becomes apparent that they are far more talented and better prepared than most of their big-city peers:

> When we enrolled in Toussaint L'Ouverture Grammar School, we were struck by the ignorance of our schoolmates and the rudeness of our teachers. Only the vastness of the building impressed us; not even the white school in Stamps was as large.
>
> The students, however, were shockingly backward. Bailey and I did arithmetic at a mature level because of our work in the Store, and we read well because in Stamps there wasn't anything else to do. We were moved up a grade because our teachers thought that we country children would make our classmates feel inferior—and we did. Bailey would not refrain from remarking on our classmates' lack of knowledge. At lunchtime in the large gray concrete playground, he would stand in the center of a crowd of big boys and ask, "Who was Napoleon Bonaparte?" "How many feet make a mile?" It was infighting, Bailey style. (63)

This passage efficiently illustrates many of the ways in which references to schools contribute to the characterization and key motifs of Angelou's narrative. Any school, of course, is deliberately and inevitably a site of competition, and Maya and Bailey are bonded by their shared sense of superiority not only to the Stamps students but especially to the St. Louis students. Their academic skills allow them to feel less alienated and less insecure in the new city than they might have felt otherwise; their academic talent gives them a self-confidence they might not otherwise have possessed, especially as poor rural blacks. Their skills win them the respect of adults (even if those adults themselves are not especially worthy of respect), and those same skills elevate their status among their peers.

One of the most interesting aspects of this passage, however, is how little credit it gives to the school in Stamps, or any specific teachers there, for the academic excellence Maya and her brother display. Early in the book, Maya and Bailey both express pride in their rural school when talking in front of Uncle Willie (10), but in the passage quoted above their arithmetical skill is attributed to their "work in the Store," while they are said to read well "because in Stamps there wasn't anything else to do." No particular teacher in Stamps stands out as especially memorable in Angelou's mind; no particular classroom experience (at least none focused on actual teaching or learning) is ever given much emphasis. Instead, the Stamps school is depicted mainly as a place where Maya and Bailey interact with each other, with their friends, and with their antagonists, as in an episode that takes place on Valentine's Day (142-46).

For the most part, Angelou places little emphasis on the actual instruction or learning that occurs at school, either in Stamps or in St. Louis, nor does she remember any specific teachers in either place with any special fondness. Indeed, Miss Williams, the teacher described in the Valentine's Day episode in Stamps, sounds at least as pretentious and self-important as any Maya encountered in St. Louis: after opening the students' valentine cards and reading them aloud, Miss Williams is said to have "smirked" as she mocked the phrasing of one card. Maya tunes out the rest of the teacher's condescending comments by quoting them as follows: "blah, blah, blooey, blah" (145). Few actual, professional teachers impress Maya anywhere in *I Know Why the Caged Bird Sings* (although an important exception will be discussed later), and few actual schools in the book make much of a deep, positive impression on her. Inevitably, of course, she and Bailey learn a great deal from all their various encounters with schools, with teachers, and with other students, but often the lessons they learn are not especially positive.

II

This emphasis on the less appealing aspects of structured education is especially obvious in chapter 23, which describes at length one of the most important and memorable of all of Maya's experiences with formal schooling. This chapter vividly re-creates a sense of the importance a local school could have in a small rural town, especially as the graduation ceremony draws near. Once again, Angelou's emphasis is less on teaching and learning themselves than on the school as the site of a central social ritual, a crucial rite of passage involving the whole community. Hierarchies among the students are established, enacted, and reaffirmed (169-70), and indeed even "teachers were respectful of the now quiet and aging seniors, and tended to speak to them, if not as equals, as beings only slightly lower than themselves" (170). The students and faculty are depicted as behaving at graduation time "like an extended family" (170), and that sense of familiarity and togetherness extends to (and involves) Stamps as a whole. Nowhere else in the text does Angelou describe more precisely—or at greater length—the appearance of the Stamps school or the conduct and interactions of the teachers, the students, and the students' families than when she describes the preparations for graduation (170-77). Indeed, nowhere else in the narrative are any experiences with formal schooling detailed so extensively.

Chapter 23 is in many ways the crucial episode in Angelou's various depictions of schools and schooling, and that is why the irony of this episode is so stunning and painful. During what should be the highlight of young Maya's educational career up to that point, a high-ranking white educational administrator, a guest speaker from out of town named Mr. Donleavy, spoils the day by addressing the assembled students, teachers, and community members in highly condescending and patronizing terms. After detailing the educational improvements planned for a local white high school, he implies that the main function of Maya's school is merely to train potential athletes. "The white kids," Angelou comments, "were going to have a chance to become Galileos and Madame Curies and Edisons and Gauguins, and our boys (the girls weren't even in on it) would try to be Jesse Owenses and Joe Louises" (179). The effect of Donleavy's words on the assembled audience of blacks is instantly demoralizing:

> Graduation, the hush-hush magic time of frills and gifts and congratulations and diplomas, was finished for me before my name was called. The accomplishment was nothing. The meticulous maps, drawn in three colors of ink, learning and spelling decasyllabic words, memorizing the whole of *The Rape of Lucrece*—it was for nothing. Donleavy had exposed us.
> We were maids and farmers, handymen and washerwomen, and anything higher that we aspired to was farcical and presumptuous. (180)

Ironically, then, the most important event in Maya's formal education up to this point is spoiled by a professional educator, and there may be even further irony, since Donleavy may actually be sincerely well intentioned but have no idea of the devastating impact of his words. It is possible, of course, that he is deliberately and consciously racist, but the bitter paradox of the scene is even stronger if we assume that he actually means well. In fact, as a politician running for election and seeking black votes (181), it is not in his pragmatic interest to insult his audience intentionally, and so his speech seems consciously (if paradoxically) designed to curry favor. In any case, his words unleash what may be Maya's darkest and most bitter thoughts in the book. Indeed, Liliane K. Arensberg calls Maya's response here "far and away the most dramatic instance" of a "revenge theme" that appears in the text (119). Maya wishes not only that Donleavy himself might die but that all whites, all blacks, and indeed all humans might be violently exterminated (180-81). Her response to Donleavy is far more angry and vehement than her reaction, for instance, to Mr. Freeman, the man who raped her, for whom she actually felt a kind of pity. No one else in the book provokes the kind of bitterness and disgust in Maya—the blatant and unmitigated hatred, not only for him but for herself and for all of humanity—that Donleavy provokes.

The fact that Donleavy is a professional educational administrator, whose job is to promote the welfare of children and set a good example for them, makes Maya's reaction all the more powerfully ironic. Donleavy teaches a powerful and memorable lesson and makes a vivid, long-lasting impact, but all in ways he probably never intended. He leaves the auditorium before the ceremony ends, but the bad taste he leaves behind sticks with Maya forever. As Mary Jane Lupton notes, Donleavy helps make Maya regard her school—at least for the moment—as a kind of prison (66). Moreover, as Joanne Megna-Wallace observes, disagreement among African Americans regarding the aims of people like Donleavy was hardly unusual at the time (66).

Fortunately, all is not lost, thanks in part to the inspired response of Henry Reed, the young black student who had been selected to give the valedictory address. That address, which he had long been rehearsing, is based on Hamlet's "To Be or Not to Be" soliloquy, and, as Maya half listens to it, she is disgusted by the ironies it now seems to contain. Suddenly, however, Henry begins singing (and leading the crowd in singing) the inspiring hymn "Lift Ev'ry Voice and Sing," known as the Negro national anthem (183). Maya remarks: "Every child I knew had learned that song with his ABC's and along with 'Jesus Loves Me This I Know.' But I personally had never heard it before. Never heard the words, despite the thousands of times I had sung them. Never thought they had anything to do with me" (183). A teacher brings the kindergartners up onto the stage, and they, too, join in the song, along with all the assembled students, instructors, and adults from the community.

Significantly, teachers do have an important and positive role in this inspiring episode: teachers have taught the song to their students, a teacher leads the smallest children in singing it, and teachers are part of the larger crowd who sing along. At the very end of the chapter, however, when Angelou credits various black men and women for helping to sustain the spirit of her beleaguered race over the decades and centuries, teachers, as a specific group, are not mentioned: "If we were a people much given to revealing secrets, we might raise monuments and sacrifice to the memories of our poets, but slavery cured us of that weakness. It may be enough, however, to have it said that we survive in exact relationship to the dedication of our poets (include preachers, musicians and blues singers)" (184). Poets, preachers, musicians, and blues singers—these are the types of individuals Angelou praises for helping her people survive. All, of course, are teachers in a sense, but they are not professional educators. Indeed, in chapter 23 the most powerful of all the professional educators depicted is, unfortunately, pompous and racist, and neither the black principal nor any of the black teachers is capable of standing up to him or teaching him any kind of memorable lesson. Thus, in the one chapter in the book set almost entirely at school and featuring a crucial educational event, school seems, ironically, a far from appealing or satisfying place.

III

The same kind of disappointment with formal education seems apparent, at least initially, when Maya and her brother move away from Stamps and transfer to a large urban school, George Washington High School, in San Francisco. Suddenly, Maya, who has been an accomplished and self-confident student for most of her life, feels uneasy and intimidated:

In the school itself I was disappointed to find that I was not the most brilliant or even nearly the most brilliant student. The white kids had better vocabularies than I and, what was more appalling, less fear in the classrooms. They never hesitated to hold up their hands in response to a teacher's question; even when they were wrong they were wrong aggressively, while I had to be certain about all my facts before I dared to call attention to myself. (216)

Angelou's phrasing here is significant: the most "appalling" thing is not that the whites know more words (Maya could always catch up in that respect) but that they have a greater inherent sense of self-worth, just because they are white. The latter advantage is rooted not in their knowledge but in their race, and it is an advantage Maya is not sure she can overcome.

Significantly, however, Maya now meets the one professional educator in the entire book who really seems to stimulate and inspire her, and, ironically, that teacher is not someone close to her in age or personal experience or even a member of her own race. Rather, she is an elderly white spinster. Further ironies quickly accumulate: the teacher, known simply as "Miss Kirwin," wins Maya's respect and affection not by displaying affection herself or by showing any particular personal interest in or encouragement toward Maya (or anyone else, for that matter) but by being utterly impersonal and dispassionate. Her focus is less on her students than on the material she imparts: "Miss Kirwin was that rare educator who was in love with information. I will always believe that her love of teaching came not so much from her liking for students but from her desire to make sure that some of the things she knew would find repositories so that they could be shared again" (216). Paradoxically, it is this somewhat remote and forbidding woman who earns Maya's lifelong devotion. Maya even calls her "my Miss Kirwin" and describes her as "a brilliant teacher" (216), praise she lavishes on no other educator in the book.

Kirwin's teaching methods might strike some contemporary readers as stiff, formal, and remote, but they quickly win Maya's admiration, partly because Kirwin treats her students with the same dignity she both demands and displays:

> She greeted each class with "Good day, ladies and gentlemen." I had never heard an adult speak with such respect to teenagers. (Adults usually believe that a show of honor diminishes their authority.) "In today's *Chronicle* there was an article on the mining industry in the Carolinas [or some such distant subject]. I am certain that all of you have read the article. I would like someone to elaborate on the subject for me."
>
> After the first two weeks in her class, I, along with all the other excited students, read the San Francisco papers, *Time* magazine, *Life* and everything else available to me. (217)

Kirwin, without knowing it, functions in Angelou's book as the antitype of, and antidote to, Donleavy. Whereas Donleavy demeans his audience even as he tries to curry favor with them, Kirwin treats everyone with absolutely equal respect and is in love with her subject, not with herself. She is impressed by facts, not by her own status; in this she differs not only from Donleavy but also from many of Maya's previous teachers—even (or especially) the ones who were well intentioned and black. Kirwin feels no need to make an impression. Paradoxically, however, precisely because she feels no such need, the impression she makes is striking and permanent:

> There were no favorite students. No teacher's pets. If a student pleased her during a particular period, he could not count on special treatment in the next day's class, and that was as true the other way around. Each day she faced us with a clean slate and acted as if ours were clean as well. Reserved and firm in her opinions, she spent no time in indulging the frivolous.
>
> She was stimulating instead of intimidating. Where some of the other teachers went out of their way to be nice to me—to be a "liberal" with me—and others ignored me completely, Miss Kirwin never seemed to no-

tice that I was Black and therefore different. I was Miss Johnson and if I had the answer to a question she posed I was never given any more than the word "Correct," which was what she said to every other student with the correct answer.

Years later when I returned to San Francisco I made visits to her class-room. She always remembered that I was Miss Johnson, who had a good mind and should be doing something with it. I was never encouraged on those visits to loiter or linger about her desk. She acted as if I must have had other visits to make. I often wondered if she knew she was the only teacher I remembered. (217-18)

"The only teacher I remembered"—striking words in a lengthy book full of references to schools and schooling. Those words, of course, are not entirely accurate, at least if taken literally, since Angelou does remember or describe various other educators, for a va-riety of reasons, some good, many bad. Indeed, within a few sentences of the one just quoted, she mentions favorably—but not by name—a "forceful and perceptive" teacher of drama who "quickly and unceremoniously separated me from melodrama" when Maya began taking acting classes (218). Kirwin, however, is the only professional educator whom Maya remembers by name, with such fondness, and at such length. It speaks well of the color-blindness and high standards of both Kirwin and Angelou that the one teacher accorded this honor is an aging white spinster, a teacher with a stern demeanor and demanding style who played no favorites and who inspired devotion by being devoted to her discipline in every sense of the word.

IV

References to schooling continue as the book proceeds. At one point, for instance, Maya indicates her admiration for Daddy Clidell, her stepfather, when she reports his self-confidence, which never verged on arrogance, despite the fact that he had had only three years of formal schooling: "He was a simple man who had no inferiority complex about his lack of education and, even more amazing, no superiority complex because he had succeeded despite that lack" (221). Maya admires Daddy Clidell for many of the same reasons she admires Kirwin: both are accomplished people who take their responsibilities seriously, treat others with respect, and never develop pretensions or inflated opinions of themselves. What matters to Maya is not formal schooling per se but the kind of intelligence and humane values shown by a person who is truly thoughtful, no matter how many years that person has spent in classrooms.

Nevertheless, Maya makes a point of finishing high school herself, even though she becomes pregnant before she graduates. She refuses (supported by the advice of her beloved brother, Bailey) to tell her mother about her condition, partly because they "both knew her to be violently opposed to abortions, and she would very likely order me to quit school. Bailey suggested that if I quit school before getting my high school diploma I'd find it nearly impossible to return" (286). Neither Bailey nor Maya overestimates the value of mere schooling, nor does either simply equate time spent in school with genuine learning, but each of them has a realistic appreciation of the importance of a diploma. Maya thus delays informing her mother and stepfather of her pregnancy until she graduates:

Two days after V-Day, I stood with the San Francisco Summer School class at Mission High School and received my diploma. That evening, in the bosom of the now-dear family home I uncoiled my fearful secret and in a brave gesture left a note on Daddy Clidell's bed. It read: *Dear Parents, I am sorry to bring this disgrace on the family, but I am pregnant. Marguerite.* (288)

Fewer than twenty paragraphs after this, the book comes to an end.

The birth of Maya's baby nearly coincides with Maya's graduation from high school. One phase of her formal schooling concludes, and a new phase of her personal life begins. Maya begins the book as a child, and she ends it by bearing a child of her own. She begins the book as a student in elementary school, and she ends it as a high school graduate. The development of the plot, therefore, like the evolution of Maya's own character, is charted against a background in which teachers, schools, and schooling play recurring and important parts. Nevertheless, Angelou makes it clear that the lessons learned from teachers at school are not always the most valuable or the most inspiring. Angelou deeply values learning, but she never makes the mistake of simply equating it with mere time spent in class.

Notes

1. On Mr. Freeman as a kind of teacher, and especially on Mrs. Flowers as a teacher of an entirely different sort, see Evans.
2. I have turned up little extended discussion of this topic through key-word searches in the Modern Language Association bibliography, Google Books, or the on-line versions of the Bloom anthologies, the collection edited by Braxton, the book by Lupton, or the volume by Megna-Wallace. The last of these, however, does contain a useful chapter on segregated schools (43-86). Nero does mention the topic, but only in passing.

Works Cited

Angelou, Maya. *I Know Why the Caged Bird Sings*. 1970. New York: Bantam, 1997.

Arensberg, Liliane K. "Death as Metaphor of Self." *Maya Angelou's "I Know Why the Caged Bird Sings": A Casebook*. Ed. Joanne M. Braxton. New York: Oxford University Press, 1999. 111-27.

Bloom, Harold, ed. *Bloom's Guides: Maya Angelou's "I Know Why the Caged Bird Sings."* Philadelphia: Chelsea House, 2004.

_____. *Bloom's Notes: Maya Angelou's "I Know Why the Caged Bird Sings."* Philadelphia: Chelsea House, 1996.

_____. *Modern Critical Interpretations: Maya Angelou's "I Know Why the Caged Bird Sings."* Philadelphia: Chelsea House, 1998.

Braxton, Joanne M., ed. *Maya Angelou's "I Know Why the Caged Bird Sings": A Casebook*. New York: Oxford University Press, 1999.

Evans, Robert C. "Death, Rebirth, and Renewal in Maya Angelou's *I Know Why the Caged Bird Sings."* *Bloom's Literary Themes: Rebirth and Renewal.* Ed. Harold Bloom and Blake Hobby. New York: Chelsea House, forthcoming.

Lupton, Mary Jane. *Maya Angelou: A Critical Companion.* Westport, CT: Greenwood Press, 1998.

Megna-Wallace, Joanne. *Understanding "I Know Why the Caged Bird Sings": A Student Casebook to Issues, Sources, and Historical Documents.* Westport, CT: Greenwood Press, 1998.

Nero, Clarence. "A Discursive Trifecta: Community, Education, and Language in *I Know Why the Caged Bird Sings.*" *Langston Hughes Review* 19 (Spring 2005): 61-65.

CRITICAL READINGS

Death as Metaphor of Self
in *I Know Why the Caged Bird Sings*_____

Liliane K. Arensberg

> When I think about myself,
> I almost laugh myself to death,
> My life has been one great big joke,
> A dance that's walked
> A song that's spoke
> I laugh so hard I almost choke
> When I think about myself.
>   —Maya Angelou

In 1970, at a time when most blacks and a growing number of liberal whites affirmed the ad-campaign motto that "Black Is Beautiful," Maya Angelou's autobiography was published. An unbeautiful, awkward, rather morose, dreamy, and "too-big Negro girl," young Maya Angelou seems an unlikely heroine. Neither the pretty and radiant prom queen of her all-black high school, like Anne Moody in *Coming of Age in Mississippi*, nor the acknowledged genius of her doting family like Nikki Giovanni in *Gemini*, the child Angelou writes of is unadmired, unenvied, uncoddled as she makes her precarious way (on "broad feet," she reminds us) into the world.

Spanning the first sixteen years of her life, *I Know Why the Caged Bird Sings* opens with Maya Angelou's[1] arrival, at the green age of three, in dusty Stamps, Arkansas. Her parents' marriage dissolved, Maya and her older brother, Bailey, have been sent across country from their parents' home in Long Beach, California, to Momma's, their paternal grandmother's, in Stamps. After five years of chores, books, fantasies, and escapades with Bailey, Maya rejoins her mother in teeming, gray St. Louis. There she is raped, at age eight, by her mother's lover, who in retaliation is murdered by her uncles. A guilt-ridden, terrified and bewildered "woman," Maya is again sent to Stamps. Upon her graduation from Lafayette County Training School, at fourteen Maya rejoins her mother, now living in San Francisco. She spends part of one summer at a trailer camp in Southern California with her father and his lover, Dolores. When returning with him from a jaunt into Mexico, Maya is stabbed in a quarrel with Dolores. Fearing another murderous reprisal, Maya is unwilling to return to any of her homes. Instead, she seeks refuge in a car junkyard. There "a collage of Negro, Mexican and white" youths initiate her into a redeeming vision of universal brotherhood—one that Malcolm X could only discover thousands of miles from the United States in Mecca. She returns to San Francisco, a sobered and self-possessed young woman, and challenges the racial bar to be hired as the town's first black female streetcar conductor. At the end of the book Maya becomes mother to an illegitimate son, the offspring of her "immaculate pregnancy."

This brief sketch, though excluding some very crucial personalities and episodes in her youth, emphasizes the rootlessness of Maya Angelou's early years. Angelou herself underscores this pattern of mobility in the opening phrase of her introduction:

"What you looking at me for?
I didn't come to stay. . . ."[2]

Indeed, geographic movement and temporary residence become formative aspects of her growing identity—equal in importance to experiences and relationships more commonly regarded as instrumental in forming the adult self. Appropriately, this poetic phrase becomes the young girl's motto or "shield" (p. 58) as Angelou calls it, Maya's means of proclaiming her isolation while defending against its infringement.

Shuttled between temporary homes and transient allegiances, Maya necessarily develops a stoic flexibility that becomes not only her "shield," but, more important, her characteristic means of dealing with the world. This flexibility is both blessing and curse: it enables her to adapt to various and changing environments, but it also keeps her forever threatened with loss or breakdown of her identity, as will presently be shown.

Indeed, Angelou's descriptions of her younger self seem almost entirely comprised of negatives: she is not wanted by her parents who hold over her the unspoken, but ever-present, threat of banishment; she is not beautiful or articulate like her brother, Bailey; she is too introverted and passive to assert herself on her environment; and, finally, she is a child in a world of enigmatic adults, and a black girl in a world created by and for the benefit of white men.

Furthermore, Maya's geographic worlds are each separate and self-contained. There is the world of Momma and her store in Stamps, a puritan world of racial pride, religious devotion and acquiescence to one's worldly lot. And there is her "wild and beautiful" mother's world of pool halls, card sharks, fast dancing, fast talking and fast loving. Combining and transcending both is the private and portable world of Maya's imagination.

If there is one stable element in Angelou's youth it is this dependence on books. Kipling, Poe, Austen, and Thackeray, Dunbar, Johnson, Hughes, and Du Bois, *The Lone Ranger, The Shadow,* and *Captain Marvel* comics—all are equally precious to this lonely girl. Shakespeare, whose Sonnet 29 speaks to Maya's own social and emotional alienation, becomes her "first white love" (p. 11). As it does for Mary Antin, Anaïs Nin, and other female autobiographers, the public library becomes a quiet refuge from the chaos of her personal life. "I took out my first library card in St. Louis" (p. 64), she notes. And it is the public library she attempts to reach after her rape. Later, when running away from her father, she hides in a library. Indeed, when her life is in crisis, Maya characteristically escapes into the world of books.

As artifacts creating complete and meaningful universes, novels and their heroes become means by which Maya apprehends and judges her own bewildering world. Thus, Louise, her first girlfriend, reminds Maya of Jane Eyre; while Louise's mother, a domestic, Maya refers to as a governess. Mrs. Flowers, who introduces her to the magic of books, appeals to Maya because she was like "women in English novels who walked the moors . . . with their loyal dogs racing at a respectful distance. Like the women who sat in front of roaring fireplaces, drinking tea incessantly from silver trays full of scones and crumpets. Women who walked the 'heath' and read morocco-bound books and had two last names divided by a hyphen." Curiously, it is this imaginative association with a distant, extinct, and colonial world that makes Mrs. Flowers one who "made me proud to be Negro, just by being herself" (p. 79).

But the plight of lovers, madmen, and poets is also Maya's problem. "The little princesses who were mistaken for maids, and the long-lost children mistaken for waifs," writes Angelou, "became more real to me than our house, our mother, our school or Mr. Freeman" (p. 64). She is so consummately involved in the world of fantasy that even while being raped she "was sure any minute my mother or Bailey or the Green Hornet would burst in the door and save me" (p. 65).

As in this quotation, the style by which Angelou describes her youth seems in counterpoint to the meaning of her narrative. It is written with a humor and wry wit that belies the personal and racial tragedies recorded. Since style is such a revealing element in all autobiographies, hers, especially, seems a conscious defense against the pain felt at evoking unpleasant memories. Moreover, wit operates as a formidable tool of the outraged adult; by mocking her enemies, Angelou overcomes them. Thus the gluttonous Reverend Thomas gets his just deserts at church when, "throwing out phrases like home-run balls," he loses his dentures in a scuffle with an overzealous parishioner; the self-serving condescension of "fluttering" Mrs. Cullinan is ridiculed in a "tragic ballad" on "being white, fat, old and without children" (so, too, with the vanity and carelessness of her mother's "lipstick kisses" and her father's pompous "*ers* and *errers*" as he struts among Stamps's curious "down-home folk.") The adult writer's irony retaliates for the tongue-tied child's helpless pain.

The primary object, however, for Angelou's wit is herself. At times maudlin, always highly romantic and withdrawn, the young Maya is a person the older writer continually finds comic. Her idolatrous attachment to Bailey, her projections of fantasy upon reality, her reverence of her mother's stunning beauty, her strained attempts at sympathy for her self-enamoured father, her ingenuous attitude toward sexuality—these are but a few of the many and recurring aspects of her younger self the adult mocks.

The basic motive for writing one's autobiography, some believe, is to be understood, accepted, and loved. Angelou's willingness to ridicule former self-deceptions—more precisely, her former self—indicates the adult's fearlessness of the reader's judgments and her own critical stance toward herself. If Angelou's voice in re-creating her past is, therefore, ironic, it is, however, supremely controlled.

Nevertheless, despite the frankness of her narrative, Angelou avoids charting a direct path to her present self. Unlike *Gemini* or *Coming of Age in Mississippi* or *The Autobiography of Malcolm X* or Richard Wright's *Black Boy*—books in the same genre—Angelou's autobiography barely mentions the emergent woman within the girlish actor. Although Roy Pascal believes that "the autobiographer must refer us continually outwards and onwards, to the author himself and to the outcome of all the experiences,"[3] Maya Angelou proves an exception to the rule.

Because Angelou's apprehension of experience and, indeed, herself, is essentially protean and existential, it is difficult to find one overriding identity of the adult self controlling her narrative. For what connects the adult and the child is less a linear development toward one distinct version of the self through career or philosophy than an ever-changing multiplicity of possibilities. It is, in fact, her mutability, born of and affirmed through repeated movement, reorientation and assimilation, that becomes Angelou's unique identity, her "identity theme,"[4] to use Heinz Lichtenstein's more precise term. And if "work, in man, serves the maintenance of the individual's identity theme,"[5] as Lichtenstein asserts, then the numerous careers of the adult Angelou—as dancer, prostitute, S.C.L.C. organizer, actor, poet, journalist, and director—document restlessness and resilience.

The unsettled life Angelou writes of in *I Know Why the Caged Bird Sings* suggests a sense of self as perpetually in the process of becoming, of dying and being reborn, in all its ramifications. Thus death (and to some extent its companion concept, rebirth) is the term by which her "identity theme" operates. It is the metaphor of self that most directly and comprehensively communicates Angelou's identity. Moreover, the compulsion to repeat—a necessary instrument for the maintenance of any "identity theme"[6]—adds credence to the power of this major motif in Angelou's narrative. For, while the book's tone is predominantly witty, even light, resonating just below the surface of almost every page of Angelou's autobiography is the hidden, but ever-present, theme of death.

Angelou introduces *I Know Why the Caged Bird Sings* with an anecdote. It is Easter Sunday at the Colored Methodist Episcopal Church in Stamps. In celebration of the event, Momma has prepared a lavender taffeta dress for Maya. Believing it to be the most beautiful dress she has ever seen, Maya attributes to it magical properties: when worn, the dress will change Maya into the lovely, blond and blue-eyed "sweet little white girl" she actually believes herself to be.

But on Easter morning the dress reveals its depressing actuality: it is "a plain, ugly cut-down from a white woman's once-was-purple throwaway." No Cinderella metamorphosis for Maya; instead she lives in a "black dream" from which there is no respite. Unlike Christ, whose resurrection from death the church is celebrating, Maya cannot be reborn into life. Overcome with the impossibility of her white fantasy, she escapes the church "peeing and crying" her way home. Maya must, indeed, lose control of her body and feelings. "It would probably run right back up to my head," she believes, "and my poor head would burst like a dropped watermelon, and all the brains and spit and tongue and eyes would roll all over the place" (p. 3). By letting go of her fantasy—physically manifested by letting go of her bladder—Maya will not "die from a busted head."

But, to "let go," as Erik Erikson observes in *Childhood and Society*, "can turn into an inimical letting loose of destructive forces."[7] For, on this Easter Sunday Maya Angelou comprehends the futility of her wish to become "one of the sweet little white girls who were everybody's dream of what was right with the world." "If growing up is painful for the Southern Black girl," the adult writer concludes, "being aware of her displacement is the rust on the razor that threatens the throat." Although she acknowledges the "unnecessary insult" of her own white fantasy, Angelou nevertheless puts the rust on the razor by her awareness of its insidious and ubiquitous presence.[8]

The form an autobiography takes is as revealing as its style and content. By placing this anecdote before the body of her narrative, Angelou asserts the paradigmatic importance of this particular event on her life. The atemporality of this experience (Maya's age remains unmentioned), coupled with the symbolic setting of Easter Sunday, suggests a personal myth deeply imbedded in Angelou's unconscious. One could, indeed, speculate that this event, introducing Maya Angelou's autobiography, is the "epiphanic moment" of her youth. For this short narrative presents the two dynamic operatives that circumscribe Angelou's self: her blackness and her outcast position.

Immediately striking in the anecdote is Maya's fantastic belief that "I was really white," that "a cruel fairy stepmother, who was understandably jealous of my beauty" (p. 2) had tricked Maya of her Caucasian birthright. The fairy-tale imagery employed to depict her creation is characteristic of the imaginative and impressionable girl, but the meaning of her tale cannot be overlooked. For, according to her schema, Maya's identity hinges on the whims of this fairy stepmother. If benevolent, she will transform Maya back into a pretty white girl; if she remains cruel, her spell over Maya will rest unbroken. When her dress does not produce the longed-for results, Maya is forced to contend with her blackness. But if she acknowledges this blackness, Maya must also acknowledge the existence of an arbitrary and malevolent force beyond her control that dictates her personal and racial identity.

As if mourning the death of the lovely white body beyond her possession, Maya describes her dress as sounding "like crepe paper on the back of hearses" (p. 1). Maya's body indeed becomes a symbolic hearse, containing not only her dead dream but also a life whose very existence is threatened by the whims of a murderous white culture.

Angelou's highly personal confession of racial self-hatred is, unfortunately, not unique in Afro-American experience. Many works of contemporary black novelists and autobiographers—from Ralph Ellison and Imamu Baraka/LeRoi Jones to Richard Wright and Malcolm X—assert that invisibility, violence, alienation, and death are part and parcel of growing up black in a white America. Likewise, psychological and sociological studies affirm that the first lesson in living taught the black child is how to ensure his/her survival. "The child must know," write Grier and Cobbs, "that the white world is dangerous and that if he does not understand its rules it may kill him."[9] It is, then, pitifully understandable for Maya to wish herself white, since blackness forebodes annihilation.

Of equal significance in this introductory anecdote is Maya's belief that a stepmother has put her under this spell and then abandoned her. Her image of herself, for at least the first five years of life, is that of an orphan. Even later, when forced to recognize the existence of both her parents, she still clings to this orphan identity. Although acknowledging that Bailey, by dint of beauty and personality, is his parents' true son, she describes herself as "an orphan that they had picked up to provide Bailey with company" (p. 45).

While her father is as culpable as her mother in Maya's abandonment, it is nevertheless her mother whom Maya most yearns for and consequently blames. No real mother would "laugh and eat oranges in the sunshine without her children" (p. 42), Maya reflects bitterly when first confronted with her mother's existence. No proper mother should let her child so profoundly mourn her passing as Maya has done.

I could cry anytime I wanted by picturing my mother (I didn't know what she looked like) lying in her coffin. Her hair, which was black, was spread out on a tiny little pillow and her body was covered with a sheet. The face was brown, like a big O, and since I couldn't fill in the features I printed M O T H E R across the O, and tears would fall down my cheeks like warm milk. (p. 43)

Maya's image of her dead mother is deeply comforting to the child. The protective and nurturing maternal love Maya yearns for is symbolically created through her own tears: they "would fall down my cheeks like warm milk." Consider then, the shock, the affront to her tottering self-image as well as to the image of her dead mother, when Maya receives her mother's first Christmas presents. Not only is her mother alive, but Maya herself must have been as good as dead during those early years of separation.

Adding insult to injury are the "awful presents" themselves: "a tea set—a teapot, four cups and saucers and tiny spoons—and a doll with blue eyes and rosy cheeks and yellow hair painted on her head" (p. 43). Symbols of a white world beyond Maya's reach or everyday experience, these toys not only evidence her mother's exotic and alien life but also intimate questions of guilt and banishment no five-year-old can answer. The doll, especially, whose description so closely parallels Maya's own wished-for physical appearance, is an intolerable presence. It serves as an effigy of her mother by virtue of being female and her gift, as well as of Maya's impossible fantasy; Maya and Bailey "tore the stuffing out of the doll the day after Christmas" (p. 44).

Abandonment by a dead mother is forgivable, but abandonment by a living one evokes a rage so threatening that it must undergo massive repression. Thus, Maya becomes passive, inhibiting her deep anger and hostility. The fear of abandonment, even when living with her mother in St. Louis, never abates. "If we got on her nerves or if we were disobedient, she could always send us back to Stamps. The weight of appreciation and the threat, which was never spoken, of a return to

Momma were burdens that clogged my childish wits into impassivity. I was called Old Lady and chided for moving and talking like winter's molasses" (p. 57). Maya's fears come true; after her rape she is again banished to Stamps.

Nevertheless, Maya repeatedly protests fondness for her mother. Beautiful, honest, gay, and tough, Vivian Baxter leaves her daughter awestruck. "I could never put my finger on her realness," Angelou writes. "She was so pretty and so quick that . . . I thought she looked like the Virgin Mary" (p. 57). So much is Vivian Baxter idealized that Angelou capitalizes "Mother" in her narrative, while "father" remains in lowercase. But Vivian Baxter is diametrically opposite to the brown-faced nurturing mother Maya had mourned and yearned for in Stamps. Her beauty and animation keep Maya suspicious of their consanguinity.

Maya's ambivalence about her mother—her fear and love, her rage and need for her, her isolation and her desire for closeness—is never fully resolved. Although she insists verbally on this love, her affect reveals sullenness, resignation, depression, and overwhelming passivity. Maya's aggression against her mother is well-defended, and thus specific suggestions of hostility toward her are rare. But the proliferating references to death in Angelou's autobiography provide another route for releasing Maya's (and Angelou's) repressed violent aggression.

This aspect of death's overdetermined significance is important but by no means the only level of reference; at least five subthemes, each bearing on the major theme of death, emerge in *I Know Why the Caged Bird Sings*. The first is the most obvious: the realistic fear of whites that Momma and the Southern black community have drummed into Maya. Momma, Angelou writes, "didn't cotton to the idea that whitefolks could be talked to at all without risking one's life" (p. 39). The white lynchers whom Uncle Willie hides from in the vegetable bin, the taunting "powhitetrash" girls, the bloated dead man fished out of the river— all are daily proof of a predatory white world. This fact leads Angelou to a bitter conclusion: "the Black woman in the South who raises sons, grandsons and nephews had her heartstrings tied to a hanging noose" (p. 95).

The daily fear of murder at the hands of whites leads the Southern black community into the haven of religion and the belief of a blessed reward in "the far off bye and bye." Thus, Southern black religion celebrates death, since life itself is too precarious to pin one's hopes on. Even at the revival meeting attended by members from a variety of Southern churches, death continually asserts its presence: the cardboard fans flourished by the worshippers advertise Texarkana's largest Negro funeral parlor. "People whose history and future were threatened each day by extinction," comments Angelou, "considered that it was only by divine intervention that they were able to live at all" (p. 101).

Balancing this image of a white world threatening her own and her people's lives is Maya's revenge fantasy of murdering the offending whites. When Dentist Lincoln refuses to treat her toothache, Maya creates an elaborate revery wherein a Herculean Momma has the cowering dentist pleading for his life: "Yes, ma'am. Thank you for not killing me. Thank you, Mrs. Henderson" (p. 162).

Far and away the most dramatic instance of this revenge theme occurs the day of Maya's graduation from Lafayette County Training School. Unable to stand the invited white speaker's "dead words," which systematically destroy the dreams and aspirations of the black children and their elders, Maya wills them all dead.

Then I wished that Gabriel Prosser and Nat Turner had killed all whitefolks in their beds and that Abraham Lincoln had been assassinated before the signing of the Emancipation Proclamation, and that Harriet Tubman had been killed by that blow on her head and Christopher Columbus had drowned in the *Santa Maria*.

It was awful to be Negro and have no control over my life. It was brutal to be young and already trained to sit quietly and listen to charges brought against my color with no chance of defense. We should all be dead. I thought I should like to see us all dead, one on top of the other. A pyramid of flesh with the whitefolks on the bottom, as the broad base, then the Indians with their silly tomahawks and teepees and wigwams and treaties, the Negroes with their mops and recipes and cotton sacks and spirituals sticking out of their mouths. The Dutch children should all stumble in their wooden shoes and break their necks. The French should choke to death on the Louisiana Purchase (1803) while silkworms ate all the Chinese with their stupid pigtails. As a species, we were an abomination. All of us. (pp. 152-53)

Operating on a more personal level is the violence Maya witnesses within the members of her own family. Angelou introduces her Uncle Willie by describing his method of pushing her and Bailey onto the Store's red heater if they neglect their lessons. Momma, too, does not spare the rod when she believes her grandchildren remiss in hygiene, schooling, manners, or piety. But this corporal punishment—executed more in love than in rage—is small matter, indeed, when compared to the fundamental brutality of Maya's maternal relations in St. Louis. Her maternal grandfather and uncles revel in their own "meanness": "They beat up whites and Blacks with the same abandon" (p. 56). Even her mother is not immune from her family's violent streak. Once, in retaliation for being cursed, Vivian Baxter, with the aid of her brothers, "crashed the man's head with a policemen's billy enough to leave him just this side of death" (p. 55). Later Vivian Baxter, again in response to an insult, shoots the partner of her gambling casino.

As the climax of this familial violence, Mr. Freeman's rape is performed under the threat of death: "If you scream, I'm gonna kill you. And if you tell, I'm gonna kill Bailey" (p. 65). But her family's response to Maya's subsequent withdrawal into silent passivity is itself another form of violence. "For a while I was punished for being so uppity that I wouldn't speak; and then came the thrashings, given by any relative who felt himself offended" (p. 73). The rape itself is the most flagrant example of her maternal family's characteristic combination of aggression and neglect. Not only is Mr. Freeman her mother's lover, but mother and children all live under his roof. Ruthless in her quest for material comfort, Vivian Baxter is not above taking full advantage of Freeman's obvious adoration. Already at eight a sagacious observer, Maya responds with mixed emotions to her mother's relationship with Freeman. "I felt sorry for Mr. Freeman. I felt as sorry for him as I had felt for a litter of helpless pigs born in our backyard sty in Arkansas. We fattened the pigs all year long for the slaughter on the first good frost, and even as I suffered for the cute little wiggly things, I knew how much I was going to enjoy the fresh sausage and hog's headcheese they could give me only with their deaths" (p. 60).

Of course, Maya's sympathy for Freeman has another cause: she feels as neglected by Vivian Baxter as he does. And while Freeman's motives in the earlier masturbatory episodes and even the rape itself probably stem as much from revenge against the mother as easy access to the daughter, Maya's own need for attention and physical closeness cannot be overlooked. After the first of these episodes, Angelou writes, "came the nice part. He held me so softly that I wished he wouldn't ever let me go. I felt at home. From the way he was holding me I knew he'd never let me go or let anything bad ever happen to me. This was probably my real father and we had found each other at last" (p. 61). Pitifully unable to distinguish lust from paternal love (never having experienced the latter), Maya projects onto Freeman this physical warmth missing from all her relationships with adults. "I began to feel lonely for Mr. Freeman and the encasement of his big arms," Angelou recalls. "Before, my world had been Bailey, food, Momma, the Store, reading books and Uncle Willie. Now, for the first time, it included physical contact" (p. 62).

Freeman's subsequent murder (he was kicked to death by her uncles) evokes overwhelming guilt in Maya. At Freeman's trial Maya gives false testimony about their encounters, and now "a man was dead because I lied" (p. 72). Associating her spoken word with death, Maya stops talking.

Maya as bearer of death is the fourth dimension of death and violence in Angelou's narrative. In disgrace with God because "I had sold myself to the Devil and there could be no escape," Maya conceives herself to be the cursed instrument of violent death. This conviction is part of the pattern of self-rejection and inferiority well-established within Maya's psyche; it lies but one small step beyond a personal sense of inherent gross repulsiveness. Introjecting this repulsiveness—which she believes everyone except Bailey feels toward her—Maya generalizes on her role in Freeman's death and perceives herself as death's tool. "The only thing I could do," she reasons, "was to stop talking to people other than Bailey. Instinctively, or somehow, I knew that because I loved him so much I'd never hurt him, but if I talked to anyone else that person might die too. Just my breath, carrying my words out, might poison people and they'd curl up and die like the black fat slugs that only pretended" (p. 73).

In this psychic state Maya conceives of her own body mythically as a Pandora's Box containing a degeneracy so virulent that, if left uncontrolled, will contaminate the universe. So profound is her hatred and rage, she recalls, that "I could feel the evilness flowing through my body and waiting, pent up, to rush off my tongue if I tried to open my mouth. I clamped my teeth shut, I'd hold it in. If it escaped, wouldn't it flood the world and all the innocent people" (p. 72). As a vessel containing a death-inducing fluid, Maya must control the physical force within her with all the strength and will she can muster. Thus, her resolve not to speak, and her consequent impassivity become outward manifestations of an inner struggle no less cosmic than Jacob and the Angel's. This same struggle is the one that opens Angelou's autobiography.

Upon her return to Stamps, Maya projects her own deathlike inertness on the whole town. It is described as "exactly what I wanted, without will or consciousness. . . . Entering Stamps, I had the feeling that I was stepping over the border lines of the map and would fall, without fear, right off the end of the world. Nothing more could happen, for in Stamps nothing happened" (p. 74).

An outcast in a community of outcasts, Maya avoids emotional ties with others. In fact, for six years, until Louise befriends her, Maya is without an intimate friend her own age. It is not surprising, then, that when Mrs. Bertha Flowers takes an active interest in her, Maya describes her as "the lady who threw me my first life line" (p. 77). Nor is it surprising that Maya turns to the safety of books for the exciting relationships shunned in real life.

Yet this pathological paralysis that inhibits Maya's ability to express her resentment and anger also opens the door to a gratification of her desire for a union with her mother. For Maya's passivity and obsession with death serve more than one unconscious need. While keeping her emotionally isolated from, and invulnerable to, others, they also gratify her regressive strivings for her mother.

Indeed, Maya's decision to lie at Freeman's trial was motivated not simply by mortal terror of her maternal clan and by fear of revealing her own complicity in the sexual episodes but, more important, by her desire for her mother's warmth and approving love.

I couldn't say yes and tell them how he had loved me once for a few minutes and how he had held me close before he thought I had peed in my bed. My uncles would kill me and Grandmother Baxter would stop speaking, as she often did when she was angry. And all those people in the court would stone me as they had stoned the harlot in the Bible. And Mother, who thought I was such a good girl, would be so disappointed. . . .

. . . I looked at his heavy face trying to look as if he would have liked me to say No. I said No.

The lie lumped in my throat and I couldn't get air. . . . Our lawyer brought me off the stand and to my mother's arms. The fact that I had arrived at my desired destination by lies made it less appealing to me. (pp. 70-71)

When Maya's attempts at physical closeness with her mother—pathetically by way of Mr. Freeman's arms and her lie—prove unsuccessful, she reverts to the most primitive of all longings: to die. If death is "the condition in which identification with mother can be achieved," as Barchelon and Kovel postulate about *Huckleberry Finn*, then its "ultimate expression is passivity, of doing nothing." Thus, "in the unconscious, death can be represented as that dissolution of self necessary for reunion with the source of life, as a recapitulation of that self-less time in the womb."[10] Consequently, for a major portion of her autobiography, Maya Angelou evokes the notion of her willful dissolution— still another dimension in her book of the death-motif.

Thanatos, or the unconscious drive toward dissolution and death, exists in Angelou's narrative before the crucial episode of her rape and courtroom lie. Indeed, it first emerges when Maya is confronted with recognizing the existence of her parents. Deeply attached to the image of her dead mother, her indecision about joining the living one in St. Louis evokes the thought of suicide. "Should I go with father? Should I throw myself into the pond, and not being able to swim, join the body of L. C., the boy who had drowned last summer?" (pp. 46-47). Even her choice of method—death by water—calls up her yearning for a return to the source of all life, the mother.

Although her second residence in Stamps includes episodes wherein Maya considers her own death, these are generally handled more with humor than pathos. At any rate, the very abundance of references to her own extinction, regardless of Angelou's tone, is evidence of this theme's powerful hold over both the actor's and the author's unconscious. Three examples out of many will suffice. When cautioned by Mrs. Flowers to handle her books well, Maya can only imagine the most extreme punishment if she proves negligent: "Death would be too kind and brief" (p. 82). Later, having survived to see the day of her graduation, Angelou relates that "somewhere in my fatalism I had expected to die, accidentally, and never have the chance to walk up the stairs in the auditorium and gracefully receive my hard-earned diploma. Out of God's merciful bosom I had won reprieve" (p. 147). Again, referring to the overwhelming sway books had over hers and

Bailey's imaginations, Angelou writes that "ever since we read *The Fall of the House of Usher*, we had made a pact that neither of us would allow the other to be buried without making 'absolutely, positively sure' (his favorite phrase) that the person was dead" (p. 166).

Included in this part of her experience is Angelou's first conscious cognizance of her own mortality. So crucial an aspect of her identity is this awareness, that Angelou devotes an entire chapter to it. Beneath the mock-Gothic melodrama of Mrs. Taylor's funeral and her posthumous nocturnal returns to visit her husband (neither of whom are mentioned again in the book), exists Maya's real and growing apprehension of her own mortal state: "I had never considered before that dying, death, dead, passed away, were words and phrases that might be even faintly connected with me" (p. 135).

This deathward drift is arrested and altered when Maya moves to California. Just as Stamps reflects Maya's impassivity, so does San Francisco evoke her resiliency; while Stamps projects the worst side of Maya, so San Francisco affirms the best: "The city became for me the ideal of what I wanted to be as a grownup. Friendly but never gushing, cool but not frigid or distant, distinguished without the awful stiffness" (p. 180). In San Francisco Maya's own identity happily merges with her environs. "In San Francisco, for the first time, I perceived myself as part of something," writes Angelou. "I identified . . . with the times and the city. . . . The undertone of fear that San Francisco would be bombed which was abetted by weekly air raid warnings, and civil defense drills in school, heightened my sense of belonging. Hadn't I, always, but ever and ever, thought that life was just one great risk for the living?" (p. 179).

Death in its many manifestations is, indeed, pivotal to Maya Angelou's sense of self. But the life instinct, Eros, coexists with Thanatos in her autobiography, as it does in life. In fact, the tension between Maya's quest for a positive, life-affirming identity and her obsession with annihilation provide the unconscious dynamism affecting all aspects of her narrative, and endowing it with power and conviction.

Thus, the ultimate challenge to death is Maya's own active assertion of self and her willingness to face annihilation and overcome it. The remainder of Angelou's autobiography addresses itself to this end. It is not until she visits Mexico with her father that Maya tenaciously struggles for her life. Leaving Maya to her own wits in a Mexican *cantina*, Bailey Johnson, Sr., takes off with his Mexican lover. When he finally returns, intoxicated beyond help, Maya must drive them both home. Although she has never driven, Maya defies and masters the bucking Hudson.

> The Hudson went crazy on the hill. It was rebelling and would have leaped over the side of the mountain, to all our destruction, in its attempt to unseat me had I relaxed control for a single second. The challenge was exhilarating. It was me, Marguerite, against the elemental opposition. As I twisted the steering wheel and forced the accelerator to the floor I was controlling Mexico, and might and aloneness and inexperienced youth and Bailey Johnson, Sr., and death and insecurity, and even gravity. (pp. 202-03)

But, as in the incident of Freeman's rape, the fatal pattern of reversal again appears. Maya's temporary safety is followed by Dolores's stabbing. When, in order to save face, Johnson hides Maya at a friend's home rather than bring her to a hospital, Maya is again confronted with the specter of her own death. She survives the night, however, sleeping "as if my death wish had come true" (p. 212). But morning presents the inevitable questions: "What would I do? Did I have the nerve to commit suicide? If I jumped in the ocean wouldn't I come up all bloated like the man Bailey saw in Stamps?" (212). Although she has evoked her childish alternative of death by water and its unconscious wish for a return to mother, this time Maya resolves to make it on her own.

The decision not to retreat to her mother's home becomes the turning-point in Maya Angelou's autobiography. "I could never succeed in shielding the gash in my side from her," she argues. "And if I failed to hide the wound we were certain to experience another scene of violence. I thought of poor Mr. Freeman, and the guilt which lined my heart, even after all those years, was a nagging passenger in my mind" (p. 213). With this gesture, Maya not only triumphs over her regressive longing for death and mother, but also, by sparing her father and Dolores, overcomes her sense of herself as death's tool.

Employing the same simile she had earlier used to describe her mother—"She was like a pretty kite that floated just above my head—" (p. 54)—Maya now describes herself as "a loose kite in a gentle wind floating with only my will for anchor" (p. 214). Put more plainly, Maya rises in her own estimation, incorporates the best of her mother and becomes her own guardian. It is only then that Maya is ready to return to the human fold.

The outcast children of the dead-car junkyard where she seeks refuge eliminate Maya's "familiar insecurity," especially in relation to her mother. She learns "to drive . . . to curse and to dance" (p. 215), with the best of them. But of signal importance is that these children disprove the racial prejudice—and its concurrent death fantasies—of her earlier experiences.

After hunting down unbroken bottles and selling them with a white girl from Missouri, a Mexican girl from Los Angeles and a Black girl from Oklahoma, I was never again to sense myself so solidly outside the pale of the human race. The lack of criticism evidenced by our ad hoc community influenced me, and set a tone of tolerance for my life. (p. 216)

That Angelou concludes her autobiography with the birth of her son is final evidence of the substantive power of death as metaphor of self in *I Know Why the Caged Bird Sings*.[11] Her body, which she had earlier described as not only ugly and awkward but also contaminated with a death-inducing power, brings forth a living child. But the vestiges of her former self-image are not so easily excised. When her mother brings to Maya's bed her three-week-old baby, Maya is terror-stricken: "I was sure to roll over and crush out his life or break those fragile bones" (p. 245). But later, when her mother wakens her, the apprehensive Maya discovers her son safe: "Under the tent of blanket, which was poled by my elbow and forearm, the baby slept touching my side"(p. 246).

This final picture of Vivian Baxter as a confident and compassionate mother lovingly bent over her daughter's bed, evokes the brown, nurturing figure of Maya's childhood fantasy. By asserting her faith in Maya's instinctive, preserving motherhood, Vivian Baxter not only qualifies the book's implicit image of her as cruel stepmother, but also consummates Maya's growing sense of herself as an adult, life-giving woman.

When writing one's autobiography one's primary concern is the illumination of personal and historical identity while giving shape and meaning to the experiences out of which that identity has developed. Through the abyss of social and emotional death, Angelou emerges as a tenacious and vital individual. Indeed, in keeping with her death-and-rebirth fantasy, Maya Angelou is reborn: once, into a life-affirming identity recorded within the pages of her narrative, and again, when she re-creates that life as author of her autobiography. If one must enter a dark night of the soul in order to emerge radiant, then Maya Angelou's "terrible beauty" shines clear to the sky.

From *College Language Association Journal* 20, no. 2 (December 1976): 273-291. Copyright © 1976 by College Language Association. Reprinted by permission of College Language Association.

Notes

1. In the autobiography Angelou calls herself Maya or Marguerite Johnson, her given name. But, to avoid undue confusion, I have limited myself to the writer's signature. I do distinguish the child from the writer, however, and refer to the child as "Maya" and to the adult as "Angelou."

2. Maya Angelou, *I Know Why the Caged Bird Sings* (New York: Bantam Books, 1970), 1. Subsequent page references are to this edition.

3. Roy Pascal, *Design and Truth in Autobiography* (London: Routledge & Kegan Paul Ltd., 1960), 163.

4. Heinz Lichtenstein, "Identity and Sexuality: A Study of Their Interrelationship in Man," *Journal of the American Psychoanalytic Association* 9 (1961): 208.

5. Ibid., 253.

6. Ibid., 235.

7. Erik H. Erikson, *Childhood and Society* (New York: W. W. Norton & Company, 1963). 251.

8. All quotations referring to the anecdote are from pp. 1-3 of *I Know Why the Caged Bird Sings.*

9. William H. Grier and Price M. Cobbs, *Black Rage* (New York: Bantam Books, 1968), 51.

10. Jose Barchelon and Joel S. Kovel, "*Huckleberry Finn*: A Psychoanalytic Study," *Journal of the American Psychoanalytic Association* 22 (1966): 785.

11. Although the second volume of her autobiography, *Gather Together in My Name*, also contains the theme of death, it does not "open up" the book the way it does her first. This supports (conveniently?) my contention that much of this theme is resolved in *I Know Why the Caged Bird Sings*. On the other hand, her book of verse *Just Give Me a Cool Drink of Water 'fore I Diiie* contains nineteen poems, out of a total thirty-eight, in which death is directly mentioned. Moreover, the theme of "mutability" echoes throughout her later works. One's "identity theme" is, indeed, irreversible.

Breaking the Silence:
Symbolic Violence and the Teaching of Contemporary "Ethnic" Autobiography_____

Martin A. Danahay

The question of what constitutes resistance to hegemony and what accommodation to existing power relations has provoked much critical discussion recently in a variety of disciplines. Works such as James C. Scott's *Weapons of the Weak* and *Domination and the Arts of Resistance* in anthropology, and in education Paul Willis's *Learning to Labour*, have suggested that acts of resistance at the local level do not threaten large-scale hegemony, but rather confirm existing distributions of power. Literary criticism books such as Jim Merod's *The Political Responsibility of the Critic*, Richard Ohmann's *Politics of Letters*, and Gerald Graff's *Professing Literature* have explored the issue of the profession's complicity with or resistance to hegemony in its critical practices. In a recent special issue of *College Literature* on "The Politics of Teaching Literature," Barbara Foley has addressed directly the "rhetoric of subversion" operative in the academy, asking whether critical readings of "marginal" texts really challenge hegemony within the university, let alone in the wider social arena. Taken as a whole, these works suggest that resistance and accommodation are mutually affirming categories, and that what looks from one perspective like resistance may in a larger context appear simply an adjustment to hegemony.

This article explores issues of resistance and accommodation through examples drawn from Maya Angelou's *I Know Why the Caged Bird Sings* (1970), Maxine Hong Kingston's *The Woman Warrior* (1976), and Richard Rodriguez's *Hunger of Memory* (1982). In drawing on these texts my primary purpose is not to present a systematic reading of each as a complete work, but to use the texts to illuminate problems in the teaching of "ethnic" literature in the classroom. In other words, thematic discussion is deliberately subordinated to the theoretical elaboration of the ways in which these texts present challenges to the critic as teacher within the university. Each of these texts presents the teacher with an image of education as a form of "symbolic violence" that reflects upon the institutional context within which pedagogical authority is being exercised. Each of these texts can be mobilized by the teacher as part of a general critique of the university as a hegemonic institution.

I derive the term "symbolic violence" from the work of Pierre Bourdieu and J. C. Passeron, who in *Reproduction in Education, Society and Culture* suggest that such practices as the withholding of emotional support by a teacher represent a form of domination. Education in Bourdieu and Passeron's analysis reinforces power relations while mystifying its role in the reproduction of social class. Education in this sense encompasses not only the formal site of institutionalized schooling, but also more informal sites of socialization in which power relations are reproduced. Education as symbolic violence "enables a group or class to produce and reproduce its intellectual and moral integration without resorting to external repression or physical coercion" (36). Like Antonio Gramsci's concept of hegemony, Bourdieu and Passeron's analysis of "symbolic violence" in education invites consideration of the ways in which subjects are simultaneously coerced and seduced into fashioning themselves in the image of social power relations. The question that animates this article, given Bourdieu and Passeron's definition of education as "symbolic violence," is how one may differentiate resistance from accommodation to hegemony, both in texts and in the realm of pedagogical practice.

The categories of "resistance" and "accommodation" cannot be easily separated in either arena. George Yúdice has suggested that "*écriture* is not an unproblematic liberatory practice" for ethnic autobiographies, but on the contrary is "riddled with ambiguity, contradiction, even bad faith" (224). Yúdice's comments help underscore the dangers of a simple dichotomizing of liberation and oppression (or domination and resistance) in the study of texts. His invocation of Jacques Derrida's term "*écriture*" rather than "writing" indicates how useful a construction of such oppositions can be in this context. In his essay "Violence and Metaphysics" Derrida has stressed that philosophy itself is involved in issues of violence and oppression. Objectivity is "a displacement of technico-political oppression in the direction of philosophical discourse" (92). Violence and oppression are not, in Derrida's view, extrinsic to the philosophical or any other text; he deconstructs simple binary oppositions such as speech/writing or violence/nonviolence. Derrida suggests that "the limit between violence and nonviolence is perhaps not between speech and writing but within each of them" (102). There are therefore no "inside" and "outside" in this question, no privileged, pristine spaces for the author or critic to occupy.

Even silence may be interpreted as violent; Derrida at one point defines violence as "the solitude of a mute glance, of a face without speech" (99). It is therefore impossible simply to equate silence and resistance. Derrida's comments raise the possibility that silence itself may be a mute marker of violence. Similarly, Angelou's silence, Kingston's breaking of silence, and Rodriguez's ambivalence toward silence subvert any simple connection of silence and resistance, or any separation of silence from violence. The power of these texts resides in the way the authors resist any straightforward equation between silence and resistance, or *écriture* and violence.

To link violence and silence is to subvert a current critical orthodoxy. Silence in a text has hitherto been interpreted as a sign of victimization. While there has been a great deal of critical interest in the idea of silence in the context of writings by women and ethnic minorities, such analysis has tended to read silence univocally as the product of hegemony and as a sign of resistance.[1] Whether hegemony is named as patriarchy or as a broader form of oppression, these studies valorize silence as the locus of a counter-hegemonic critical position. This approach romanticizes certain texts as purely resistant, as if they were immune from contamination by hegemony.[2]

Silence is certainly one locus of a text's potential resistance to hegemony. However, the act of writing text, as a means of breaking that silence, is inextricably bound up with the very forces it wishes to oppose. The idea of breaking a silence underscores the implicit violence in the act of writing, a violence that I wish to highlight in this analysis of ethnic autobiography. José Rabesa has advanced the proposition that "discourse is violence" (132); a similar proposition informs this article. In each of these texts, the act of writing is a breaking of silence that becomes embodied within the narrative itself: for Angelou the self-inflicted silence after her rape, for Kingston the silence enjoined on her by her culture and family, and for Rodriguez the silence of those excluded from the academy to which he gained entrance.

Defining discourse as violence avoids the temptation to romanticize the author's position as purely counter-hegemonic. It is an alluring idea that texts have an unproblematic political status as "resistant" literatures. As Foley points out, there is a widespread critical belief in studying what has come to be called "ethnic" literature that "these voices, because excluded, must somehow constitute a significant threat to the hegemony of dominant social groups" (67). However, even to designate autobiographies such as the ones in this study as "ethnic" and therefore marginal or excluded raises troubling issues. To analyze autobiographies as "ethnic" for a critic in the current political and social climate is to risk becoming party to the symbolic violence aimed at minorities, a violence that both appropriates and silences them. To designate texts as "ethnic" is to risk marginalizing them at the outset. In *Beyond Ethnicity: Consent and Descent in American Culture*, Werner Sollors has suggested that the category of the ethnic is itself the product of a dominant culture that seeks to marginalize those who do not fit the norm. Similarly, Roberta Rubenstein contends that "both gender and ethnic status render [writers] 'speechless' in patriarchy" (8). The way in which these texts are labeled at the outset consigns them to a borderland with an ambiguous relationship to a single, "dominant" culture.

I therefore read the texts in this article not as "ethnic" autobiographies that represent a marginalized group, but as products of American culture. One of the hallmarks of that culture, along with apple pie and flags, is violence. In registering the effects of violence, these texts are simply reproducing a preeminent American trait, a trait that is evident in the way that newspapers and television news focus so relentlessly on crime, especially murder, and in the amount of naturalized and unremarked violence in "entertainment" from Hollywood movies to children's cartoons. These texts are noteworthy not because of their "ethnic" status but because of the way in which they problematize the relationship of the subject to violence. They simultaneously record the effects of violence, representing the position of the victim, and enact violence themselves, taking the position of the victimizer. They therefore eschew neat categories such as violent/nonviolent, and suggest the ways in which the subjects themselves are implicated in violence.

An example of the troubling romanticization of ethnic texts to which I refer occurs in Michael M. J. Fischer's "Ethnicity and the Postmodern Arts of Memory." In this article Fischer characterizes ethnic autobiographies as a "postmodern" genre, linking them to a decentered and fragmented subjectivity. He invokes the image of a general social breakdown of cultural identities and promotes ethnic autobiography as the most graphic representation of this "postmodern" sensibility. Because ethnic autobiographies construct a bifocal identity such as "Chinese-American," or other similar hyphenated conditions, Fischer sees within them the possibility of a "multidimensional" subjectivity: "In part, such a process of assuming an ethnic identity is an insistence on a pluralist, multidimensional, or multifaceted concept of self; one can be very many different things, and this personal sense can be a crucible for a wider social ethos of pluralism" (196).

There is obviously some truth to Fischer's position. For authors of ethnic autobiography, identity can never be taken for granted. They cannot simply assume any of the terms for group identity proffered them, because none of them quite fits this hyphenated condition. However, Fischer moves rapidly from a discussion of the subjectivity constructed in a text to an analysis of the social context, and it is here that the most troubling elision takes place. Fischer ascribes to these texts a univocally positive political message and then implies that they are a model of "pluralism" for society at large. Such a view sounds all too rosy given the complex range of attitudes expressed in ethnic texts (not all of which are necessarily conducive to "pluralism") and their existence in an American culture that is in theory pluralist but in practice hostile to minorities.

As Yúdice has pointed out, "marginality" is now central to contemporary thought, but critics may appropriate this marginality in troubling ways (214). He cites Wayne C. Booth's use of "dialogism" as a way of addressing feminist criticism that inadvertently subsumes a feminist voice. By downplaying conflict, Booth appropriates other voices within a benevolent pluralism "in which everything is allowed in its proper place . . . so long as it engages in a congenial, or if not 'congenial,' a 'shared conversation,' one that, of course, utterly changes the tenor of Bakhtin's notion of a conflictive 'dialogue'" (215). Lost in both Fischer's and Booth's pluralism is Mikhail Bakhtin's concept of "monologism," a universal trope that represents the hegemonic power of a centralized and normative bureaucratic State. As Bakhtin emphasizes, there is no such thing as a purely "dialogic" text; every text participates simultaneously in the monologic and the dialogic.[3]

The Bakhtinian category of the monologic raises the possibility of language as "coerced speech," a use of language implicated in ideas of power and domination.[4] A pluralist approach, on the other hand, tries to deny or repress violence and conflict in favor of an image of "shared conversation." Rather than presenting speech as "conversation," the texts in this study represent it in terms of coercion and domination. For instance, *I Know Why the Caged Bird Sings* begins with an image of "coerced speech." Angelou is forced to recite a memorized text in front of a congregation. To speak, to break the silence, becomes in this context fraught with anxiety. Dramatizing her own ambivalent position as writer of an autobiographical text, Angelou begins with a moment of failed speech in which memory eludes her. She cannot remember the lines she is supposed to recite, and flees from the church in embarrassment. As she runs out she hears the congregation repeat the lines for her in a communal voice (3).

This moment contains multiple layers of significance. In particular, the scene recalls Angelou's being forced to testify at the trial of her rapist. At this crucial moment, as in the church, she finds herself unable to speak (70-71). Angelou is initially afraid that if she speaks the rapist, Mr. Freeman, will kill her family. After she reveals the rape to her brother, her fear becomes focused on herself rather than on Mr. Freeman. Angelou feels forced by the weight of the expectations of the courtroom audience to lie about her relationship with her attacker. When she hears the next day that Mr. Freeman is dead, she becomes convinced that her lie caused his death. It is at this moment that she resolves to remain silent, because speech is identified in her mind with violence, lies, and murder: "The only thing I could do was stop talking to people other than Bailey. . . . Instinctively, or somehow, I knew . . . if I talked to anyone else that person might die too. Just my breath, carrying my words out, might poison people and they'd curl up and die like the black fat slugs that only pretend" (73).

Angelou internalizes the violence of the rape and turns herself into the source of violence rather than its victim. In an embodiment of Rabesa's formulation that "discourse is violence," Angelou fears that speech is an inherently aggressive act. Her speech has killed once, and could do it again. She now voluntarily assumes the silence that Mr. Freeman had imposed on her when he forbade her to reveal the rape to anyone else. She internalizes a hegemonic definition of women (even prepubescent girls) as sexual and therefore dangerous. Angelou had felt compelled to lie because the crowd in the court expected her to say that Mr. Freeman had not touched her before the rape. Having to lie about these events forces her to accept an image of herself as poisoned and made poisonous by her encounter with adult sexuality.

The rape and its effects make breaking the silence a dangerous and violent act. The text enacts a dialectic between "discourse as violence" and silence as the narrator retreats into muteness. Angelou does not represent herself as entirely a victim, however, in that she sees herself as the potential source of a "flood" of violence that would engulf the world if she were to let it go: "I could feel the evilness flowing through my body and waiting, pent up, to rush off my tongue if I tried to open my mouth. I clamped my teeth shut, I'd hold it in. If it escaped, wouldn't it flood the world and all the innocent people?" (72).

This "flood" finds its analogue in the release of urine with which the autobiography opens as Angelou runs peeing from the church. Like the figurative "flood" above, this release indicates Angelou's resolve to speak even at the risk of violence. Violence is a potential within both speech and silence, and the equation of water and violence expresses metaphorically Angelou's dialectic of containment and release. In the opening pages of the autobiography, containing or holding back the figurative violence of speech becomes a more self-violating option than letting it go:

> I stumbled and started to say something, or maybe to scream, but a green persimmon, or it could have been a lemon, caught me between the legs and squeezed. I tasted the sour on my tongue and felt it on the back of my mouth. Then before I reached the door, the sting was burning down my legs and into my Sunday socks. I tried to hold, to squeeze it back, to keep it from speeding but when I reached the church porch I knew I'd have to let it go, or it would probably run right back up to my head and my poor head would burst like a dropped watermelon, and all the brains and spit and tongue and eyes would roll all over the place. (3)

Speech, sexuality, and violence are all figuratively invoked and con- nected in this passage. The violence of the rape is prefigured in this passage by the violent force that "squeezes" her between her legs. The "coerced speech" of the courtroom scene is prefigured in the symbol of the lemon: just as the juice is forced from a lemon, liquid/speech is coerced from her. However, to contain the force is also to "burst" and turn the violence inward on her own body, fracturing her identity into a decomposed mass of spit, tongue, and eyes. Angelou therefore represents her involuntary eruption into speech as a liberation from the internalized violence of her enforced silence: "I laughed anyway, partially for the sweet release; still, the greater joy came not only from being liberated from the silly church but from the knowledge I wouldn't die from a busted head" (3).

The release of speech/urine therefore is a liberation from oppressive forces, including the "silly church" and the "nasty children" of Stamps, Arkansas. The "sweet release" is also a response to the symbolic violence of growing up as a poor black woman in the South. Angelou's knowledge of her position adds to the bitterness of the situation. Her alienation from the life of Stamps makes her doubly victimized: "being aware of her displacement is the rust on the razor that threatens the throat" (3). *I Know Why the Caged Bird Sings* records not only the literal violence of the rape, but also the symbolic violence of a white cultural hegemony that metaphorically threatens Angelou's intellectual as well as physical existence. Cultural hegemony is the "razor" of symbolic violence against which she struggles in the text.

Angelou escapes from silence by turning her existence in Stamps into a novel and conferring value on her experience in terms of its relation to the literary. Thus Mrs. Flowers, a literate and educated woman whom she admired and who helped her end her silence after the rape, is described as a woman from a novel: "She appealed to me because she was like people I had never met personally. Like women in English novels who walked moors (whatever they were) with their loyal dogs racing at a respectful distance. Like the women who sat in front of a roaring fireplace, drinking tea incessantly from silver trays full of scones and crumpets" (79). Angelou fits Mrs. Flowers into archetypal images drawn from these novels, even as she parenthetically acknowledges their inappropriateness to her life in Stamps. They provide her with models of value, yet are also a distraction from seeing people as they really are. Just as Mrs. Flowers is an ideal because of her association with English novels, so Angelou's friend Louise appears interesting because she is "genteel" and "reminded me of Jane Eyre" (118). Within the cultural hierarchy of the United States, a kind of *Masterpiece Theatre* image of things English operates even in Stamps.

One of the most obviously disturbing effects of the kind of cultural hegemony embodied in novels about upper-class English life is the way they alienate Angelou even further from her social context, from which she felt distant in the first place. Her reading underscores her sense of estrangement from the people around her. The inhabitants of Stamps are interesting only if they have in some way been fictionalized and have had value conferred on them by their association with English novels. A further effect of this class-based form of cultural hegemony is apparent in Angelou's response to a white acquaintance who remarks, "Why, you were a debutante!" when told that Angelou's grandmother was the only African American to own a grocery store in Stamps. Reacting to being described as a "debutante," Angelou muses on the socialization of herself and her friends:

> Negro girls in small Southern towns, whether poverty-stricken or just munching along on a few of life's necessities, were given as extensive and irrelevant preparations for adulthood as rich white girls shown in magazines. Admittedly the training was not the same. While white girls learned to waltz and sit gracefully with a tea cup balanced on their knees, we were lagging behind, learning the mid-Victorian values with very little money to indulge them. (Come see Edna Lomax spending the money she made picking cotton on five balls of ecru tatting thread.) (87)

There is a complex process of identification and differentiation going on in this passage. Angelou expresses a sense of the gulf between Southern whites and blacks, but also a sense of solidarity in terms of gender. Underlying both issues, however, is the role of class. It is the *rich* white girls who make it into the magazines, and the poor who bankrupt themselves living up to a cultural ideal that is not only irrelevant but destructive. Angelou expresses cultural value in terms of an upper-class English Victorian lifestyle that, as her ironic commentary indicates, is irrelevant at best to life in Stamps. The effect of the class system here is to force poor Southerners to spend their slender resources on irrelevant finery. Just as Malcolm X describes how he conked his hair and bought expensive shoes to imitate white fashions, Angelou records the destructive effect of white upper-class cultural hegemony.

However, the effect of English novels is not entirely destructive. *I Know Why the Caged Bird Sings* is peppered with references to *Jane Eyre* (1847). For example, Angelou comments that "there was going to be a storm and it was a perfect night for rereading *Jane Eyre*" (129). Her story itself is a contemporary reenactment of Charlotte Brontë's novel as she refuses the names imposed on her and asserts her own identity and independence. Angelou reads *Jane Eyre* as a text authorizing resistance, finding within the values of the dominant culture a justification for her own resistance. Novels help her emerge from the cocoon of silence in which she envelops herself after the rape. Her reading of these novels thus embodies cultural hegemony and resistance simultaneously. The novels warp her relationship to other people in Stamps and impose false values (so that she fails to recognize that the cultured Mrs. Flowers and her grandmother are "as alike as sisters—"[78]), but also provide her with models of resistance against oppression.

Angelou's text dramatizes her ambivalent attitude to her socialization. On the one hand, she finds reading English fiction an escape from the barrenness of Stamps and the trauma of her rape. On the other hand, the novels help reproduce a race- and class-based system of oppression that identifies the preeminent cultural values as rich and white. Novels can thus be instruments of cultural hegemony and reinforce the symbolic violence of "the razor that threatens the throat," the oppression of one social group by another. Her reading cannot be separated from her own social context, but raises troubling issues of domination and resistance to cultural hegemony, just as do Kingston's and Rodriguez's texts. Angelou's text in particular forces consideration of the relationship of American students to the class-based ideologies of nineteenth-century novels. Her remarks show the way in which the teaching of nineteenth-century novels could function as a means of reproducing class and race hierarchies in contemporary America. Such issues surface even more overtly in Kingston's *Woman Warrior* and Rodriguez's *Hunger of Memory*.

Much has been written about Kingston's breaking of the injunction "don't tell" imposed on her by her mother and her culture.[5] Less has been said about a very painful moment in the text where the young Kingston tries to break the silence of another girl, tormenting a Chinese-American in the bathroom of her school. Unlike Kingston, who has overcome her initial silence, this is the "one girl who could not speak up even in Chinese school" (172). As Sidonie Smith points out, Kingston identifies with this girl and also plays out some of her own guilt at breaking away from Chinese culture's prohibitions against speaking out. Like other girls, Kingston has "found some voice, however faltering. We invented an American-feminine speaking personality" (172). Kingston tries to coerce the silent girl into speech, and in doing so replicates the effect of education on her.

This episode records the effects of both resistance and accommodation to hegemony. As King-Kok Cheung has pointed out, Kingston fears silence because it is linked with victimization, so that in this scene "she cannot help linking utterance and coercion" (164). Her attempt to make the other girl speak is a double move—both an escape from victimization and a turning of the other girl into a victim. She both cajoles the girl into speech and tells her, "Don't you dare tell anyone I've been bad to you" (181). She thus enforces the injunction not to speak, just as it was imposed on her by her culture. The silent Chinese girl functions as a nightmare double for Kingston, who tries to exorcise her through an act of violence of her own. This incident reenacts the symbolic violence of the American educational system that both gave her a voice and forced her to speak.

Kingston's American education both empowers her and alienates her from other Chinese women who don't find a voice. Her victimization of the girl in the bathroom enacts the violent aspects of her own education. To become educated is in some ways to take up the position of the oppressor and reenact the repression of the state-sponsored hegemony of education.

Kingston's text raises the issue of women and violence particularly acutely because, as the book's title indicates, she identifies herself with the legend of the "woman warrior." The central essay in the book, "White Tigers," is a revenge fantasy in which Kingston imagines herself to be the mythic "woman warrior" Fa Mu Lan. The image of the woman warrior resonates with particular force in the context of the increasing feminization of the military. Where the military was once gendered masculine, and its innocent victims often presented as women and children, this simple dichotomy no longer holds. As anxious debates in the media have shown, and images from the Persian Gulf conflict confirmed, the contemporary high-tech United States military has made warfare an equal-opportunity employer. Kingston's book registers the increasing possibility that women can be the originators as well as the victims of violence.

This is not to deny that in American culture women are far more likely to be victims of overt violence than men. However, it does suggest that the effects of violence have to be seen in a cross-gender perspective, not in a dichotomized view where one gender is violent and the other the victim. As the scene in the school bathroom shows, Kingston can impose violence as well as endure it. Furthermore, this scene names education explicitly as symbolic and reproducible violence.

At the conclusion of "White Tigers," Kingston links writing with violence under the rubric of revenge. Remarking that "the swordswoman and I are not so dissimilar," she claims that "the reporting is the vengeance" (53); that is, writing her book and reporting the symbolic violence she has suffered is a revenge similar to Fa Mu Lan's military exploits. Fa Mu Lan and Kingston "have in common . . . the words at our backs" (53), the record of oppression inscribed on their bodies. Like Angelou's razor at the throat, oppression in Kingston's text is represented as a symbolic violence to which the writing of the text is a response.

The image of the "woman warrior" raises the questions of the function of the literary in relation to hegemony, and of how far the text combats the oppression to which it is opposed. Before imagining herself as the woman warrior, Kingston reports an incident in which her own quiet resistance to racism costs her a job. In her "bad, small-person's voice that makes no impact" Kingston refuses to type invitations to a restaurant accused of racist practices (48). This small act of resistance subverts the force of the fantasy that accompanies it. In reality Kingston is not the woman warrior; she can combat racism and oppression only on a small scale. *The Woman Warrior* constantly problematizes the relationship between stories, both familial and cultural, and the reality to which they refer. It is not clear at the end of the essay whether the "woman warrior" story is a compensation for Kingston's real lack of power, or the literary predecessor that authorizes the small act of resistance. Like the English novels in Angelou's text, Chinese stories present a contradictory blend of models of resistance and accommodation to cultural hegemony, made particularly problematic in the context of Chinese culture's attitude toward women, which on one level defines them as "useless" (52). In the university context these two texts pose with particular urgency the question of the relationship between hegemony and literature. Both suggest that literary texts can be, but are not necessarily, counter-hegemonic forces.

Kingston's image of education as coerced speech in *The Woman Warrior* resonates with particular force in the context of *Hunger of Memory*. Subtitled "The Education of Richard Rodriguez," this text addresses directly the role of education as cultural hegemony. Rodriguez claims, like Kingston, to be breaking an injunction to silence in writing his autobiography; Rodriguez is "writing about the very things my mother asked me not to reveal" (175), just as Kingston represents herself as breaking her mother's injunction "Don't tell." But Rodriguez's attitude differs markedly from both Kingston's and Angelou's in the way he uses silence as a mark of oppression. His book ends with an image of his father's silence, which, like the silence of other marginalized figures, "remains to oppress them" (185). As in Kingston's book, silence and oppression are linked. However, the silence is not his own, but that of other figures within his narrative who have not learned to speak English, such as "*los pobres.*"

Rather than record with ambivalence his separation from his family and his community, Rodriguez celebrates his learning of English as a sign of his gaining of autonomy and a public identity. Like Kingston, by learning English he has apparently escaped oppression. Rodriguez's text is not written in opposition to the cultural hegemony of education; he claims that his education was fundamentally a benign exercise turning him into a citizen of the United States. Education gave him a voice. This education was also explicitly a matter of class, as he uses "American" and "middle-class" as synonyms. He calls his narrative "an American story" (5) and a "middle class pastoral" (6). Rodriguez's text, unlike Angelou's and Kingston's, apparently does not record any kind of resistance. When Rodriguez writes, "I had grown culturally separated from my parents" (72), he is describing what he sees as a natural and all-American process of turning the lower-class immigrant kid into a middle-class American citizen.

The most striking silence in *Hunger of Memory* is that of "*los pobres,*" Mexican immigrants in the United States who cannot speak the "public" language that Rodriguez has learned. Rodriguez is haunted by the image of the laborers he meets when he works on a construction site for the summer and finally comes face to face with "*los pobres,*" who had always been figures of both fear and desire for him. He finds he has nothing to say to them, and they can say nothing to him.

As he explains, "Their silence stays with me" (139). Rodriguez has reached a gulf neither he nor his language can bridge.

The silence of *"los pobres"* is the most troubling aspect of the text. Rodriguez realizes that without access to the language he has learned, "cultural minorities are least able to defend themselves against social oppression, whatever its form" (149-50). It is this silence that records most graphically the cost of the educational process that he celebrates in his book. As he writes, "Their silence is more telling" (138). The word "telling" resonates especially deeply in this context, for unlike Rodriguez, *"los pobres"* can never "tell their story" in the way that he does and are thus doomed to a perpetual silence. Their silence is "telling" because it betrays the true cost of the educational process he has undergone.

Yúdice places the attitude of this text to *"los pobres"* within a Bakhtinian context when he characterizes Rodriguez's middle-class American identity as "wrested, stolen, extorted from the heteroglossia of sociality at the cost of the 'marginalized'" (224). Yúdice goes too far in his castigation here, however, since Rodriguez himself is aware of his troubled relationship with *"los pobres"*; it is partly guilt that fuels his fascination with them. Nevertheless, as Yúdice correctly points out, *"los pobres"* show how Rodriguez's education depends upon the marginalization and exclusion of other groups. Rodriguez aligns himself with the "monoglossia" of English (and most disturbingly with the xenophobia of such legislation as Florida's recent designation of English as its official language) in advocating that all education be carried out in English and that other languages be confined to the home. This is not all that the text does, however.

Rodriguez mounts a thoroughgoing critique of affirmative action within the university, and it is a critique informed by the silence of *"los pobres."* He claims that those who have benefited most from affirmative action were those "culturally, if not always economically, of the middle class" (145). In other words, the kind of reform embodied in affirmative action in the university does not reach *"los pobres"* but people like Rodriguez who had already been transformed by the cultural hegemony of education. Groups such as "*los pobres*" are effectively excluded from the university, so that this kind of reform never reaches them.

The image of the silent workers stands as a reminder within Rodriguez's text of the class basis of education. He himself does not resist cultural hegemony. As he notes, "I had been submissive . . . willing to re-form myself in order to become 'educated'" (160). He is, however, the most explicit of all three autobiographers about education's costs. Like the silence in Kingston's and Angelou's texts, the silence in his text stands as a testimony of victimization. It is not Rodriguez's own victimization, because he does not view himself as a victim in the same way as Kingston and Angelou.[6] Rather, "*los pobres*" function as a silent mark of victimization. Rodriguez makes it impossible to ignore the class basis of cultural hegemony because he is so insistent upon this aspect himself. As he writes of the use of the term "minority" in the 1960s, "It became easy to underestimate, even to ignore altogether, the importance of class" (149). Rodriguez makes the class issue impossible to ignore.

Just as in the ethnic autobiographies I have analyzed it is impossible to separate hegemony and resistance, so in any act of writing it is impossible to escape the interrelated categories of the violent and the nonviolent. To speak for texts, to break their silence, is itself an act of appropriation and, in Derrida's terms, an act of violence. This is why it is not enough simply to celebrate the heteroglossic and decentered subjectivity of ethnic autobiographies. If we take seriously the messages of these texts, a critical analysis must be linked to a wider political program that acknowledges the exclusionary nature of a class-based educational system. As Rodriguez points out, what is needed is not affirmative action, but a much wider redistribution of social resources that addresses housing and jobs (152). Ultimately any analysis of ethnic autobiography cannot be divorced from an acknowledgment of the social inequities that give rise to the labels "ethnic" and "marginal" in the first place, and the way in which these categories serve as evasions of the word "class." The implication of this for oppositional critics is that a literary analysis of ethnic autobiography should also be part of a wider program of political action to remedy the social imbalances of power that the university itself reflects.

The problem for literary criticism that I am raising here is that of complicity. The impulse to celebrate certain texts as intrinsically resistant that I critiqued in the opening pages of this article reflects a desire on the part of literary critics to escape implication in systems of violence and oppression. The desire to find an unproblematically counterhegemonic literature is an understandable reaction to the obvious widespread social oppression in American society. However, like Foley I am troubled by the implication that "writers, simply by virtue of their race and/or gender positioning, necessarily articulate a counterdiscourse that is intrinsically subversive of dominant power relations" (67). As Rodriguez's text shows, an "ethnic" writer can take a stance that supports such monologic and hegemonic initiatives as the various attempts in California and Florida to make English the official language of the state.

This is not to say that *Hunger of Memory* is simply a monologic text. Rodriguez's book raises most directly of the three texts in question here the issues treated theoretically by Bourdieu and Passeron in *Reproduction*. Rodriguez records directly the effects upon him and upon others of education as symbolic violence. Although he celebrates his deracination, his poignant descriptions of the plight of the "scholarship boy" record the personal cost of his class transformation. His descriptions of "*los pobres*" also reveal the wider social and cultural violence of American Anglo education. As Bourdieu and Passeron point out, it is not enough simply to study education in terms of its internal protocols. Since education is a systematic process of selection and exclusion, it is necessary also to consider those ejected from the system and the reason for their exclusion.

Merely adding texts such as those analyzed in this article to the canon is not enough. A committed and engaged criticism cannot content itself with simply giving a voice to texts without acknowledging the teacher's implication in an educational system that is itself exclusive and hegemonic. The critic and teacher's own "breaking of silence," like the breaking of silence in these texts, opens up questions of dominance and violence that should not be ascribed to an impersonal power. The teacher is also implicated as subject to and initiator of "symbolic violence." Henry Giroux has called for a critical pedagogy in which teachers function as "transformative intellectuals," as "cultural workers engaged in the production of ideologies and social practices" (*Rethinking* 42). However, Giroux suggests that teachers as transformative intellectuals "distance themselves from those power relations that subjugate, oppress, and diminish other human beings" (42). This is an appealing notion, but one that depends upon the ability to separate an "inside" and an "outside" of oppression, thus removing the threat of complicity. Derrida's meditation upon philosophy and violence demonstrates that such distinctions do not hold, and that a truly "critical pedagogy" would identify the teacher's own complicity in "power relations that subjugate, oppress, and diminish other human beings" as readily as that teacher denounces those at work in the wider social realm.

While complicity is an uncomfortable issue to consider, to avoid it is to risk reproducing the very cultural hegemony that the oppositional critic wishes to combat. Bourdieu and Passeron emphasize that part of the work of education is to mystify existing power relations. The teacher's position depends upon a notion of Pedagogical Authority (PA) that itself confirms the social order. Teaching is simply one in an array of "symbolic forces" that reproduce existing hierarchies: "Every power to exert symbolic violence, i.e. every power which manages to impose meanings and to impose them as legitimate by concealing the power relations which are the basis of its force, adds its own specifically symbolic forces to those power relations" (4).

In other words, when teachers or critics "impose meanings" on a text, they are complicit in symbolic violence and the process of confirming and reproducing power relations. This is not to say that every exercise of PA confirms existing power relations; rather it implies that unless the basis upon which meanings are imposed is denaturalized, the teacher/critic runs the risk of reproducing symbolic violence. It is the idea of a natural "legitimacy," an unquestioned authority, that makes such practices suspect. The teacher or critic must unmask the "cultural arbitrary" that is being imposed as natural order upon the students. Breaking the silence of these texts and speaking for them as the legitimate interpreter of meaning is as much a problematic exercise for the critic as writing them is for the authors.

In the final analysis, however, Bourdieu and Passeron's argument that education reproduces hegemony may well be overly deterministic. As Giroux has pointed out in *Theory and Resistance in Education*, Bourdieu and Passeron leave no room for human agency and provide no theoretical basis for "unravel[ing] the way in which cultural domination and resistance are mediated through the complex interface of race, gender, and class" (90). The texts I have analyzed above provide a useful corrective to this aspect of *Reproduction* by showing how domination is mediated through their authors' particular race, class, and gender positions. In my analysis of the three texts, I have suggested some of the ways in which both domination and resistance are encoded in the moments of "symbolic violence" in the text. Whether these texts serve to resist cultural hegemony or reproduce symbolic violence ultimately depends upon what the teacher does with them in the classroom. In their representation of the contradictory and conflicted nature of cultural hegemony, they at least open up a space for the discussion of symbolic violence within the context of the higher educational system itself. In their representation of education as symbolic violence, they provide an opening for the kind of "critical pedagogy" that Giroux has called for. Whether the ideal of "critical pedagogy" can be realized will depend on teachers' everyday classroom practices.

Notes

1. This criticism should perhaps be put in the past tense. Jan Clausen has argued that the "feminist metaphor of silence as repression, either political or psychological repression," is being revised within feminism. Now that feminist poetry is "more professionalized," such premises are no longer valid (216). See also Duvall; Kitch; Miner.

2. In using the term "hegemony" I am of course drawing upon the work of Gramsci. In my use of "cultural hegemony" I am drawing upon Merod's elaboration of Gramsci's concept in *The Political Responsibility of the Critic*.

3. In *Discourse in the Novel* Bakhtin maintains that "processes of centralization, of unification and disunification" intersect in the utterance of every speaking subject (272). In other words, the forces of the monologic and dialogic are inseparably implicated in one another in every text.

4. I derive the term "coerced speech" from Aaron Fogel's "Coerced Speech and the Oedipus Dialogue Complex."

5. See for instance Smith; Cheung.

6. The differences between these autobiographies in terms of gender bear out the characterization of the differences between male and female autobiography by Shari Benstock and Domna C. Stanton.

Works Cited

Angelou, Maya. *I Know Why the Caged Bird Sings*. New York: Bantam, 1971.

Bakhtin, M. M. "Discourse in the Novel." *The Dialogic Imagination: Four Essays*. Trans. Caryl Emerson, ed. Michael Holquist. Austin: U of Texas P, 1981. 259-422.

Benstock, Shari. *The Private Self: Theory and Practice of Women's Autobiographical Writings*. Chapel Hill: U of North Carolina P, 1988.

Bourdieu, Pierre, and J. C. Passeron. *Reproduction in Education, Society, and Culture*. Beverly Hills: Sage, 1977.

Cheung, King-Kok. "'Don't Tell': Imposed Silences in *The Color Purple* and *The Woman Warrior*." *PMLA* 103.2 (March 1988): 162-74.

Clausen, Jan. "Mending the Silences: New Directions for Feminist Poetry." *Books and Life*. Columbus: Ohio State UP, 1989. 216-24.

Derrida, Jacques. "Violence and Metaphysics: An Essay on the Thought of Emmanuel Levinas." *Writing and Difference*. Trans. Alan Bass. Chicago: U of Chicago P, 1978. 79-153.

Duvall, John N. "Silencing Women in 'The Fire and the Hearth' and 'Tomorrow.'" *College Literature* 16.1 (Winter 1989): 75-82.

Fischer, Michael M. J. "Ethnicity and the Postmodern Arts of Memory." *Writing Culture: The Poetics and Politics of Ethnography.* Ed. James Clifford and George E. Marcus. Berkeley: U of California P, 1986. 194-293.

Fogel, Aaron. "Coerced Speech and the Oedipus Dialogue Complex." *Rethinking Bakhtin: Extensions and Challenges.* Ed. Gary S. Morson and Caryl Emerson. Evanston: Northwestern UP, 1989. 173-96.

Foley, Barbara. "Subversion and Oppositionality in the Academy." *College Literature* 17.2/3 (June/October 1990): 64-79.

Giroux, Henry A. "Rethinking the Boundaries of Educational Discourse: Modernism, Postmodernism, and Feminism." *College Literature* 17.2/3 (June/October 1990): 1-50.

_____. *Theory and Resistance in Education: A Pedagogy for the Opposition.* South Hadley: Bergin, 1983.

Graff, Gerald. *Professing Literature: An Institutional History.* Chicago: U of Chicago P, 1987.

Kingston, Maxine Hong. *The Woman Warrior: Memoirs of a Girlhood among Ghosts.* New York: Random House, 1976.

Kitch, Sally L. "Gender and Language: Dialect, Silence and the Disruption of Discourse." *Women's Studies* 14.1 (1987): 65-78.

Merod, Jim. *The Political Responsibility of the Critic.* Ithaca: Cornell UP, 1987.

Miner, Madonne M. "Lady No Longer Sings the Blues: Rape, Madness, and Silence in *The Bluest Eye.*" *Conjuring: Black Women, Fiction, and Literary Tradition.* Ed. Marjorie Pryse and Hortense J. Spillers. Bloomington: Indiana UP, 1985. 176-91.

Ohmann, Richard M. *Politics of Letters.* Middletown: Wesleyan UP, 1987.

Rabesa, José. "Dialogue as Conquest: Mapping Spaces for Counter-Discourse." *Cultural Critique* 6 (Spring 1987): 131-59.

Rodriguez, Richard. *Hunger of Memory: The Education of Richard Rodriguez.* New York: Bantam, 1983.

Rubenstein, Roberta. *Boundaries of the Self: Gender, Culture, Fiction.* Urbana: U of Illinois P, 1987.

Scott, James C. *Domination and the Arts of Resistance: Hidden Transcripts.* New Haven: Yale UP, 1990.

_____. *Weapons of the Weak: Everyday Forms of Peasant Resistance.* New Haven: Yale UP, 1985.

Smith, Sidonie. *A Poetics of Women's Autobiography: Marginality and the Fictions of Self-Representation.* Bloomington: Indiana UP, 1987.

Sollors, Werner. *Beyond Ethnicity: Consent and Descent in American Culture.* New York: Oxford UP, 1986.

Stanton, Domna C. *The Female Autograph.* Chicago: U of Chicago P, 1987.

Willis, Paul. *Learning to Labour.* Westmead: Saxon, 1977.

Yúdice, George. "Marginality and the Ethics of Survival." *Universal Abandon? The Politics of Postmodernism.* Ed. Andrew Ross. Minneapolis: U. of Minnesota P, 1988. 214-36.

Reembodying the Self:
Representations of Rape in
Incidents in the Life of a Slave Girl and
*I Know Why the Caged Bird Sings*_____

Mary Vermillion

A study of a woman's written record of her own rape can illustrate the dual consciousness that Susan Stanford Friedman identifies as a primary characteristic of female life-writing. According to Friedman, a woman's alienation from her culturally defined self motivates the creation of an alternate self in her autobiography.[1] Because patriarchal cultural definitions of a woman center on her body and sexual status, the rape victim not only becomes painfully aware of her culturally defined self, but she also confronts a hideous paradox as she tries to construct an alternate self. In trying to perceive herself as whole and untouched, the rape victim runs the risk of fragmenting her identity, of excluding her body from what she considers as the rest of her self. Such negation of her body is a natural continuation of the actual rape: the victim tells herself that *she* was not there during the rape—it was not *she* whom he raped. Unanswerable questions then loom. If she was not there, then who was? Who is this "she," this "self" who exists bodiless?[2]

The rape victim's uncertainties about her own subjectivity stem in part from a long tradition in Western patriarchal thought—what Elizabeth Spelman terms "somatophobia," fear of and disdain for the body. Spelman demonstrates that patriarchal thinkers from Plato onward have channeled most of this disdain toward the female body.[3] I will briefly examine the partnership of misogyny and somatophobia in Shakespeare's *The Rape of Lucrece* because his poem influenced the two autobiographers whom I examine in the second and third parts of this essay. Maya Angelou specifically refers to the poem, and it shaped the novels of seduction that Harriet Jacobs critiques in her autobiography.[4] Shakespeare describes the raped Lucrece as privileging her innocent mind over her violated body: "Though my gross blood be stain'd with this abuse, / Immaculate and spotless is my mind."[5] Stephanie Jed describes how somatophobia springs from such a Platonic duality between body and mind: "Implicit in every construct of a chaste or integral mind is the splitting off of the body as the region of all potential contamination."[6] The dire but logical consequences of this splitting off emerge when Lucrece views her violated body through patriarchy's eyes. Perceiving her body as her husband's damaged property, she gives the following rationale for killing herself:

> My honor I'll bequeath unto the knife
> That wounds my body so dishonored.
> 'Tis honor to deprive dishonor'd life,
> The one will live, the other being dead.
> So of shame's ashes shall my fame be bred,
> For in my death I murther shameful scorn:
> My shame so dead, mine honor is new born.[7]

Informing Lucrece's deadly resolution are somatophobia and two other key aspects of patriarchal ideology: the identification of the female with her body and the equation of female "honor" and chastity. The destruction of Lucrece's body perpetuates these patriarchal conceptions of womanhood.[8]

The woman who records her own rape must—if she does not wish to do with her pen what Lucrece does with her sword—close the distance between her body and whatever her society posits as a woman's integral self (i.e., sexual reputation, mind, soul, desire, or will). She must reclaim her body. While this written reclamation is difficult for any woman, it presents a special problem for the black woman because of the meanings that hegemonic white cultures have assigned to her body. According to Spelman, somatophobia supports both sexist and racist thinking because these hegemonic cultures have posited women as more bodylike than men and blacks as more bodylike than whites.

Within these two hierarchical relationships, the black woman is implicitly perceived as the most bodylike, and this perception fosters her oppression in somatophobic societies.[9] Numerous scholars have demonstrated that both the institutions of slavery and antebellum writing constructed the black woman as the sum total of her bodily labor and suffering. Antebellum writers—including abolitionists and black males—depicted the black woman as breeder, wet nurse, field laborer, and, most significant, sexually exploited victim. So pervasive were these images of the black woman's body that the National Association of Colored Women's Clubs, founded in 1896, targeted for its most vehement attacks negative stereotypes of black women's sexuality.[10] Angela Davis and bell hooks illustrate how these nineteenth-century stereotypes inform twentieth-century racist images of the black woman as promiscuous and bestial.[11] Because of this long history of negative stereotypes, the black woman who records her own rape faces the arduous task of reaffirming her sexual autonomy without perpetuating the racist myths that associate her with illicit sexuality. She must recover and celebrate her body without reinforcing racist perceptions of her as mere body.

This task is, of course, also a crucial project for contemporary black feminists. Reviewing Spike Lee's film *She's Gotta Have It* (1986)—in which a black woman, Nola Darling, is raped—hooks writes:

> She [Darling] has had sex throughout the film; what she has not had is a sense of self that would enable her to be fully autonomous and sexually assertive, independent and liberated. . . . A new image, the one we have yet to see in film, is the desiring black woman who prevails, who triumphs, not desexualized, not alone, who is 'together' in every sense of the word.[12]

How two black women who have suffered rape (or its threat) begin to construct this "new image" will be my focus as I examine Harriet Jacobs's and Maya Angelou's autobiographies.

* * *

Jacobs, in *Incidents in the Life of a Slave Girl* (1861), adopts the pseudonym Linda Brent and describes how, as a young enslaved girl, she coped with the threat of rape from her master, Dr. Flint.[13] In order to escape this threat, as well as slavery itself, Brent deliberately chooses to have sexual relations with another white man, Mr. Sands. Many critics have argued that Jacobs's narration of these events echoes and subverts various components of nineteenth-century sentimental discourse—particularly the seduction plot and the basic tenets of "true womanhood" (piety, purity, submissiveness, and domesticity).[14] In my examination of these subversions, I will focus on how Jacobs critiques somatophobia and degrading images of the black female body. Brent's decision to have sexual relations with Sands marks a turning point in Jacobs's reembodying strategies. Before this point, she obscures her own corporeality in order to counter negative stereotypes about black women, and after this point, she begins constructing new positive images of the black female body.

For over one hundred years preceding Jacobs's writing of her autobiography, sentimental novelists portrayed both raped and seduced heroines as believing, like Shakespeare's Lucrece, that their sexual activities sever their integral selves from their bodies. In Susanna Rowson's *Charlotte Temple* (1791), for instance, when the eponymous heroine leaves her paternal home with her seducer, she mourns, "It seemed like the separation of soul and body."[15] Sentimental heroines who undergo such a separation (i.e., lose their "sexual purity")—be it by their own choice or not—face a bout of madness or muteness usually followed by a slow, painful death.[16] Inscribing the "fallen" woman's body as damaged male property, the sentimental novel identifies the female with her body and promotes somatophobia. Furthermore, in dishing out the same "punishment" to both raped and seduced heroines, the sentimental novel as a literary mode obscures seduction's crucial difference from rape: seduction requires a contest of wills, while rape requires the mastery of one will over another. In disguising this difference, the sentimental novel erases female volition. Jacobs, I believe, must have recognized that such an erasure reinforced the slaveholder's negation of the enslaved woman's will.[17] In order to reclaim her own volition, she appropriates the sentimental novel's obfuscation of rape and seduction. By portraying in the language of seduction her former master's legally sanctioned threat to rape her, Jacobs refutes his idea that she was his property, "subject to his will in all things."[18]

Jacobs further accentuates her own volition by depicting the unequal contest between Brent's and Flint's bodies as an equal contest of words. Observing that Jacobs's autobiography contains more reconstructed dialogue than any male-authored slave narrative, William Andrews maintains that Brent's and Flint's dialogues pivot on arguments of the slave woman's rights to define herself.[19] I want to argue that Jacobs also uses dialogue to challenge the hegemonic culture's perception of her as mere body. Flint tries to control Brent by whispering foul words into her ear, and Jacobs writes that he "*peopled* my young mind with unclean images, such as only a vile monster could think of" (27, emphasis added). With the choice of the word "peopled," Jacobs merely hints that Flint would like to "people" his plantation through Brent's body. She portrays the sexual threat that Flint poses as a predominantly psychological/spiritual one and thus lessens her reader's tendency to associate her body with illicit sexuality. Jacobs continues to mystify her former master's physical power and legal right to rape her by confining it to verbal expressions. She primarily depicts his economic mastery over Brent not as his ability to overpower her physically but as his power to perpetuate her slavery in his last will and testament. Jacobs further confines Flint's power to words as she portrays him sending Brent letters, making speeches, and, ironically, promising to make her a lady, a category from which black women were excluded by the white planter culture.[20] Even after Brent runs away, it is Flint's words, and not his body, that threaten her. In her first hiding place the sight of Flint gives her a "gleam of satisfaction" (100), but the sound of his voice "chills her blood" (103). Brent's differing reactions to Flint highlight Jacobs's primary strategy in recording his threat to her body. As Flint's body nears Brent's, as he enters the house she hides in, Jacobs describes him as a mere voice. In recording Flint's attempts to disembody her, she disembodies him.

In thus obscuring the corporeality of Flint's threat of rape, Jacobs minimizes her own body and thereby strikes a blow against the racist stereotype of the black woman as sexually exploited victim. The pen with which she strikes, however, is double-edged, and like Lucrece's dagger, annihilates her own body. In the early part of her autobiography, Jacobs, like Lucrece, privileges an interior self over her body and nearly erases its presence in her text.

Brent's decision to have sexual relations with Sands, however, begins Jacobs's rewriting of her body into her life story. Most feminist readers of Jacobs's narrative interpret her discussion of this incident as her most powerful rejection of sentimental discourse and "true womanhood."[21] I want to emphasize that Jacobs's reversals of the seduction plot's conventions also enable her to reject the body/mind duality that promotes somatophobia. When Flint asks if she loves the father of her unborn child, she retorts, "I am thankful that I do not despise him" (59). Unlike the stock seduced maiden, Brent has no uncontrollable passion for Sands. Reasoning that he will buy and free her and the children they have, Brent exerts her own will to escape Flint's. "It seems," she states, "less degrading to give one's self, than to submit to compulsion. There is something akin to freedom in having a lover who has no control over you except that which he gains by kindness and attachment" (56). Mary Helen Washington calls this declaration "the clearest statement of . . . the need for control over one's female body."[22] Jacobs, I believe, seizes this control by insisting upon a connection between her sexuality and autonomy: "I knew what I did, and I did it with deliberate calculation" (55). By thus emphasizing that Brent willed her sexual activity, Jacobs critiques the somatophobic sentimental convention that severs an unchaste woman's body from her integral self, and she inscribes Brent's union with Sands as a union of her own body and will.

After Brent escapes Flint's plantation, his pursuit of her is so rigorous that she is forced to hide for seven years in a crawl space in her grandmother's attic. Of these years in hiding Andrews writes that "her disembodied presence in patriarchal society lets her become for the first time Dr. Flint's manipulator instead of his tool."[23] While I acknowledge this power shift, I want to further explore Andrews's use of the word "disembodiment." Confined to a coffin-like space and temporarily losing the use of her limbs, Brent is indeed disembodied in her situation. Yet it is, I maintain, in describing this very disembodiment that Jacobs embodies herself in her text. Her descriptions of Brent's physical sufferings in the attic reinforce the bond between her body and her will. Jacobs engages a pattern of first cataloging Brent's physical ills and then comparing them favorably to her state as a slave:

> I was eager to look on their [her children's] faces; but there was no hole, no crack through which I could peep. This continued darkness was oppressive. It seemed horrible to sit or lie in a cramped position day after day, without one gleam of light. Yet I would have chosen this, rather than my lot as a slave. (114)

Here Brent's physical suffering accentuates not only her ability to choose but also the reason behind her choice—her children's freedom.

Jacobs also emphasizes this connection between Brent's will, body, and children by juxtaposing her agony in hiding with the pain of the slave mother whose children have been sold (122). This recurrent figure who has lost both her will and the fruit of her body represents the completely disembodied black woman. She is Jacobs's antitype and has no wish to continue her life. "Why *don't* God kill me?" asks one (16). "I've got nothing to live for now," says another (70). In chapter 13, "The Church and Slavery," Jacobs uses the disembodied slave mother to demonstrate how the somatophobic privileging of an interior self over the body disembodies the black race. In this scene not only does the childless woman voice her suffering and loss, but Jacobs also minutely records her physical torment. The woman stands and beats her breast, then sits down, "quivering in every limb." The white constable who presides over the Methodist class meeting disregards her longing for her sold children, her physical suffering, and the many enslaved people who weep in sympathy with her. He stifles a laugh and says, "Sister, pray to the Lord that every dispensation of his divine will may be sanctified to the good of your poor needy soul" (70). This "spiritual" advice disembodies the woman and her friends, leaving them only their singing voices: "Ole Satan's church is here below./ Up to God's free church I hope to go" (71). While these words disparage the white constable, they also confirm his privileging of soul over body. Critiquing the slaveholder's religion within her rewriting of the seduction plot, Jacobs juxtaposes the "Christian" slaveholder's devaluation of the black body with the sentimental novel's devaluation of the female body and thereby unveils the somatophobia in both discourses.[24]

She further contests both of these disembodying discourses with her descriptions of Brent's activities in her attic hideaway. It is in this part of the text that Brent—tearful, hysterical, and sleepless—most resembles the sentimental heroine. Brent's crawling exercises, her drilling of peepholes, her sewing, reading, and letter writing oddly mimic domestic industriousness. During the second winter, in which cold stiffens her tongue, Brent's muteness and delirium echo that of a "fallen" and dying sentimental heroine. Jacobs thus parallels Brent's attic with the private space that usually confines the sentimental heroine: the kitchen, the parlor, the upstairs chamber, the deathbed, and the grave. Jane Tompkins calls such female space "the closet of the heart" and observes that sentimental fiction "shares with the evangelical reform movement a theory of power that stipulates that all true action is not material, but spiritual."[25] Jacobs challenges this stipulation by emphasizing the drastic material change that Brent works from within her "closet of the heart." As Valerie Smith observes, Brent "uses to her advantage all the power of the voyeur."[26] She prevents her own capture by embroiling Flint in an elaborate plot to deflect his attention, and she meets with Sands to secure his promise to free her children. In her hiding place she not only has a mystical vision of her children, but she actually succeeds in gaining their freedom from slavery.

This uniting of spiritual and material action reenacts Jacobs's earlier textual union of Brent's body and will, and it situates her maternity as a powerful symbol of her autonomy.[27] In her autobiography, Jacobs transforms her body from a site of sexual oppression to a source of freedom—freedom from slavery for herself and her children and freedom from somatophobic racist ideologies that demean the black female body. With one of Brent's early experiences in the North, however, Jacobs suggests that her maternity is not the only cause for celebrating her body. Brent sees portraits of her friend Fanny's children and remarks, "I had never seen any paintings of colored people before, and they seemed to me beautiful" (162). With this statement, Jacobs subtly indicates that her readers must likewise see the black race anew. Jacobs's autobiography, like Fanny's portraits, insists that the value and worth of the black female body exists outside of its functions in a patriarchal slaveholding society.

* * *

Important differences obviously exist between Jacobs's antebellum autobiography and Maya Angelou's twentieth-century record of her rape at age eight in *I Know Why the Caged Bird Sings*. One important difference is the way in which somatophobia manifests itself in their texts. Because Angelou does not have to contend with the nineteenth-century patriarchal ideology of "true womanhood," she is freer to portray her rape, her body, and her sexuality. Yet Jacobs describes herself as beautiful and sexually desirable, while Angelou, as a child and young adult, sees herself as ugly. Jacobs posits somatophobia outside herself and critiques it as part of slaveholding culture, while Angelou portrays her younger self internalizing and finally challenging the somatophobia inherent in twentieth-century racist conceptions of the black female body. Despite these differences, Angelou's text contains reembodying strategies similar to those of Jacobs. Both women contest somatophobia by questioning religious ideologies, rewriting white literary traditions, and celebrating their bodies and motherhood as symbols of their political struggles. In order to challenge racist stereotypes that associate black women with illicit sexuality, both writers obscure their corporeality in the early part of their texts by transforming the suffering connected with rape into a metaphor for the suffering of their race. In Jacobs's text rape is a metaphor for the severed body and will of the slave, and Angelou similarly uses her rapist's violation of her body and will to explore the oppression of her black community.

Angelou first connects her rape with the suffering of the poor. "The act of rape on an eight-year-old body," she writes, "is a matter of the needle giving because the camel can't."[28] In this description, Angelou subtly links her rapist with the wealthy man whom Jesus warned would have a difficult time getting into heaven, and she reinforces this link by alluding to Jesus's words in her ironic description of a black revival congregation's sentiments: "The Lord loved the poor and hated those cast high in the world. Hadn't He Himself said it would be easier for a camel to go through the eye of a needle than for a rich man to enter heaven?" (108). As she continues to imagine the congregation's thoughts, Angelou makes the connection between her rape and the plight of the poor in class society more racially explicit, and, like Jacobs, she also demonstrates that privileging a future world over the present perpetuates black oppression:

> They [the congregation] basked in the righteousness of the poor and the exclusiveness of the downtrodden. Let the whitefolks have their money and power and segregation and sarcasm and big houses and schools and lawns like carpets, and books, and mostly—mostly—let them have their whiteness. (110)

With the image of the camel and the needle, Angelou transforms her rape into a symbol of the racism and somatophobia that afflict Maya and her race throughout much of *Caged Bird*.

Rape in Angelou's text, however, primarily represents the black girl's difficulties in controlling, understanding, and respecting both her body and her words in a somatophobic society that sees "sweet little white girls" as "everybody's dream of what was right with the world" (1). Angelou connects white definitions of beauty with rape by linking Maya's rape with her first sight of her mother, Vivian Baxter. Angelou's description of Vivian echoes that of the ghostlike whites who baffle young Maya. Vivian has "even white teeth and her fresh-butter color looked see-through clean" (49). Maya and her brother, Bailey, later determine that Vivian resembles a white movie star. Angelou writes that her mother's beauty "literally assailed" Maya and twice observes that she was "struck dumb" (49-50). This assault by her mother's beauty anticipates the physical assault by Mr. Freeman, her mother's boyfriend, and Maya's muteness upon meeting her mother foreshadows her silence after the rape. With this parallel Angelou indicates that both rape and the dominant white culture's definitions of beauty disempower the black woman's body and self-expression.

Angelou further demonstrates the intimate connection between the violation of Maya's body and the devaluation of her words by depicting her self-imposed silence after Freeman's rape trial. Freeman's pleading looks in the courtroom, along with Maya's own shame, compel her to lie, and after she learns that her uncles have murdered Freeman, she believes that her courtroom lie is responsible for his death. Angelou describes the emotions that silence Maya: "I could feel the evilness flowing through my body and waiting, pent up, to rush off my tongue if I tried to open my mouth. I clamped my teeth shut, I'd hold it in. If it escaped, wouldn't it flood the world and all the innocent people?" (72). Angelou's use of flood imagery in this crucial passage enables her to link Maya's inability to control her body and her words. Throughout the text Maya's failure to keep her bodily functions "pent up" signals the domination of her body by others. The autobiography's opening scene merges her inability to control her appearance, words, and bodily functions. Wanting to look like a "sweet little white girl," Maya is embarrassed about her own appearance and cannot remember the words of the Easter poem she recites. With her escape from the church, Angelou implicitly associates Maya's inability to rule her bladder with her inability to speak:

> I stumbled and started to say something, or maybe to scream, but a green persimmon, or it could have been a lemon, caught me between the legs and squeezed. I tasted the sour on my tongue and felt it in the back of my mouth. Then before I reached the door, the sting was burning down my legs and into my Sunday socks. I tried to hold, to squeeze it back, to keep it from speeding. (3)[29]

Maya's squeezing back in this passage anticipates her stopping the flood of her words after the rape, and Angelou also connects this opening scene of urination with one of Freeman's means of silencing Maya. After ejaculating on a mattress, he tells her that she has wet the bed, and with this lie, he denies her knowledge about her own body and confounds her ability to make a coherent story out of his actions.

This inability to create a story about her body pervades the remainder of *Caged Bird* as Maya struggles to cope with her emerging womanhood. Angelou, however, is not content to let the mute, sexually abused, wishing-to-be-white Maya represent the black female body in her text. Instead, she begins to reembody Maya by critiquing her admiration for white literary discourse. An early point at which Angelou foregrounds this critique is in Maya's meeting with Mrs. Bertha Flowers. Presenting this older black woman as the direct opposite of young Maya, Angelou stresses that Flowers magnificently rules both her words and her body. Indeed Flowers's bodily control seems almost supernatural: "She had the grace of control to appear warm in the coldest weather, and on the Arkansas summer days it seemed she had a private breeze which swirled around, cooling her" (77). She makes Maya proud to be black, and Maya claims that Flowers is more beautiful and "just as refined as whitefolks in movies and books" (79). Although Maya begins to respect and admire the black female body, white heroines still provide her standard for beauty, and Angelou pokes fun at the literary discourse that whitens Maya's view of Bertha Flowers and womanhood:

> She [Flowers] appealed to me because she was like people I had never met personally. Like women in English novels who walked the moors (whatever they were) with their loyal dogs racing at a respectful distance. Like the women who sat in front of roaring fireplaces, drinking tea incessantly from silver trays full of scones and crumpets. Women who walked over the 'heath' and read morocco-bound books. (79)

This humorous passage demonstrates that Maya's self-perception remains dangerously regulated by white culture. Angelou treats such regulation less comically when Flowers breaks Maya's self-imposed silence by asking her to read aloud. The first words Maya speaks after her long spell of muteness are those of Charles Dickens.

Angelou dramatizes the danger that a borrowed voice poses to Maya in her description of Maya's relationship with Viola Cullinan. Maya makes fun of this white woman, whose kitchen she briefly works in, until she discovers that Cullinan's husband has two daughters by a black woman. Then Maya—in a gesture of sisterhood and empathy that is never returned by Cullinan—pities her employer and decides to write a "tragic ballad" "on being white, fat, old and without children" (91). Such a ballad would, of course, completely exclude Maya's own experience: black, thin, young, and (near the end of her autobiography) with child. Through Maya's speculation that Cullinan walks around with no organs and drinks alcohol to keep herself "embalmed," Angelou implies that Maya's potential poetic identification with Cullinan nearly negates her own body. Cullinan's empty insides echo Maya's own perception of herself after the rape as a "gutless doll" she had earlier ripped to pieces (72).

Angelou's most complex and subtle examination of Maya's attachment to white literary discourse occurs when she lists as one of her accomplishments the memorization of Shakespeare's *The Rape of Lucrece*. Christine Froula maintains that Maya's feat of memory suggests the potential erasure of black female reality by white male literary discourse.[30] More specifically, I believe, Angelou's reference to *Lucrece* subtly indicates that Maya's propensity for the verbal and the literary leads her to ignore her own corporeality. After their rapes both Maya and Lucrece turn to representations of suffering women. Maya reads about Lucrece, and Lucrece, finding a painting of the fall of Troy, views Hecuba's mourning the destruction of her city and husband, King Priam. Unlike Lucrece, Maya seeks strength not from pictorial representations of female bodies but from print, and this preference for the verbal over the pictorial suggests her tendency to privilege literature over her own physical reality. Lucrece decides to speak for the mute sufferers in the painting, and Shakespeare writes, "She lends them words, and she their looks doth borrow."[31] Maya's situation is an inversion of Lucrece's lending of words and borrowing of looks. The once mute Maya can borrow Lucrece's words, but she must somehow lend these words her own "looks" if she does not wish Shakespeare's equation of Lucrece's virtue and whiteness to degrade her own blackness.[32] In remembering *The Rape of Lucrece* Maya must also remember or reconstruct her own body.

One of the ways that she accomplishes this is by celebrating the bodies of other black women. In the only story Maya creates within *Caged Bird*, she augments her grandmother's physical and verbal powers. After a white dentist refuses to treat Maya because she is black, Maya imagines her grandmother ten feet tall, arms doubling in length. As this fantasy grandmother orders the dentist out of town and commands him to quit practicing dentistry, her words, too, metamorphose: "Her tongue had thinned and the words rolled off well enunciated. Well enunciated and sharp like little claps of thunder" (161). With Maya's brief fantasy, Angelou demonstrates how her own autobiography functions. Maya's story, which empowers her grandmother's body and speech, attacks the dentist's derogatory behavior; Angelou's autobiography, which celebrates Maya's body and words, critiques the rape and racial oppression she suffers.

Maya finds, however, that her body and words exist uneasily together. While in the early part of the narrative Maya depends heavily on literature,[33] in the text's final San Francisco section, all words, particularly those packaged as literature, fail to account for her adolescent body's changes. Reading Radclyffe Hall's *The Well of Loneliness* (1928) leads Maya to mistakenly interpret these changes as signals that she is becoming a lesbian. When Maya confronts her mother with this fear, Angelou further demonstrates the inability of the verbal to explain the physical. Vivian's requiring Maya to read aloud the dictionary definition of the word "vulva" echoes strangely Flowers's asking Maya to read aloud from Dickens. Unlike Dickens's prose, however, Noah Webster's and Vivian's words lose their soothing power as soon as Maya is confronted with a stronger physical reality—her own admiration for her girlfriend's fully developed breasts. This scene in which Maya shifts her attention from words to bodies paves the way for Angelou's concluding celebration of the black female body.

Seeking physical rather than verbal knowledge of her sexuality, Maya determines to have sex with one of "the most eligible young men in the neighborhood" (239). Their encounter, which "is unredeemed by shared tenderness" (240), leaves sixteen-year-old Maya pregnant and alone. The young man quits talking to her in her fourth month, and Maya's brother, who is overseas, advises her not to tell her parents until she graduates from high school. Yet it would be wrong to see Maya's motherhood as "a tragic way to end the book and begin life as an adult."[34] While Angelou portrays the pain and confusion resulting from Maya's pregnancy, she places a far greater emphasis on her newfound autonomy. Even Maya's naive style of seduction accentuates her feminist stance. She asks the young man, "Would you like to have a sexual intercourse with me?" (239). In posing this straightforward question, Maya claims control of her body and her identity for the first time in the text. Just as Jacobs describes Brent's union with Sands as a union of her body and will, Angelou celebrates Maya's encounter with the young man. She accentuates Maya's reclamation of her body and volition by ironically alluding to the violation she suffered as an eight-year-old. "Thanks to Mr. Freeman nine years before," asserts Angelou, "I had had no pain of entry to endure" (240).

By detailing how the pregnant Maya copes with her isolation, Angelou pays further tribute to Maya's increased autonomy and acceptance of her own body. Beginning to reject the literary myths that led her to deny her own agency, Maya accepts complete responsibility for her pregnancy: "For eons, it seemed, I had accepted my plight as the hapless, put-upon victim of fate and the Furies, but this time I had to face the fact that I had brought my new catastrophe upon myself" (241). This acceptance of responsibility also leads Maya to a greater acceptance of her own body's powers: "I had a baby. He was beautiful and mine. Totally mine. No one had bought him for me. No one had helped me endure the sickly gray months. I had had help in the child's conception, but no one could deny that I had had an immaculate pregnancy" (245). Angelou's use of the word "immaculate" not only challenges racist stereotypes that associate black women with illicit sexuality, but it also suggests that Maya has shed her earlier conceptions of her body as "dirty like mud" (2) and "shit-colored" (17). Because the eight-year-old Maya perceives her own mother as looking like the "Virgin Mary" (57), the word "immaculate" also indicates that the teenage Maya begins to see in herself the power and beauty she sees in Vivian.

Maya's lack of confidence in her body briefly returns, however, in the autobiography's final paragraphs. Vivian's suggestion that Maya sleep with her child accentuates her worry that she is too clumsy to handle a baby. Vivian banishes this fear by waking Maya and showing her the baby sleeping under a tent that Maya unconsciously formed with her body and a blanket. "See," Vivian whispers, "you don't have to think about doing the right thing. If you're for the right thing then you do it without thinking" (246). Presenting the mother/child bond as a symbol of Maya's newfound autonomy, this closing scene reverses her earlier privileging of the verbal over the physical and celebrates the harmonious interaction of her body and will.

* * *

Rape can destroy a woman's autonomy and self-image, yet Jacobs and Angelou transform this potentially destructive event into an opportunity to celebrate their resistance to somatophobia and negative stereotypes about the black female body. An early scene in *Caged Bird* serves as a synecdoche for the reembodiment both Angelou and Jacobs accomplish in recording their experiences of rape. Three "powhitetrash" girls ape the posture and singing of Maya's grandmother, yet she emerges victorious and beautiful from this degradation and calms the enraged Maya. Afterward Maya rakes away the girls' footprints in the lawn and creates a new pattern: "a large heart with lots of hearts growing smaller inside, and piercing from the outside rim to the smallest heart was an arrow" (27). These connected hearts, which represent the bond between Maya and her grandmother, encapsulate Angelou's and Jacobs's celebration of black motherhood as a sign of personal autonomy. In the grandmother's triumph over the white girls who mock and caricature her body, and in young Maya's erasure of their footprints, I see Angelou's and Jacobs's refutation of negative stereotypes about their bodies. Maya's newly raked pattern resembles their autobiographies—their writings (or rightings) of the black female body outside of dominant cultural definitions.

Notes

1. Susan Stanford Friedman, "Women's Autobiographical Selves: Theory and Practice," in *The Private Self: Theory and Practice of Women's Autobiographical Writings*, ed. Shari Benstock (Chapel Hill: Univ. of North Carolina Press, 1988), 37.

2. Susan Griffin argues that even the fear of rape causes women to negate their bodies: "The fear of rape permeates our lives. . . . the best defense against this is not to be, to deny being in the body." See *Rape: The Power Of Consciousness* (New York: Harper, 1979), qtd. in Jacquelyn Dowd Hall, "'The Mind That Burns in Each Body': Women, Rape, and Racial Violence," in *Powers of Desire: The Politics of Sexuality*, ed. Ann Snitow, Christine Stansell, and Sharon Thompson (New York: Monthly Review Press, 1983), 333.

3. Elizabeth V. Spelman, *Inessential Woman: Problems of Exclusion in Feminist Thought* (Boston: Beacon Press, 1988), 30, 126-31. While I assume that disdain for the female body is inherent in patriarchal ideology, I do not perceive this ideology as monolithic, and I discuss somatophobia's differing manifestations in Shakespeare's, Harriet Jacobs's, and Maya Angelou's times.

4. Ian Donaldson provides a detailed analysis of the role of the Lucretia myth in Samuel Richardson's *Clarissa* (1747-48), a novel that greatly influenced American novels of seduction before and during Jacobs's time. See *The Rapes of Lucretia: A Myth and Its Transformations* (Oxford: Clarendon, 1982), 57-82.

5. William Shakespeare, *The Poems*, ed. F. T. Prince (London: Methuen, 1974), 1655-56.

6. Stephanie H. Jed, *Chaste Thinking: The Rape of Lucretia and the Birth of Humanism* (Bloomington: Indiana Univ. Press, 1989), 13.

7. Shakespeare, 1184-90. Shakespeare's sources similarly privilege an integral self over the body.

8. There are many good feminist readings of *Lucrece*. My reading is most influenced by Coppelia Kahn, "The Rape in Shakespeare's *Lucrece*," *Shakespeare Studies* 9 (1976): 45-72.

9. Spelman, 126-32.

10. Darlene Clark Hine, "Rape and the Inner Lives of Black Women in the Middle West: Preliminary Thoughts on the Culture of Dissemblance," *Signs* 14 (1989): 917-20. In examining dissemblance, Hine also states that antebellum black women had to "collectively create alternative self-images and shield from scrutiny these private empowering definitions of self" in order to function in white patriarchal America (916). I will show how Jacobs and Angelou make their empowering self-definitions public in their autobiographies.

11. Because of the vast scholarship on negative stereotypes about the black woman's body, I will cite only those works that most strongly informed this essay. bell hooks, *Ain't I a Woman: Black Women and Feminism* (Boston: South End Press, 1981), 15-86; Angela Y. Davis, *Women, Race and Class* (New York: Random House, 1981); Hazel V. Carby, *Reconstructing Womanhood: The Emergence of the Afro-American Woman Novelist* (New York: Oxford Univ. Press, 1987), 20-61; Barbara Christian, *Black Feminist Criticism: Perspectives on Black Women Writers* (New York: Pergamon

Press, 1985), 1-30; Christian, *Black Women Novelists: The Development of a Tradi-tion, 1892-1976* (Westport: Greenwood Press, 1980); Sondra O'Neale, "Inhibiting Midwives, Usurping Creators: The Struggling Emergence of Black Women in Ameri-can Fiction," in *Feminist Studies/Critical Studies*, ed. Teresa de Lauretis (Blooming-ton: Indiana Univ. Press, 1986), 139-56; Sander L. Gilman, "Black Bodies, White Bodies: Toward an Iconography of Female Sexuality in Late Nineteenth-Century Art, Medicine, and Literature," in *"Race" Writing, and Difference*, ed. Henry Louis Gates, Jr. (Chicago: Univ. of Chicago Press, 1985), 223-61; Barbara Omolade, "Hearts of Darkness," in *Powers of Desire: The Politics of Sexuality*, ed. Ann Snitow, Christine Stansell, and Sharon Thompson (New York: Monthly Review Press, 1983), 350-70; Frances Foster, "'In Respect to Females . . .': Differences in the Portrayals of Women by Male and Female Narrators," *Black American Literature Forum* 15 (1981): 66-70; Hall; and Hine.

12. hooks, *Talking Back: Thinking Feminist, Thinking Black* (Boston: South End Press, 1989), 140. hooks's challenge is indeed a difficult one. As Barbara Christian ob-serves, "The garb of uninhibited passion wears better on a male, who after all, does not have to carry the burden of the race's morality or lack of it" (*Novelists*, 40).

13. All the names in Jacobs's text are pseudonyms. Dr. Flint is a fictitious name for Jacobs's former master, James Norcom. In this paper I will refer to the author of the au-tobiography as Jacobs, and to the actor within it as Brent. In order to avoid confusion, I will call the other people Jacobs writes about by their pseudonyms.

14. For the basic tenets of "true womanhood" see Barbara Welter, *Dimity Convic-tions: The American Woman in the Nineteenth Century* (Columbus: Ohio State Univ. Press, 1976), 21. For discussions of Jacobs's subversion of sentimental discourse see Carby, 20-61; Jean Fagan Yellin, "Texts and Contexts of Harriet Jacobs' *Incidents in the Life of a Slave Girl*: Written by Herself" in *The Slave's Narrative*, ed. Charles T. Davis and Henry Louis Gates, Jr. (New York: Oxford Univ. Press, 1985), 262-82; Yellin, introduction, *Incidents in the Life of a Slave Girl*, by Harriet Jacobs, ed. Yellin (Cambridge: Harvard Univ. Press, 1987), xiii-xxxiv; Valerie Smith, *Self-Discovery and Authority in Afro-American Narrative* (Cambridge: Harvard Univ. Press, 1987), 35-43; Joanne M. Braxton, "Harriet Jacobs' *Incidents in the Life of a Slave Girl*: The Re-Definition of the Slave Narrative Genre," *Massachusetts Review* 27 (1986): 379-87; Claudia Tate, "Allegories of Black Female Desire; or, Rereading Nineteenth-Cen-tury Sentimental Narratives of Black Female Authority," *Changing Our Own Words: Essays on Criticism, Theory, and Writing by Black Women* (New Brunswick: Rutgers Univ. Press, 1989), 108-11; and Mary Helen Washington, *Invented Lives: Narratives of Black Women 1860-1960* (Garden City: Doubleday, 1987), 3-15.

15. Susanna Rowson, *Charlotte Temple*, ed. Clara M. and Rudolf Kirk (New Haven: College and Univ. Press, 1964), 117. For an excellent discussion of how eighteenth-century English novels represented a split between the rape victim's body and mind see Frances Ferguson, "Rape and the Rise of the Novel," *Representations* 20 (1987): 88-110.

16. Welter, 23.

17. As Susan Staves observes, the idea of seduction is incomprehensible "if women have no rights over their own bodies but are simply the property of men to use as they

will, as female slaves were the property of slaveowners." See "British Seduced Maidens," *Eighteenth-Century Studies* 14 (1981): 116.

18. Harriet Jacobs, *Incidents in the Life of a Slave Girl*, ed. Jean Fagan Yellin (Cambridge: Harvard Univ. Press, 1987), 27. Future references to this text will be inserted parenthetically.

19. William L. Andrews, "Dialogue in Antebellum Afro-American Autobiography," in *Studies in Autobiography*, ed. James Olney (New York: Oxford Univ. Press, 1988), 94. Braxton observes that Brent "uses 'sass' the way Frederick Douglass uses his fists and his feet, as a means of expressing her resistance" (386).

20. Carby's second chapter in *Reconstructing Womanhood*, "Slave and Mistress: Ideologies of Womanhood under Slavery" (20-39), is an excellent study of how nineteenth-century conceptions of "lady" and "womanhood" depended upon the exclusion of black women.

21. Carby, 57-59; Yellin, introduction, xxx-xxxi; Tate, 108-09; Washington, xxiii, 6-7.

22. Washington, xxiii.

23. Andrews, *To Tell a Free Story: The First Century of Afro-American Autobiography 1760-1865* (Urbana: Univ. of Illinois Press, 1986), 259.

24. For a discussion of how privileging a discrete spiritual realm increased patriarchal authority's control over the bodies of enslaved people and white women in antebellum America, see Karen Sanchez-Eppler, "Bodily Bonds: The Intersecting Rhetorics of Feminism and Abolition," *Representations* 24 (1988): 49-50.

25. Jane Tompkins, *Sensational Designs: The Cultural Work of American Fiction* (New York: Oxford Univ. Press, 1985), 150-51.

26. Valerie Smith, 32.

27. For discussions of Jacobs's depiction of her motherhood as a source of her personal autonomy, see Carby, 40-61; Tate, 107-10; and Braxton, *passim*.

28. Maya Angelou, *I Know Why the Caged Bird Sings* (New York: Bantam Books, 1969), 65. Future references to this text will be inserted parenthetically. I will refer to the author of *Caged Bird* as Angelou, and to the actor within it as Maya. In my reading of the early part of Angelou's autobiography, I am indebted to Sidonie Smith's discussion of Maya's quest after her "self-accepted black womanhood," to Liliane K. Arensberg's analysis of Maya's dependence on books, and to Françoise Lionnet's exploration of how Angelou makes her body the source and model of her creativity. See Smith, "The Song of the *Caged Bird*: Maya Angelou's Quest for Self-Acceptance," *Southern Humanities Review* 7 (1973): 365-75; Arensberg, "Death as Metaphor of Self in *I Know Why the Caged Bird Sings*," *CLA* 20 (1970): 275-76; Lionnet, *Autobiographical Voices: Race, Gender, Self-Portraiture* (Ithaca: Cornell Univ. Press, 1989), 130-68. I differ from these readers in that I discuss the somatophobia and racism in white literary discourse as significant obstacles that Maya must overcome before she can begin to recover from her rape and take pride in her body.

29. For another examination of this opening scene and for a consideration of Angelou's other images of flowing liquids and rhythms, see Lionnet, 134-35, 146. Unlike Lionnet, I emphasize Maya's attempts to control her body and words.

30. Christine Froula, "The Daughter's Seduction: Sexual Violence and Literary History," *Signs* 11 (1986): 673.

31. Shakespeare, 1498. He devotes over two hundred lines to Lucrece's viewing of this painting (1367-1569) and contrasts the muteness of the painted Hecuba with Lucrece's venting of grief and outrage at her rape:

> On this sad shadow [Hecuba] Lucrece spends her eyes,
> And shapes her sorrow to the beldame's woes,
> Who nothing wants to answer her but cries,
> And bitter words to ban her cruel foes;
> The painter was no god to lend her those,
>   And therefore Lucrece swears he did her wrong,
>   To give her so much grief, and not a tongue. (1457-64)

32. The following lines typify the many times Shakespeare makes this equation throughout his poem: "This heraldry in Lucrece' face was seen,/ Argued by beauty's red and virtue's white" (64-65).

33. Arensberg, 275-76, and Lionnet, *passim*. Neither critic discusses Maya's dependence on literature in the San Francisco section of *Caged Bird*.

34. Stephanie A. Demetrakopoulos, "The Metaphysics of Matrilinearism in Women's Autobiography: Studies of Mead's *Blackberry Winter*, Hellman's *Pentimento*, Angelou's *I Know Why the Caged Bird Sings*, and Kingston's *The Woman Warrior*," in *Women's Autobiography: Essays in Criticism*, ed. Estelle C. Jelinek (Bloomington: Indiana Univ. Press, 1980), 189.

I Know Why the Caged Bird Sings:
"Childhood Revisited" _____

Lyman B. Hagen

The title of Angelou's first long book, *I Know Why the Caged Bird Sings* (1970), was suggested by Abbey Lincoln Roach. The appropriateness of this borrowed line is most apparent when it is considered in its original presentation. It is taken from a line in Paul Laurence Dunbar's poem, "Sympathy." Asked by an interviewer why does the caged bird sing, Angelou replied,

> I think it was a bit of naivete or braggadocio . . . to say I know why the caged bird sings! I was copying a Paul Laurence Dunbar poem so it's all right. I believe that a free bird . . . floats down, eats the early worm, flies away, and mates . . . . But the bird that's in a cage stalks up and down, looking constantly out . . . and he sings about freedom. Mr. Paul Laurence Dunbar says,

> > I know why the caged bird sings, ah me,
> >   when his wing is bruised and his bosom sore,—
> > When he beats his bars and he would be free;
> > It is not a carol of joy or glee,
> >   But a prayer that he sends from his heart's deep core,
> > But a plea, that upward to Heaven he flings—
> > I know why the caged bird sings![1]

The book's title cleverly attracts readers while subtly reminding of the possibility of losing control or being denied freedom. Slaves and caged birds chirp their spirituals and flail against their constrictions.

I Know Why the Caged Bird Sings was an immediate commercial and critical success. Hailed as a "contemporary classic," it belongs in the "development genre,"—work in the tradition of *Bildungsroman*— a subcategory of literature that focuses on growth and psychological development of the central figure. Transformation is the work's dominating theme, a metamorphosis of one who went from "being ignorant of being ignorant to being aware of being aware."[2] Throughout her writings, Angelou leaves a trail of overcoming parental and societal betrayal without espousing judgmental condemnations. Her maturation is shown by her responses to life's challenging situations.

According to Ernece B. Kelly, *Caged Bird* is a "poetic counterpart of the more scholarly *Growing up in the Black Belt: Negro Youth in the Rural South* by Charles S. Johnson."[3] Kelly calls *Caged Bird* an autobiographical novel rather than an autobiography for good reason: it reads like a novel. It has characters, plot, suspense, and denouement, although the form is episodic. Kelly believes, "On balance, *Caged Bird* is a gentle indictment of white American womanhood."[4] But Kelly's interpretation is too narrow. The stories, anecdotes, and jokes in *Caged Bird* do tell a dismaying story of white dominance, but *Caged Bird* in fact indicts nearly all of white society: American men, sheriffs, white con artists, white politicians, "crackers," uppity white women, white-trash children, all are targets. Their collective actions precipitate an outpouring of resentment from the African-American perspective. This suggests a thesis for examining *Caged Bird* through the lens of folklore and humor. It identifies the far broader picture of black America than its depicted focus.

Reviews of *Caged Bird* praise its use of words. E. M. Guiney wrote that "Angelou is a skillful writer, her language ranges from beautifully lyrical prose to earthy metaphor, and her descriptions have power and sensitivity. This is one of the best autobiographies of its kind that I have read."[5] And R. A. Gross writes that "Her autobiography regularly throws out rich, dazzling images which delight and surprise with their simplicity."[6] Angelou's style demonstrates an obvious ease with vibrant language deployed for the most dramatic impact. A strong sense of the theatrical enriches the most pedestrian passages.

As of the mid 1980s, *Caged Bird* had gone through twenty hardback printings and thirty-two printings in paperback. Angelou's appearance at the 1993 Presidential Inauguration sent the book back to the top of the *New York Times* best-seller lists and resulted in another round of printings. In fact, *Caged Bird* has never been out of print since first issued, nor, it seems, have any of her other books. That *Caged Bird* was once a selection of the Book of the Month Club, the Ebony Book Club, and also nominated for the National Book Award testifies to its appeal and broad popularity. *Caged Bird* alone would assure Angelou a place amongst America's most popular authors.

Angelou told Claudia Tate in an interview in 1983 that the occasion leading to the writing of *Caged Bird* was a dinner party in the late 1960s of Maya Angelou, James Baldwin (a much admired friend), and *Village Voice* cartoonist Jules Feiffer and his wife, Judy, at Feiffer's New York apartment.[7] After a night of swapping anecdotes, someone suggested that Angelou had the material for a book from her experiences while growing up in Arkansas, Missouri, and California. The next day Judy Feiffer called an editor at Random House—Robert Loomis—to ask if he knew the poet Maya Angelou, who might be able to write an interesting book. Loomis called Angelou, who demurred; she was tied up with a television project ("Black, Blues, Black"). Loomis called a few more times. When Angelou remained reluctant, Loomis conceded that perhaps it was just as well she did not attempt a book since autobiography was a most difficult form to handle, and it probably would be impossible to write one with any literary significance. This is a ploy that Angelou cannot resist, she has said. If someone suggests that she can't do something, she considers it a challenge and immediately accepts the proposal. She responded as expected to the reverse psychology and promised Loomis she would prepare a manuscript. Angelou wound up in London, closeting herself to work on the project. Nearly two years later, at a breakfast table, she confronted her good friend Jessica Mitford with a completed text. The two women spent the day poring over the manuscript, which Mitford found fascinating. *Caged Bird* was the resultant book. Over the years, Angelou has maintained a good working relationship with Robert

Loomis, and he continued to serve as editor for all her Random House books. Loomis has made very few public comments on Angelou, as befits a professional editor, but in one instance did show an admiration for her craftsmanship by noting that she could completely reverse material, put the ending as the beginning, with no trouble whatsoever.

Memory plus distance equals true autobiography, the cliché reads. Benvenuto Cellini recommended that "all men of every sort should set forth their lives with their own hand; . . . But they should not commence so noble an undertaking before they have reached the age of forty years."[8] Since Angelou was almost forty when she undertook writing *Caged Bird*, she conforms to Cellini's caveat. According to Marcel Proust, memory can be a powerful weapon against mortality; for Angelou it is also a powerful weapon against bigotry.

With a mind filled with memories, Angelou recaptures her youth. She demonstrates an impressive recall of what it is like to be a child while diligently striving to maintain perspective. Some critics have questioned the point of view as being overly influenced by adult perception. Angelou has publicly addressed this difficulty and feels confident about her presentation. She structures her story into three parts: arrival, sojourn, and departure, geographically and psychologically. The narrative opens with a flashback to an Easter Sunday church scene in the early 1930s, shortly after her arrival from California. This scene constitutes a three-page prologue which establishes the insecurity and lack of status felt by the child Marguerite. She initially recreates the embarrassment she feels at her inability to remember the four-line poem she recites before the congregation, a situation often experienced by youngsters in like circumstances. As R. A. Gross says, Angelou "opens her autobiography and conveys the diminished sense of herself that pervaded much of her childhood."[9] Angelou recalls preparing for church and struggling with her troublesome body image. She is dressed in a discarded "ugly cut-down from a white woman's once-was-purple throwaway" (*CB* 2), which to her childish perception symbolizes her unacceptable being. She daydreams of having "real" hair and blue eyes, which, in her young mind, denote affluence and accept-ability. A tone of "displaced" frustration pervades this introductory section, and the reader is immediately won over and becomes a sympa-thetic confidante. This beginning initiates the journey to establish a worthwhile self-concept.

Following the church incident, Angelou begins the narrative proper and proceeds chronologically from her sojourn at Stamps to her intro-duction to San Francisco. The book ends with the birth of her son, sym-bolic of the end of childhood. However, this closing door opens a new status for the important women of *Caged Bird*. Angelou moves to the level of a mother; Vivian to that of grandmother; and Momma, while losing none of her wisdom, is less effective upon current life. A certain increase in worthiness accompanies motherhood and is an affirmation of Maya's value as a person. Angelou fleshes out the narrative of her very young days with stories that depict the humiliation and struggles resulting from the racism then practiced. Angelou recounts how diffi-cult it was for hard-working African Americans to survive in an eco-nomically depressed and racially oppressed area. She intentionally in-corporates incidents that show her community, in spite of its marginal existence, had moments of fun and laughter, and a significance as an entity.

In *I Know Why the Caged Bird Sings*, Angelou acknowledges that many strong memories of her childhood were of unpleasant happen-ings. However, she knows what a good solid sense of humor can con-tribute to the success of stories, and relies on her humor to soften her recollections. Making the difficult palatable allows for the incorpora-tion of subtle judgments on the inequities of black, communal life. Thus while the comedy in *Caged Bird* and in her other writings is often dark humor emerging from hurt, it is woven into her narratives to do more than lighten them. Angelou's mother, Vivian, on a car ride to San Francisco, "strung humorous stories along the road like a bright wash and tried to captivate us" (*CB* 172). This bridging with humor by Vivian attempts to close the gap caused by her rather haphazard record of mothering. The many jokes, stories, anecdotes, and amusing incidents in Angelou's writings testify to a native humor and its bonding effect. Outsiders feel like insiders when they chuckle and smile together.

In a rather long and very impressive article, Elizabeth Schultz examines the classification of many African-American autobiographies. She particularly looks at the blues mode featured in these writings. Maya Angelou's *Caged Bird* is naturally included by Schultz as a blues genre autobiography, as discussed in a previous chapter. Schultz does state that "Black autobiography has a testimonial as well as a blues mode."[10] Thus there is a blending of two differing approaches to autobiography by most black writers, particularly of more recent times, according to Schultz. The single, individual voice is seen to expand and reflect a communal tone to impact upon the reader. Testimonial autobiographies often shift chronology, as Angelou does with her church-scene opening of *Caged Bird*, to affect later experiences. The mixture of blues and testimonial offers a counterpoint presentation of personal convictions and confrontations balanced against the innate wit and grace essential to survival. The dependence upon a black-generated folklore and humor has already been explored. Schultz goes on to note that blues autobiographers are involved in a process of self-discovery.[11] They are too involved with life events and responses for reflection, but their readers are drawn into this relationship.[12] Angelou is perceived as writing from a "perch of time," allowing her a perspective of maturity.[13] The vision of the black autobiographer, particularly in the blues mode, is shaped by the writer's experience in his community and a discovery of a personal consciousness, according to Schultz.[14] This approach depends upon a level of maturity for assessing the good and the bad and expressing the hope that the good will prevail.

Angelou's style in *Caged Bird* reflects the inflections and rhythms and natural metaphors of the blues which creates a sense of community with her readers, but she also incorporates prose identifiable with African-American sermonizing. This, too, signifies to her particular audience.[15] An essential blues characteristic of ironic understatement serves as a vehicle for enduring the contradictions of life. Yet, conscious overstatement of episodic details allows a focus upon the extreme emotional responses.[16] Angelou permits herself flights of fantasy and exaggeration to express an intensity of feeling.[17] This is particularly pertinent to *Caged Bird*, where a major goal is self-determination.

Caged Bird chronicles approximately ten years that Angelou and her brother Bailey, Jr., live with their paternal grandmother, Mrs. Annie Henderson, who owns the store in the segregated section of Stamps, Arkansas. Marguerite and Bailey, Jr., had been tagged and shipped by their parents by rail from California to Arkansas to live with Momma. Mrs. Henderson's world "was bordered on all sides with work, duty, religion, and 'her place'" (*CB* 47). "Momma" Henderson and her views on life provide what little stability Maya experiences.

In 1935, "without warning," father Bailey Johnson, Sr., swoops into town from California, and Marguerite and Bailey, Jr., are again up-rooted and taken to live with their mother in St. Louis. Here Angelou meets the maternal side of her family and finds these relatives to be an extremely close-knit group: "Grandfather had a famous saying that caused great pride in his family: 'Bah, Jesus, I live for my wife, my children and my dog'" (*CB* 50). Angelou actively advocates family strength and cohesion as often as possible. Her maternal grandmother, a quadroon or an octoroon, raised in a German setting, is an active force in local politics. Grandfather Baxter was a dark West Indian native in stark contrast to his wife's nearly white visage. Each had the distinctive dialect of their backgrounds. However, the grandmother's German upbringing and light appearance made her more acceptable to the local power structure and assured her a position of significance.

But the urban high-life differs diametrically from the fundamentalist structure of rural Stamps. In St. Louis, Marguerite is raped by her mother's current paramour while she is under his care. The detailed recall of the rape itself and the searing memory of it inform the reader of the tremendous impact both mental and physical upon the innocent victim. On the courtroom stand at the trial of the accused, a Mr. Freeman, Angelou hides previous advances made by him—some innocent and some not-so-innocent—still fearful of his threats. As a result, he is given a reduced sentence. The rape of a black child is apparently not of great concern to the judicial system of that time and place. The lifetime impact upon the small victim apparently does not warrant serious punishment. But his immediate release proves to be his undoing. Street justice is exercised with no ensuing legal recourse. He is found dead, possibly kicked to death by Angelou's "mean and ugly" uncles, righting a family wrong and asserting its status. The eight-year-old child associates his death with her lack of truthfulness and therefore blames herself. She takes upon herself the guilt for the lawless act of retribution. Speech causes tragedy, she concludes simplistically, so to avoid further harm to anyone, Marguerite decides to stop talking except to her trusted brother, Bailey. Her mother mistakes this retreat into silence for impudence, however, and ships the two children back to Stamps and the strict discipline and uncomplicated protection of Grandmother Henderson.

Shortly thereafter, in the General Store Marguerite meets Mrs. Flowers, her community's anointed intellectual, who becomes Angelou's "first life line" (*CB* 77). Momma solicits her aid with the mute Maya, and at her sanctuary-like home Mrs. Flowers gently and graciously draws out Marguerite and encourages her to continue an interest in literature. Mrs. Flowers extols the value of poetry: "Poetry is music written for the human voice. Until you read it (aloud), you will never love it."[18] Through this device, reciting poetry aloud to herself, Angelou regains her use of speech. A love of literature and literacy deepens at this time and continues throughout her life. According to Françoise Lionnet-McCumber, Angelou makes reference to over 100 different literary characters in her autobiographies,[19] attesting to her familiarity with conventional literature. Angelou's devotion to learning—to literacy—addresses what Robert B. Stepto says is "the central myth of black culture in America: 'the quest for freedom and literacy.'"[20] African Americans hungered for these goals and strove mightily in many subtle ways to attain them.

The pursuit of knowledge in Angelou's early development, according to George E. Kent, draws on "two areas of black life: the religious and the blues traditions." Her grandmother represents the religious influence: Black Fundamentalism, the Christian Methodist Episcopal (CME) Church. Her mother, on the other hand, stands for the "blues-street tradition," the fast life.[21] Françoise Lionnet-McCumber in her dissertation adds a third term to this comparison: "the literary tradition, all the fictional works that the narrator reads avidly."[22] *Caged Bird* draws heavily upon these elements: the hundred references noted above, a couple of dozen biblical quotes, and the music felt throughout.

Following Angelou's re-awakening and emergence under the guidance of her mentor, Mrs. Flowers, *Caged Bird*'s narrative moves forward, incorporating stories that show what it is to be black in the American South. Angelou's rural family associations are typical of the time and place. She tells of an ecumenical church revival meeting that reflects the religious cooperation and involvement of the entire community. Familiar evening entertainments often revolved around ghost stories which were told to both skeptical and supportive superstitious listeners. The folkloric derivations of these activities have been previously addressed in detail. Other reports of daily activities reflect life for African Americans in Stamps, Arkansas, and the hundreds of other Stampses.

In 1940, Angelou is graduated with honors from Lafayette County Training School. She recalls with considerable dismay that the commencement speaker—a white politician—promises academic improvements for white schools and the continuation of athletic programs for blacks: "The white kids were going to have a chance to become Galileos and Madame Curies and Edisons and Gauguins, and our boys (the girls weren't even in on it) would try to be Jesse Owenses and Joe Louises" (*CB* 151). A graduation scene appears in many autobiographies as signifying survival and achievement. Angelou finds her graduation experience once again points to how opportunity for African Americans is limited and stereotyped by the white patriarchal society. However, the singing of the Negro national anthem, James Weldon Johnson's "Lift Ev'ry Voice and Sing," expresses a unity and portends hope for the future.

Soon thereafter, an increasingly venturesome teenage Bailey, Jr., encounters his first slain black man. Momma Henderson decides it would be safer and timely for the children to be with their parents in California. So Marguerite departs for California with Momma, Bailey to follow. Maya, Bailey, and Momma live together briefly in Los Angeles. Vivian takes the children to Oakland, and Momma returns to Stamps. Vivian remarries and the family resettles in San Francisco. Angelou attends George Washington High School days and studies dance at the California Labor School at night. Maya goes to spend some time with her father and his lady in southern California. She accompanies Bailey, Sr., on a wild jaunt to a Mexican village where he seems to be known. When he becomes too drunk to drive back home, Marguerite takes the wheel, even though she had no driving instruction. She somewhat successfully maneuvers the two of them to the border, where Bailey, Sr., revives and can again take over. This incident furthers her growing awareness that she can indeed do anything she sets her mind to, as Mother Vivian regularly extols.

After a run-in with her father's mistress, Angelou leaves their home and strikes out on her own. She lives for a time in a junkyard with other homeless adolescents. They—"a collage of Negro, Mexican and White—" become her family. The great importance of this "family," Liliane K. Arensberg finds, is "that these children disprove the racial prejudice—and its concurrent death fantasies—of her earlier experiences."[23] Angelou becomes aware that an African American can survive and bond with like-kind of other races. The unquestioning support of each other in this group allows Angelou to reach beyond her former boundaries and attitudes. One of the group lives in a real home and allows its use by the entire band for periodical, personal hygiene. Rules are practical and accepted by all. They share a common goal of survival. This sharing required for survival was tested by Thor Heyerdahl, the explorer, when he deliberately mixed varied ethnic personalities on one of his expeditions. He found their only differences arose from minor personal traits rather than their ethnicity. They were able to adjust to the common bounds of necessity. A former sequestered juror from a major murder trial when questioned about racial problems in the jury room replied that the only problems arose from irritating personal traits, not race, thus further attesting to the ability of diverse persons to form bonds when faced with a common situation.

Angelou eventually returns to San Francisco to live again with her mother. As a maturing teenager, she begins to awaken sexually. Uncertain about her sexuality and fearful of being unwomanly, she turns to her mother, who tries to reassure her. But her lack of development and new, unfamiliar emotional responses leave her still curious and ambivalent. So Angelou challenges her womanhood forthrightly by instigating a casual sexual encounter. She becomes pregnant, keeps her situation hidden from all for over eight months, and just as she graduates from high school announces her condition to her family. School records show her dropping out of school one semester but returning to graduate from Mission High School after a summer session. Very shortly thereafter she gives birth to her son, Clyde (Guy).

The characters on the pages of *Caged Bird* are fully developed and three-dimensional. The only perceivable distortion might be that literary license seems to embellish them somewhat to larger-than-life personalities. However, they are real-life flesh and blood people who were a part of the life of Maya Angelou. Angelou, the principal personage of *Caged Bird*, assumes two personae: the voice of "Ritie" (a diminutive of Angelou's first name, Marguerite) who describes poignantly the incidents in her childhood and adolescence; and the voice of Maya, the near adult who is somewhat introspective, more objective and less personal. Angelou uses the second voice to make general observations or to editorialize. For example, when Uncle Willie hides from the prowling klansmen, the Maya voice objects to the lack of police protection for African Americans against obviously lawless activities.

In Jungian archetypal terms, Angelou is the anima. The animus—the male part of her make-up—is represented by her brother Bailey. Bailey Johnson, Jr., is a firm, rather free-spirited youngster who because of being male, is able to move about in his segregated world with fewer restrictions than sister Maya. The two children are very close, probably because of their life situations as much as from their shared experiences and interests. They are both highly literate and adaptable. Bailey is protective of Maya, yet each appears to be very independent. Bailey must face greater dangers in the larger white-dominated world and is taught early on of the risks of being an African-American man. He does not allow this to prevent his functioning as a typical bright, energetic boy. He, more than any other character, with his outgoing personality and natural curiosity, seems to exemplify Angelou's contention regarding blacks and whites: that they are more alike than unalike; that there are more similarities than differences. Bailey likes reading, comic books, movies, sportscasts, following around his St. Louis uncles and a little strutting. He idolizes his attractive, devil-may-care mother. All of these things could be said about any boy of his age. However, the promise of Bailey the boy seems to have been blunted for Bailey the man, who wound up in prison. This is a sad, unfortunate development, but is not openly attributed to race. His embracing the street-style is accepted as a matter of circumstance and choice.

In addition to Bailey, whom the young Angelou acclaims the greatest person in her world, most male characters in *Caged Bird* receive exceptionally sympathetic treatment: there are the "dirt-disappointed" field workers, whose efforts weren't enough "no matter how much cotton they had picked" (*CB* 7); there is Daddy Clidell, a successful businessman; Grandfather Baxter, a family man of stature who had "mean" (tough) but not cruel sons; Uncle Willie, handicapped physically but not mentally; and Mr. McElroy who owned property. He was an "independent Black man, a near anachronism in Stamps" (*CB* 17). Even Mr.

Freeman, the rapist of a child, had worldly status and held an important position with the railroad. In an interview with Claudia Tate, Angelou said that she "wanted people to see that the man was not totally an ogre." These men all evidence strength and some attainment, even the worst of them. This would appear to be a conscious effort to minimize popular negative images of the African-American male.

Angelou's father, Bailey, Sr., does not fare so well. Here the personal outweighs the general. She confesses that "[her] father had not shown any particular pride in [her] and very little affection" (*CB* 195). Thus he is a "stranger" to her and someone to whom she did not feel any loyalty. His betrayal of the children was evidenced by his appearance in their lives only at times of moving them around—out of his way and responsibility. Her father lived in a fast lane characteristic of "hipster" types. In *Caged Bird* and in a later book, Angelou ridicules her father's speech habit of "er-er-ing" and his tendency to posture. Bailey, Sr., has all the earmarks of a blowhard. He wheels in and out of her early life with a lot of "pizazz," but little substance. He does not fill a major role, as a father should, but is seen more as a biological acknowledgment. Even he, however, survives and flourishes in his world, despite Angelou's low opinion of him. This lack of regard for Bailey, Sr., did not prevent Angelou from acknowledging the importance of a father figure to a family. Until her son is accepted as a grown man, she searches unsuccessfully for a man who would be a proper father and role model for him. She encounters only more betrayal.

Angelou's treatment of female role models in *Caged Bird*—of her Mrs. Flowers and of her mother and grandmothers—is even more positive than her treatment of African-American males. Since it is generally accepted that children of her era developed stronger bonds with their mother than their father, it is not surprising to find Angelou emphasizing the importance of mother and grandmothers. Such emphasis on mothers is, according to Stephanie A. Demetrakopoulos, "typical in women's autobiography due to the innate and archetypal aspects of the women's psyche, celebrated and codified long ago as the Eleusinian

Mysteries."[24] These archetypal aspects may be incorporated in women's autobiographies, but it does not seem to be done consciously by Angelou. What she does do consciously, however, is to make an effort to counter unflattering female types described in the earlier literature by James Fenimore Cooper and Washington Irving. In this literature, grandmother matriarchs are depicted as silent, post-forty, corpulent and passively working in the kitchen.[25]

Compared to these earlier female stereotypes, Angelou's paternal grandmother, Mrs. Henderson, is a symbol of strength; she is in no way a weak, passive personality. She is not silent. She is the moral center and the voice of authority in *Caged Bird*. She is an Earth Mother, a figure who is good, kind, nurturing, and protecting. Angelou calls her "Momma" and in fiction she would be the "Madonna" figure, one who stands for love and home. Her love for Angelou is unconditional and maternal. This love contrasts markedly with the paternal, in which love is more conditional and is usually earned and given only if one is obedient and attractive. In Angelou's extended family an atmosphere of warmth and love prevails that is not bestowed as a result of obedience or something earned. The strong maternal instinct enveloped all.

Momma Henderson, for all her matriarchal positioning, is a total realist. If she ever failed to do her duty or did not observe her place as a lower class citizen, she knows the white power structure would soon find a way to express its displeasure. Those in control are generally more interested in order than in justice. Momma's firm leadership while still being forced to keep her place, sends a mixed message to the younger generation that required a good deal of maturity and distancing for them to understand. It was some time before Angelou expressed, particularly in her poetry, the courage and patience of those who kept quiet and saw to the survival of those in whom the future rested.

Two other characteristics of Momma contrast with the matriarchs found in early American literature. Inasmuch as there were few or no opportunities in the professions, many women turned to religion as a means of escape from the confinement of their defined roles. Thus, Momma, a natural leader, became an important figure in her church. Moreover, Momma was an entrepreneur, a female rarity in the 1930s and unheard of one hundred years earlier. Her business acumen helped her family survive the depression and keep off relief; she preserved their independence. This would not be a role natural to her predecessors.

In addition to her praise of Momma Henderson, Angelou expresses great pride in her maternal grandmother, Mrs. Baxter, who did not take a back seat to anybody. As previously noted, she was very light-skinned and probably could have easily passed as white. She chose to remain a part of a black community. She and her family spoke standard English and provided important liaison with the local white power structure. She was a political activist who wielded considerable clout in her neighborhood in St. Louis, thus giving the lie to the myth that African Americans could not participate effectively in the political arena. Power blocs delivered votes and reaped the rewards. The Baxters understood the strength of unity.

Similarly, Angelou's mother, Vivian Baxter Johnson, emerges as an extremely vital personality. She is Angelou's role model. Angelou absorbs her personal philosophy and frequently quotes her maxims of life. Mrs. Johnson's beauty and zest when she was young "made her powerful and her power made her unflinchingly honest" (*CB* 174); and "To describe (her) would be to write about a hurricane in its perfect power. Or the climbing, falling colors of a rainbow" (*CB* 49). Vivian is a city woman and sees no need in her world to conform to the subservient country folk tradition. She can sing and swing at will.

Vivian also found it too inconvenient to care for her two children or found it too incompatible with her lifestyle. She finds an excuse—a depressed Maya—to send Maya and Bailey back to Stamps. This cavalier dumping of her children appears to Stephanie Demetrakopoulos as a failure to come to terms with the matriarchate (her mother), and this treatment, Demetrakopoulos finds, is a disturbing weakness of the book. Angelou's mother is seen as "shockingly callous" and insensitive by sending the little girl back to Stamps after being raped. Maya is traumatized by events and full of unwarranted guilt. The mother's behavior here and at other times does not justify the favorable treatment she got from Angelou and this action, Demetrakopoulos says, is "puzzling and unsettling."[26] Vivian is just as guilty as Bailey, Sr., of betraying their children. But Mother Vivian is idolized by both Johnson children and neither would dream of questioning her less-than-perfect mothering. She is all that is glamorous and movie-life desirable to them. In Angelou's next book, *Gather Together in My Name*, she does question her mother's sense of responsibility. She wonders whether her mother ". . . who had left (her) with others until she was thirteen . . . (would) feel more responsibility for (her) child Guy (née Clyde) than she had felt for her own" (*GT* 3). Thus there existed an awareness of an imperfect relationship with mother as well as father. Even if not openly acknowledged, this would have a dire effect upon sense of worth. Angelou always seems to seek out her mother's wisdom and advice, however, and gives her an important role in her life. She does not seem to dwell upon any rejection or lack of love. Years later Vivian would move in with Maya, who would never abdicate family responsibility without remorse. She, like Momma Henderson, fully understood and accepted motherhood and its attendant Madonna aspects.

In *Caged Bird* and her other autobiographies, Angelou does discover herself and her capabilities and effectively conveys her personality and opinions. Her real purpose in *Caged Bird*, however, as well as in her other books, is to illuminate and explain her race's condition by protesting against white misconceptions and legitimatizing the extremes sometimes required for survival. While justifying some questionable activities, she does not judge the right or wrong of them. She wants to destroy those stereotyped images of African Americans that prevailed when she wrote *Caged Bird*. Angelou rightly resents this thinking that dehumanized her people, and which continued to be practiced despite civil rights progress. Instead of writing an argumentative response or preaching to protest, Angelou chose the traditional form of autobiography to dramatize the conditions, presenting easily understood counter-examples. The reader can relate and conclude that the stereotype image is false and destructive. Forces beyond control dictate actions determined to be antisocial. Given equal opportunities, Angelou believes that like reactions would be demonstrated by blacks and whites. Later she acted this out as the white queen in Genet's *The Blacks*.

Caged Bird ends with Angelou facing the adult world full of "Mother Wit" and determination. She accepts enthusiastically the challenge of sustaining herself and her son. Her focus is that of a mature, responsible young woman. She will do better than her predecessors and enhance the mantle of motherhood. She has gained strength from her adversities, and increased status as a mother gives her added confidence for the future. The Maya character in *Caged Bird* addresses the author's stated themes by overcoming many obstacles, establishing some sense of self as a mother, and repeatedly emphasizing the importance of literacy and education. She also serves the traditional black autobiographical themes of bondage, her dependence on others; flight, as she breaks out on her own with the junkyard group; and freedom, by taking control of her life. Thus Angelou includes all required elements in *Caged Bird* and uses it as the base for her future books.

From *Heart of a Woman, Mind of a Writer, and Soul of a Poet: A Critical Analysis of the Writings of Maya Angelou* (Lanham, MD: University Press of America): 54-73. Copyright © 1997 by University Press of America. Reprinted by permission of University Press of America.

Notes

1. Countée Cullen, *Color* (New York: Arno Press, 1969) vi.
2. "Maya Angelou." *Contemporary Literary Criticism* 35 (Detroit: Gale, 1985) 29.
3. Arthur E. Thomas, *Like It Is: Arthur E. Thomas Interviews Leaders on Black America* (New York: Dutton, 1981) 5.
4. R. B. Stepto, "The Phenomenal Woman and the Severed Daughter," *Parnassus: Poetry in Review* 8, 1 (Fall/Winter 1979) 313-15.

5. Ellen Lippman, *School Library Journal* 25 (1978): 83.

6. Janet Blundell, *Library Journal* 108 (1983): 746.

7. J. A. Avant, *Library Journal* 96 (1971): 3329.

8. S. M. Gilbert, *Poetry* (August 1976): 128-129.

9. *Choice* 9 (1972): 210.

10. Chad Walsh, *Book World* 9 (1972): 12.

11. *Publishers Weekly* 11 Feb. 1983: 59.

12. Robert Loomis, "Letter to L. B. Hagen," 3 June 1988.

13. Jeffrey M. Elliot, ed., *Conversations with Maya Angelou* (Jackson, MS: University Press of Mississippi, 1989) 155.

14. Sondra O'Neale, "Reconstruction of the Composite Self: New Images of Black Women in Maya Angelou's Continuing Autobiography," *Black Women Writers 1950-1980*, ed. Mari Evans (New York: Anchor Books/Doubleday, 1984) 28.

15. Walsh, 12.

16. Blundell, 1640.

17. "Maya Angelou," *Current Biography* (New York: H. W. Wilson, 1974) 14.

18. Stepto, 313-315.

19. Françoise Lionnet-McCumber, "Autobiographical Tongues . . ." Dissertation, University of Michigan, 1986: 74.

20. Robert B. Stepto, *From Behind the Veil* (Urbana: University of Illinois Press, 1979) ix.

21. George E. Kent, "Maya Angelou's *I Know Why the Caged Bird Sings* and Black Autobiographical Tradition," *Kansas Quarterly* 7, 3 (1975): 75.

22. Lionnet-McCumber, 74.

23. Liliane K. Arensberg, "Death as Metaphor in *I Know Why the Caged Bird Sings*," *College Language Association Journal*, December 1976, 273-91.

24. Stephanie A. Demetrakopoulos, "The Metaphysics of Matrilinearism in Women's Autobiography," *Women's Autobiography: Essays in Criticism*, ed. Estelle C. Jelinek (Bloomington: Indiana University Press, 1980), 180-205.

25. Sondra O'Neale, "Reconstruction of the Composite Self: New Images of Black Women in Maya Angelou's Continuing Autobiography," *Black Women Writers 1950-1980*, ed. Mari Evans (New York: Anchor Books/Doubleday, 1984).

26. Demetrakopoulos, 183.

Racial Protest, Identity, Words, and Form_____
Pierre A. Walker

Maya Angelou has told in interviews how Robert Loomis, her eventual Random House editor, goaded her into writing autobiography, teasing her with the challenge of writing *literary* autobiography. Considering herself a poet and playwright, she had repeatedly refused Loomis's requests that she write an autobiography until he told her that it was just as well: "He . . . said that to write an autobiography—as literature—is almost impossible. I said right then I'd do it" ("Maya Angelou," with Hitt, 211). Angelou often admits that she cannot resist a challenge; however, it was not the challenge of writing autobiography per se that Angelou could not resist (and that led to the 1970 publication of *I Know Why the Caged Bird Sings*) but the challenge implied in Loomis's remark about the difficulty of writing autobiography "as literature."[1]

Angelou does not elaborate on how she distinguishes literary autobiography from any other kind of autobiography, and of course, for a poststructuralist, the challenge to write *literary* rather than "ordinary" autobiography is meaningless because there is no difference between the two (see Eagleton, 201). For a formalist aesthetic, however, the distinctive qualities and characteristics of literary or poetic language as opposed to ordinary language are central operative concerns (see Brooks, 729-31; Shklovsky, 12; Fish, 68-96). Cleanth Brooks's belief that "the parts of a poem are related to each other organically, and related to the total theme indirectly" (730) was a primary tenet of interpretation for American New Critics, ultimately related to their determination to distinguish literary from ordinary language. Poststructuralism in its most vehemently antiformalist manifestations usually belittles Brooks's beliefs in organic unity and in the uniqueness of literary language, but criticisms of formalism and of "literature" as a distinct and privileged category, so typical of much poststructuralist theorizing, become specially problematic in relation to African-American literature.

Many African-American texts were written to create a particular political impact. As a result, one can hardly ignore either the political conditions in which the slave narratives and Richard Wright's early works, for example, were composed or the political impact their authors (and editors and publishers, at least of the slave narratives) intended them to have. Even African-American texts that are not obviously part of a protest tradition are received in a political context, as is clear from the tendency in much critical commentary on Zora Neale Hurston to demonstrate an elusive element of protest in her novels.

So important is the political to the experience of African-American literature that it comes as no surprise that the increasing incorporation of the African-American literary tradition into mainstream academic literary studies since 1980 coincides exactly with the increasingly greater significance of the political in the prevailing critical paradigm: what better for a political literary criticism to address than an overtly political literature?

The problem is that African-American literature has, on more than one occasion, relied on confirming its status as literature to accomplish its political aims. Since slavery relied on a belief that those enslaved were not really human beings, slave narrators responded by writing books that emphasized the fact that they themselves were humans who deserved to be treated as such. Since emancipation, African-American authors have used the same strategy to fight the belief in racial hierarchies that relegated them to second-class citizen status. One way to do this was to produce "high art," which was supposed to be one of the achievements of the highest orders of human civilization. African-American poetry provides many examples of this strategy: Claude McKay's and Countée Cullen's reliance on traditional, European poetic forms and James Weldon Johnson's "O Black and Unknown Bards." Cullen's "Yet Do I Marvel," for instance, relies on recognizable English "literary" features: Shakespearean sonnet form, rhyme, meter, references to Greek mythology, and the posing of a theological question as old as the Book of Job and as familiar as William Blake's "The Tyger."

Thus for a critical style to dismiss the closely related categories of form and of literature is to relegate to obscurity an important tradition of African-American literature and an important political tool of the struggle in the United States of Americans of African descent. This is clearly true in respect to *Caged Bird*, which displays the kind of literary unity that would please Brooks, but to the significant political end of demonstrating how to fight racism. Angelou wrote *Caged Bird* in the late 1960s at the height of the New Criticism, and therefore in order for it to be the *literary* autobiography Loomis referred to, Angelou's book had to display features considered at the time typical of literature, such as organic unity. This is a political gesture, since in creating a text that satisfies contemporary criteria of "high art," Angelou underscores one of the book's central themes: how undeservedly its protagonist was relegated to second-class citizenship in her early years. To ignore form in discussing Angelou's book, therefore, would mean ignoring a critical dimension of its important political work.

Because scholarly discussions of Angelou's autobiographical works have only appeared in any significant number in the last fifteen years, *Caged Bird* and her other books have avoided—or, depending on one's view, been spared—the kind of formal analysis typically associated with New Criticism or Structuralism.[2] Scholarly critics of *Caged Bird*, often influenced by feminist and African-American studies, have focused on such issues as whether the story of Angelou's young protagonist is personal or universal, or on race, gender, identity, displacement, or a combination of these. In relation to these issues, they discuss important episodes like the scene with the "powhitetrash" girls, young Maya's rape and subsequent muteness, her experience with Mrs. Flowers, the graduation, the visit to the dentist, Maya's month living in a junkyard, or her struggle to become a San Francisco streetcar conductor.[3] What they do not do is analyze these episodes as Angelou constructed them—often juxtaposing disparate incidents within an episode—and arranged and organized them, often undermining the chronology of her childhood story and juxtaposing the events of one chapter with the events of preceding and following ones so that they too comment on each other. The critics do not explore how Angelou, who has never denied the principle of selection in the writing of autobiography,[4] shaped the material of her childhood and adolescent life story in *Caged Bird* to present Maya's first sixteen years, much as a *bildungsroman* would, as a progressive process of affirming identity, learning about words, and resisting racism.[5] What scholars have focused on in *Caged Bird* does merit attention, but an attention to the formal strategies Angelou uses to emphasize what the book expresses about identity and race reveals a sequence of lessons about resisting racist oppression, a sequence that leads Maya progressively from helpless rage and indignation to forms of subtle resistance and finally to outright and active protest.

The progression from rage and indignation to subtle resistance to active protest gives *Caged Bird* a thematic unity that stands in contrast to the otherwise episodic quality of the narrative. To claim thematic unity is to argue that form and content work together, an assertion that is anathema to much current literary theory. However, the formal in *Caged Bird* is the vehicle of the political, and not analyzing this text formally can limit one's appreciation of how it intervenes in the political. Critics should not focus on the political at the expense of the formal but instead should see the political and the formal as inextricably related. Indeed, some of the most well-received works on American literature in the last decade offer compelling demonstrations of such a symbiosis of form and content. Jane Tompkins's *Sensational Designs* and Walter Benn Michaels's *The Gold Standard and the Logic of Naturalism*, for instance, are exemplary instances of new historicism or cultural criticism, but they nevertheless integrate virtuosic close formal analyses of literary texts into their overall projects.[6]

Caged Bird's commentators have discussed how episodic the book is, but these episodes are crafted much like short stories, and their arrangement throughout the book does not always follow strict chronology.[7] Nothing requires an autobiography to be chronological, but an expectation of chronology on the reader's part is normal in a text that begins, as *Caged Bird* does, with earliest memories. Nevertheless, one of the most important early episodes in *Caged Bird* comes much earlier in the book than it actually did in Angelou's life: the scene in which the "powhitetrash" girls taunt Maya's grandmother takes up the book's fifth chapter, but it occurred when Maya "was around ten years old" (23), two years after Mr. Freeman rapes her (which occurs in the twelfth chapter).

Situating the episode early in the book makes sense in the context of the previous chapters: the third chapter ends with Angelou describing her anger at the "used-to-be-sheriff" who warned her family of an impending Klan ride (14-15), and the fourth chapter ends with her meditation on her early inability to perceive white people as human (20-21). The scene with the "powhitetrash" girls follows this (24-27), indicating how nonhuman white people can be. But if that was all that motivated the organization of her episodes, Angelou could as easily have followed the meditation on white people's nonhumanity with the episode in which young Maya breaks the china of her white employer, Mrs. Cullinan. What really organizes chapters three through five is Angelou's presentation of the futility of indignation and the utility of subtle resistance as ways of responding to racism. The scene with the ex-sheriff comes at the beginning of this sequence and only leaves Maya humiliated and angry:

> If on Judgment Day I were summoned by St. Peter to give testimony to the used-to-be sheriff's act of kindness, I would be unable to say anything in his behalf. His confidence that my uncle and every other Black man who heard of the Klan's coming ride would scurry under their houses to hide in chicken droppings was too humiliating to hear. (14)

The scene with the "powhitetrash" girls causes Maya to react with the same helpless anger and humiliation, but through the response of her grandmother Henderson (whom she calls Momma) to the girls' rudeness and crudity, Maya learns there can be a better and more effective way to respond.

At first, Maya's reaction to the "powhitetrash" girls is like her reaction to the used-to-be sheriff: rage, indignation, humiliation, helplessness. When the girls ape her grandmother's posture, Maya weeps, thinks of getting her uncle's rifle, and wants to throw lye and pepper on them and to scream at them "that they were dirty, scummy peckerwoods" (24-25). When they leave and Momma politely calls good-bye to them, Maya's rage peaks:

> I burst. A firecracker July-the-Fourth burst. How could Momma call them Miz? The mean nasty things. Why couldn't she have come inside the sweet, cool store when we saw them breasting the hill? What did she prove? And then if they were dirty, mean and impudent, why did Momma have to call them Miz? (26)

But once the girls leave, young Maya realizes that her grandmother has achieved something: "Something had happened out there, which I couldn't completely understand. . . . Whatever the contest had been out front, I knew Momma had won" (26-27). Angelou claims that her ten-year-old self could not fully understand what had happened, though she did understand that there had been a contest of wills and that her grandmother had won it.

The young girl can be only vaguely conscious of how to comprehend the nature of the contest, but her next act and the organization of the whole chapter indicate nonetheless how readers should comprehend it. Angelou's description of the "powhitetrash" girls emphasizes their dirtiness. They are "grimy, snotty-nosed girls" (23), and "the dirt of [their] cotton dresses continued on their legs, feet, arms and faces to make them all of a piece" (25). In contrast to this, Maya's household is a model of cleanliness. The first thing Momma tells Maya after the "powhitetrash" girls have left is to wash her face (26). This seems appropriate because of how much Maya had been crying, but its real significance is apparent when considered in the context of the chapter's beginning and of what Maya does at the end of the chapter. The chapter begins: "'Thou shall not be dirty' and 'Thou shall not be impudent' were the two commandments of Grandmother Henderson upon which hung our total salvation," and the two subsequent paragraphs recount the ends to which Momma went to ensure her grandchildren's cleanliness (21). At first glance, this would appear to have nothing to do with the pain and humiliation of racism. But what the entire chapter demonstrates and what the ten-year-old Maya vaguely understands is that cleanliness, racism, and her grandmother's "victory" over the "powhitetrash" girls have everything to do with each other. Maya would seem to have understood this even though the adult Angelou claims she did not—for once she has washed her face, without being told to do so, she rakes the trampled front yard into a pattern that her grandmother calls "right pretty" (27).[8]

Maya and Momma demonstrate that, unlike the white trash girls, *they* are neither dirty nor impudent. This is where the victory lies. Part of it consists of Momma's resisting the white girls' attempts to goad her into descending to their level of impudence. But another part of the victory lies in maintaining personal dignity through the symbolic importance of cleanliness and politeness. The victory itself will not bring about the downfall of segregation (which is perhaps why some critics see Grandmother Henderson as ultimately helpless against racist oppression [see Kent, 76; and Neubauer, 118]), but it does allow Momma and Maya to be proud of themselves. By demonstrating their own cleanliness and politeness, Maya and her grandmother establish their family's respectability in the face of racism and subtly throw the attempt to degrade them back on their oppressors. Furthermore, there is a more effective strategy for reacting to racism and segregation than rage and indignation—a strategy of subtle resistance, what Dolly McPherson calls "the dignified course of silent endurance" (33). Later episodes demonstrate the limitations of subtle resistance, but one should not underestimate its powers: without risking harm to life, liberty, or property, Momma is able to preserve her human dignity in the face of the white girls' attempts to belittle her. It may be all that she can do in the segregated South at the time, but it is something. What is more, as Angelou subsequently shows, it serves as a basis from which Maya can later move to protesting and combating racism actively.

An important feature of the chapter is that Angelou organizes it like a short story. It begins where it ends, with cleanliness and raking the yard bracketing the scene with the white trash girls, and it leaves the reader to work out the relationship between the confrontation with the girls and the cleaning of the yard. Because of this organization, the chapter becomes more than just a narration of bigoted behavior and Momma's and Maya's responses to it: "Such experiences," says McPherson, "are recorded not simply as historical events, but as symbolic revelations of Angelou's inner world" (49). The "powhitetrash" chapter takes on the additional dimension of a lesson in the utility of endowing everyday activities such as washing, raking a yard, or minding one's manners with symbolic value as a way of resisting bigotry. Making every minute of the day a symbolic means of fighting segregation in turn means that segregation is not a helpless and hopeless situation.

Angelou organizes the fifteenth chapter, the one about Mrs. Flowers, in a similarly tight fashion, interrelating the themes of racial pride, identity, and the power of words that run throughout. The positive effect that the attention of the elegant Mrs. Flowers has on the insecurity and identity crisis of young Maya is obvious.[9] By helping Maya to begin to have some self-confidence, Mrs. Flowers contributes to the young girl's affirmation of her identity: "I was liked, and what a difference it made. I was respected . . . for just being Marguerite Johnson. . . . She had made tea cookies for me and read to me from her favorite book" (85). Such respect and affection from an older person Maya admired surely had an important positive effect on a young girl suffering from the guilt and self-loathing that resulted from being raped by her mother's boyfriend. It is no wonder Angelou feels that Mrs. Flowers "threw me my first life line" (77).

While the Mrs. Flowers chapter seems, at first glance, not to have much to do with the politics of racism, this important step in Maya's sense of identity has everything to do with race. Since she had been twice sent away by her parents to live with her grandmother, it is no surprise that Maya had an insecurity and identity problem. In the opening pages of the book, Maya suffered from a strong case of racial self-hatred, fantasizing that she was "really white," with "light-blue eyes" and "long and blond" hair (2). At that point, Maya entirely separates her sense of self from her sense of race, and this is part of her identity crisis, since she refuses to accept being who she is and hankers after a foreign identity that is a compound of received ideas of white feminine beauty. By the end of the book, the opposite is the case. When the white secretary of the San Francisco streetcar company repeatedly frustrates her attempts for a job interview, Maya is at first tempted not to take it personally: "The incident was a recurring dream, concocted years before by stupid whites. . . . I went further than forgiving the clerk, I accepted her as a fellow victim of the same puppeteer." But then Maya decides that the rebuffs, which have everything to do with her race, also have everything to do with her personally, and this is because her personal identity and her racial identity cannot be entirely separated: "The whole charade we had played out in that crummy waiting room had directly to do with me, Black, and her, white" (227). Attaining the streetcar conductor's job becomes not only a victory for civil rights, as a result, but also a personal victory for Maya's sense of self. One of the crucial transition points in this evolution over the course of the entire book from the total separation of self-image and race to the connection of the two comes in the Mrs. Flowers chapter, for not only does Mrs. Flowers make Maya feel liked and respected, but "she made me proud to be Negro, just by being herself" (79).[10] This is the first statement of black racial pride in the book, but others appear later: Joe Louis's victory, which "proved that we were the strongest people in the world" (115), and Maya's conclusion at the end of the graduation scene that "I was a proud member of the wonderful, beautiful Negro race" (156).

The Mrs. Flowers chapter emphasizes black racial pride by combining two apparently disparate episodes on the basis of their thematic affinity, much as the "powhitetrash" chapter did. Here the affinity is not cleanliness but the power of words, a theme central to African-American autobiography from the slave narratives to Richard Wright's *Black Boy* and beyond. The importance of the power of words, in themselves and in poetry, and, by implication, the importance of literature run throughout *Caged Bird*,[11] especially after the rape, when Maya fears that her lie at Mr. Freeman's trial caused his death. *Black Boy* demonstrates the negative power of words each time Wright is abused for not saying the right thing,[12] yet the book concludes on a positive note when Wright realizes that he can harness the power of words to his own artistic and political ends. Much the same thing happens in *Caged Bird*. Maya refuses to speak because she fears the potentially fatal power of words, but throughout the second half of the book she acknowledges that the imagination can harness the power of words to great ends. One of the high points in this realization comes at the end of the graduation scene, when the audience, having been insulted by a white guest speaker, lifts its morale by singing James Weldon Johnson's "Lift Ev'ry Voice and Sing" (155). Maya realizes that she "had never heard it before. Never heard the words, despite the thousands of times I had sung them," and this leads her to appreciate the African-American poetic tradition as she never had before. Angelou expresses that appreciation with an allusion to another Johnson poem: "Oh, Black known and unknown poets, how often have your auctioned pains sustained us? Who will compute the lonely nights made less lonely by your songs, or by the empty pots made less tragic by your tales?" (156). Because Johnson's words, like Angelou's story, are gathered "from the stuff of the black experience, with its suffering and its survival," to use Keneth Kinnamon's words, the singing of "Lift Ev'ry Voice and Sing" at the end of the graduation episode "is a paradigm of Angelou's own artistic endeavor in *I Know Why the Caged Bird Sings*" (132-33).

Mrs. Flowers lays the groundwork for this later appreciation of the power of the poetic word by explicitly stating the lesson of the positive power of words in her conversation with the ten-year-old Maya. (Her message is further emphasized because the main point of her invitation and attention to the mute girl is to convince her to use words again.) "[B]ear in mind," Mrs. Flowers tells Maya, "language is man's way of communicating with his fellow man and it is language alone that separates him from the lower animals. . . . Words mean more than what is set down on paper. It takes the human voice to infuse them with the shades of deeper meaning" (82). Mrs. Flowers's speech and her reading from Dickens themselves make Maya appreciate poetry—"I heard poetry for the first time in my life"(84), she says about Mrs. Flowers's reading—and the spoken word, but Angelou arranges the entire chapter to emphasize the power of words. The chapter begins with a description of Mrs. Flowers and her elegant command of standard English, which contrasts in their conversations with Momma's heavy dialect, much to Maya's shame: "Shame made me want to hide my face. . . . Momma left out the verb. Why not ask, 'How *are* you, Mrs. Flowers?' . . . 'Brother and Sister Wilcox is sho'ly the meanest—' 'Is,' Momma? 'Is'? Oh, please, not 'is,' Momma, for two or more" (78-79). As a result, Angelou has focused the chapter on the importance of words and their pronunciation, even in its very first pages, before Maya enters Mrs. Flowers's house.

The chapter's end, after Maya returns from her visit, also emphasizes the importance of words, this time in contrast to the way white people use words. When Maya tells her brother, "By the way, Bailey, Mrs. Flowers sent you some tea cookies—," Momma threatens to beat her granddaughter (85). The crime is that since "Jesus was the Way, the Truth and the Light," saying "by the way" was, in Momma's view, blasphemous (86). This episode would seem thematically unrelated to the rest of the chapter and only an example of Momma's domestic theocracy were it not for the chapter's final sentence: "When Bailey tried to interpret the words with: 'Whitefolks use "by the way" to mean while we're on the subject,' Momma reminded us that 'whitefolks' mouths were most in general loose and their words were an abomination before Christ'" (86-87). While the "by the way" episode concludes the chapter, *Black Boy* fashion, with an example of the awful power of words, this final sentence concludes both the episode and chapter just as the emphasis on cleanliness concluded the "powhitetrash" chapter: through their greater attention to details, the Henderson/Johnson clan shows itself to be superior to whites; and instead of showing Momma to be abusive and tyrannic, the "by the way" episode anticipates the affirmation later in the book of the strength blacks find in the careful— even poetic—use of words, just as Mrs. Flowers does in her reading and in her speech about words.

The internal organization of chapters, as in the "powhitetrash" and Mrs. Flowers chapters, into thematic units that would make Cleanth Brooks proud is but one of the effects Angelou uses in *Caged Bird*. Equally effective is the way Angelou juxtaposes chapters. For example, she follows the Mrs. Flowers chapter, with its lessons on the power of words and on identity, with the chapter (the sixteenth) in which Maya breaks Mrs. Cullinan's dishes because the white employer neglects to take a single but important word—Maya's name—and Maya's identity seriously. This chapter comments, then, on the previous one by showing Maya acting on the basis of what she has learned in the previous chapter about the importance of words and about affirming identity. Maya's smashing of the dishes is also an important stage in the progression of strategies for responding to racial oppression from helpless indignation to subtle resistance to active protest. No longer helplessly angered and humiliated as she was by the former sheriff and the white girls taunting her grandmother, Maya shows in the Mrs. Cullinan chapter that she has internalized the lesson of the "powhitetrash" episode and can figure out, with her brother's advice, a way to resist her white employer's demeaning of her that is subtle and yet allows her to feel herself the victor of an unspoken confrontation. After Mrs. Cullinan insists on calling her Mary instead of Margaret (which best approximates her real name, Marguerite), Maya realizes that she can neither correct her employer nor simply quit the job. Like her grandmother with the rude white girls, Maya cannot openly confront her oppressor, nor can she allow the situation to continue. Instead she breaks Mrs. Cullinan's favorite dishes and walks out, exulting as Mrs. Cullinan tells her guests, "Her name's Margaret, goddamn it, her name's Margaret!" (93).[13]

Angelou follows this chapter with a series of three chapters, the seventeenth through the nineteenth, each of which depicts subtle black resistance to white oppression. However, while the sixteenth chapter ends with Maya exulting at the efficacy of her resistance to Mrs. Cullinan, these chapters increasingly express the limitations of subtle resistance. The seventeenth chapter tells about Maya's and Bailey's viewing movies starring Kay Francis, who resembles their mother, and describes how Maya turns the stereotypical depiction of black people in Hollywood movies back onto the unknowing white members of the audience. As the whites snicker at the Stepin Fetchit-like black chauffeur in one Kay Francis comedy, Maya turns the joke on them:

I laughed too, but not at the hateful jokes. . . . I laughed because, except that she was white, the big movie star looked just like my mother. Except that she lived in a big mansion with a thousand servants, she lived just like my mother. And it was funny to think of the whitefolks' not knowing that the woman they were adoring could be my mother's twin, except that she was white and my mother was prettier. Much prettier. (99-100)

This passage works very much like Momma's victory over the white trash girls: the whites' taunts are turned back on them, though the whites may not know it. Nonetheless, this permits the black person to feel superior instead of humiliated while avoiding the kind of open confrontation that could lead to violence. What is problematic about the seventeenth chapter is that, as in the eighteenth and nineteenth chapters, the end of the chapter casts a shadow on the success achieved in the moment of subtle resistance by describing Bailey's very different reaction to the movie: it makes him sullen, and on their way home, he terrifies Maya by running in front of an oncoming train (100).

In the eighteenth and nineteenth chapters, which tell about the revival meeting and the Joe Louis fight, a black community is able to feel superior to whites. Both chapters, though, end ambiguously, with a reminder that the feeling of superiority is transitory and fragile. At the revival, the congregation thrills to a sermon that subtly accuses whites of lacking charity while reminding the congregation about the ultimate reward for their true charity. The congregation leaves the revival feeling "it was better to be meek and lowly, spat upon and abused for this little time than to spend eternity frying in the fires of hell" (110-11). Again, the oppressed are able to feel superior without risking the violence of an open confrontation. The final two paragraphs of the chapter, however, compare the gospel music at the revival with the "ragged sound" of the "barrelhouse blues" coming from the honky-tonk run by "Miss Grace, the good-time woman" (111). Like the parishioners at the revival, the customers of the suitably named Miss Grace "had forsaken their own distress for a little while." However, "reality began its tedious crawl back into their reasoning. After all, they were needy and hungry and despised and dispossessed, and sinners the world over were in the driver's seat. How long, merciful Father? How long? . . . All asked the same questions. How long, oh God? How long?" (111). Whereas the "powhitetrash" and Mrs. Cullinan chapters ended on a note of victory, this chapter ends on one that rings more of defeat. This is because the book moves through the three strategies for responding to white racist oppression—helpless indignation, subtle resistance, and active protest—and at this point is preparing the transition from the limited victories of subtle resistance to the outright victory of active protest.

The next chapter, the nineteenth, which describes the community at the store listening to a Joe Louis match, follows the same pattern as the revival chapter. Louis's victory provides his fans a stirring moment of racial pride and exaltation: "Champion of the world. A Black boy. Some Black mother's son. He was the strongest man in the world. People drank Coca-Colas like ambrosia and ate candy bars like Christmas" (114). But while Louis's victory allows his black fans to feel themselves stronger than and superior to their white oppressors, there are limits to how far the black community can rejoice in its superiority. The chapter ends by mentioning that those who lived far out of town spent the night with friends in town because "it wouldn't do for a Black man and his family to be caught on a lonely country road on a night when Joe Louis had proved that we were the strongest people in the world" (115).

Because chapters eighteen and nineteen explore the limits to subtle but passive resistance, the book has to go on to present other possible ways of responding to white oppression. The climactic response, one that consists of active resistance and outright protest, is Maya's persisting and breaking the color line of the San Francisco streetcar company, described in the thirty-fourth chapter. Since *Caged Bird* was written in the late sixties, at the height of the black power movement and at a time that was still debating the value of Martin Luther King's belief in non-violent protest, it is no surprise that this act of protest is the climactic moment of resistance to white oppression in the book, a moment that says: Momma's type of resistance was fine in its time and place, but now it is time for some real action.[14] There are at least three other episodes in the second half of *Caged Bird*, however, that explore the line between subtle but passive resistance and active, open protest: the graduation scene (chapter twenty-three), the dentist scene (chapter twenty-four), and the story Daddy Clidell's friend, Red Leg, tells about double-crossing a white con man (chapter twenty-nine).

Falling as they do between the Joe Louis chapter and the San Francisco streetcar company chapter, these three episodes chart the transition from subtle resistance to active protest. The graduation scene for the most part follows the early, entirely positive examples of subtle resistance in *Caged Bird*. The only difference is that the resistance is no longer so subtle and that it specifically takes the form of poetry, which in itself valorizes the African-American literary tradition as a source for resisting white racist oppression. Otherwise, the graduation chapter conforms to the pattern established by the "powhitetrash" and Mrs. Cullinan chapters: first, there is the insult by the white person, when the speaker tells the black audience about all the improvements that the white school will receive—improvements that far surpass the few scheduled for the black school (151). There is Maya's first response of humiliation and anger: "Then I wished that Gabriel Prosser and Nat Turner had killed all whitefolks in their beds" (152), shared now by the community: "[T]he proud graduating class of 1940 had dropped their heads" (152). Then there is the action on the part of a member of the black community—Henry Reed's improvised leading the audience in "Lift Ev'ry Voice and Sing" (155)—that at the same time avoids an irreversible confrontation with the white oppressor and permits the black community to feel its dignity and superiority: "We were on top again. As always, again. We survived" (156).

The primary difference in the graduation chapter is that because the audience sings together, the resistance is a community action. The resistance is still not exactly an outright protest, and it still avoids open confrontation since the white insulter has left and does not hear the singing. Otherwise, the scene resembles a civil rights protest two decades later. The graduation also serves as an introduction for the dentist chapter, which is similar to the graduation chapter because of the way it highlights literature as a possible source for resisting racist oppression, and which is the crucial transitional chapter from subtle resistance to active protest because it opens the door to the eventuality of open confrontation by presenting the closest instance in the book of a black person in Stamps openly confronting a racist white.

The insult in the dentist chapter occurs when Stamps's white and only dentist—to whom Maya's grandmother had lent money, interest-free and as a favor—refuses to treat Maya's excruciating toothache, telling Maya and Momma, "[M]y policy is I'd rather stick my hand in a dog's mouth than in a nigger's" (160). From this point on, though, the chapter ceases to follow the pattern of the previous examples of resistance. Instead, Momma leaves Maya in the alley behind the dentist's office and, in a passage printed in italics, enters the office transformed into a superwoman and threatens to run the now-trembling dentist out of town. Readers quickly perceive that this passage is italicized because it is Maya's fantasy, but they do have to read a few sentences of the fantasy before realizing it. The chapter ends, after Maya and Momma travel to the black dentist in Texarkana, with Angelou's explanation of what really happened inside the white dentist's office— Momma collected interest on her loan to the dentist, which pays the bus fare to Texarkana—and Angelou's remark: "I preferred, much preferred, my version" (164).

The fantasy scene bears attention because it is the only one like it in *Caged Bird*. It is the only italicized passage in the book and the only one that confuses the reader—even if only for a moment—over what is real and what is fantasy. Some critics have argued that this passage serves the purpose of underlining how limited Momma's ability to fight racism is,[15] and it is true that in a better world, Momma would have been able to exact proper and courteous care from a dentist who was beholden to her. This reading, however, does not account for either the uniqueness of the presentation of the passage or the very real pride Maya feels for her grandmother as they ride the bus between Stamps and Texarkana: "I was so proud of being her granddaughter and sure that some of her magic must have come down to me" (162-63). On the one hand, the italicized passage does highlight the contrast between what Maya wishes her grandmother could do to a racist with what little she can do, thus again demonstrating the limitations of subtle resistance as an overall strategy for responding to racist oppression. On the other hand, the fantasy passage anticipates the kind of outright confrontations between oppressed black and racist oppressor that occurred when Maya broke the streetcar company's color line and in the civil rights movement. Although it is only a fantasy, it is the first instance in

Caged Bird of a black person openly confronting a racist white and thus is the first hint that such confrontation is a possibility.

The fact that the fantasy passage is an act of imagination is also significant, since it hints that imagination and storytelling can be forms of resisting racism. It is natural to read the fantasy passage in this way because of its placement immediately after the apostrophe to "Black known and unknown poets" at the end of the graduation chapter (196). Because of this passage praising black poets, we are all the more inclined to see the imagined, italicized fantasy passage five pages later as itself an instance of poetry. For one, the apostrophe includes in the category of "poets" anyone who uses the power of the word—"include preachers, musicians and blues singers"(156). Thus, anyone who uses language to describe pain and suffering and their causes (i.e., blues singers) belongs in the category of poets. According to this definition, the author of *I Know Why the Caged Bird Sings* is a blues singer, and therefore a poet, too, since telling why the caged bird sings is an instance of describing pain and suffering and their causes, an instance of the blues. Loosely defined, poetry is also an act of imagination, and thus the italicized fantasy passage in the dentist chapter is poetic since it is an act of imagination. In fact, it is the first instance of Maya being a poet and thus the first step toward the far more monumental act of writing *I Know Why the Caged Bird Sings* itself. Poetry, in all its forms, can be an act of resistance. The graduation chapter has already made that clear, but the dentist chapter makes it clear that the victim of racial oppression can herself become a poet and use her poetry as a form of resistance. Maya had begun to learn the positive power of poetry and of words in the Mrs. Flowers chapter. Now she begins the process of harnessing the power of words to positive effect, a process that concludes with the composition almost thirty years later of the very book in hand.

The final instance of not-quite-outright resistance is the scam Red Leg tells (in chapter twenty-nine) about pulling on a white con man. This episode is not the open, active protest of Maya's integration of the streetcars since it does not involve a direct confrontation with the white racist, but it is closer to it than any of the previous examples of resistance because the white person ends up knowing that he has been had at his own game. The inclusion of the episode is at first glance irrelevant to the heroine's personal development, but Angelou's comments at the end of the chapter make clear how the passage fits with the rest of the book. For one, Angelou remarks, "It wasn't possible for me to regard [Red Leg and his accomplice] as criminals or be anything but proud of their achievements" (190). The reason for her pride is that these black con artists are achieving revenge for wrongs incurred against the entire race: "We are the victims of the world's most comprehensive robbery. Life demands a balance. It's all right if we do a little robbing now" (190-91). The scam is, therefore, another example of fighting back against white domination and racist oppression, an example that, like the others, meets with the author's approval.

The scam artist chapter ends, like so many other chapters, with a paragraph that appears to have little to do with what precedes. It tells about how Maya and her black schoolmates learned to use Standard English and dialect in their appropriate settings. This short paragraph certainly belongs to the commentary running throughout the book on appreciating the significance and power of words: "We were alert to the gap separating the written word from the colloquial" (191). It also serves to emphasize the superior ability of blacks to adapt to and get the best of circumstances and situations: "My education and that of my Black associates were quite different from the education of our white schoolmates. In the classroom we all learned past participles, but in the streets and in our homes the Blacks learned to drop *s*'s from plurals and suffixes from past-tense verbs" (191). Angelou shows here the superior adaptability of her black schoolmates (and that Maya has come a long way from her scorn of her grandmother's use of dialect): the blacks learn all the whites do and more. This lesson is entirely appropriate to the con artist chapter, since what the stories about pulling scams demonstrate is the black version of heroism, which is to make the most of what little one has—in other words, adaptability: "[I]n the Black American ghettos the hero is that man who is offered only the crumbs from his country's table but by ingenuity and courage is able to take for himself a Lucullan feast" (190).

Within strictly legal confines, such an ability is the essence of the American myth of success, and undoubtedly, at least part of the appeal of *Caged Bird* is that it corresponds both to this definition of black heroism and to the outline of a typical success story.[16] The product of a broken family, raped at age eight, Angelou was offered at first "only the crumbs" from her "country's table." She suffers from an inferiority complex, an identity crisis, and the humiliation of racist insults. By the end of the book, however, she no longer feels inferior, knows who she is, and knows that she can respond to racism in ways that preserve her dignity and her life, liberty, and property, and she knows—and demonstrates in addition through the very existence of the book itself—that she can respond by using the power of words. It may be impossible to convince a poststructuralist that there is something uniquely literary about Angelou's autobiography, but certainly part of what this autobiography is about is the power and utility of literature and its own genesis and existence as a protest against racism. One serves Angelou and *Caged Bird* better by emphasizing how form and political content work together. As Elizabeth Fox-Genovese says in respect to the general tradition of autobiographies by African-American women:

> The theoretical challenge lies in bringing sophisticated skills to the service of a politically informed reading of texts. To read well, to read fully, is inescapably to read politically, but to foreground the politics, as if these could somehow be distinguished from the reading itself, is to render the reading suspect. (67)

To neglect many of the formal ways *Caged Bird* expresses its points about identity, words, and race is to ignore the extent to which Angelou successfully met Loomis's challenge, an important aspect of her artistic accomplishment, and the potential utility of this text in literary classrooms, especially those that emphasize combining formal and ideologically based approaches to analyzing literature.

From *College Literature* 22, no. 3 (October 1995): 91-108. Copyright © 1995 by *College Literature*. Reprinted by permission of *College Literature*.

Notes

1. Angelou tells the story about how she came to write *I Know Why the Caged Bird Sings* in several interviews collected by Jeffrey M. Elliot (80, 151-52, 211). She admits having an inability to "resist a challenge" ("*Westways*," 80) in her 1983 interview with Claudia Tate ("Maya Angelou," 151-52), and in at least two interviews she discusses James Baldwin's possible role in helping Loomis use her attraction to a challenge as a ploy to get her to agree to write an autobiography ("*Westways*," 80; "Maya Angelou," with Tate, 151).

2. A search in the MLA computerized data bank reveals forty-four items on Angelou, with the oldest dating back to 1973, three years after the publication of *I Know Why the Caged Bird Sings*. Twenty-eight of these forty-four items have appeared since 1985, and only nine appeared before 1980 (and of these, two are interviews, one is bibliographic information, and one is a portion of a dissertation). There are different possibilities for interpreting these facts: on the one hand, it may be that scholarly critics have been slow to "catch up" to Angelou, slow to treat her work—and thus to recognize it—as literature worthy of their attention; on the other hand, it may be that the scholarly status of Angelou's work has risen in concert with poststructuralism's rise and has done so because poststructuralism has made it possible to appreciate Angelou's work in new ways.

3. For the significance of identity in *Caged Bird*, see Butterfield (203), Schmidt (25-27), McPherson (16, 18, 121), and Arensberg (275, 278-80, 288-90). On displacement, see Neubauer (117-19, 126-27) and Bloom (296-97). For a consideration of the personal vs. the universal, see McPherson (45-46), Cudjoe (10), O'Neale (26), McMurry (109), and Kinnamon, who stresses the importance of community in *Caged Bird* (123-33). On the "powhitetrash" scene, see Butterfield (210-12), McPherson (31-33), and McMurry (108). For an extensive consideration of the rape, see Froula (634-36). For the effect of the rape on Maya and her relationship with Mrs. Flowers, see Lionnet (147-52). For the graduation, see Butterfield (207), McMurry (109-10), Arensberg (283), and Cudjoe (14). For the visit to the dentist, see Braxton (302-04) and Neubauer (118-19). For the month in the junkyard, see Gilbert (41) and Lionnet (156-57).

4. See Angelou's interviews with Tate ("Maya Angelou," 152) and with Neubauer ("Interview," 288-89). In an interview included in McPherson's *Order Out of Chaos*,

Angelou mentions a number of incidents she omitted—some consciously, some unconsciously—from *Caged Bird* (138-40, 145-47, 157-58). O'Neale, who writes that Angelou's "narrative was held together by controlled techniques of artistic fiction" (26) and that her books are "arranged in loosely structured plot sequences which are skillfully controlled" (32), does not discuss these techniques or arrangements in any detail.

5. Angelou creates enough potential confusion about her protagonist's identity by having her called different names by different people—Ritie, Maya, Marguerite, Margaret, Mary, Sister. For the sake of consistency, I use the name "Maya" to refer to the protagonist of *Caged Bird* and the name "Angelou" to refer to its author.

6. Michaels's book is published in Stephen Greenblatt's series, "The New Historicism: Studies in Cultural Poetics," and Tompkins's book, whose subtitle is *The Cultural Work of American Fiction, 1790-1860*, emphasizes reading literature in its historical context. Tompkins's chapter, "Sentimental Power: *Uncle Tom's Cabin* and the Politics of Literary History," and Michaels's chapter on *McTeague* strike me as brilliant close literary analysis.

7. Schmidt (25) and Mcpherson (26) comment on the episodic quality of *Caged Bird*. Schmidt is the one commentator on *Caged Bird* to mention that "each reminiscence forms a unit" (25). An indication of how episodic *Caged Bird* is is how readily selections from it have lent themselves to being anthologized.

8. McMurry argues insightfully that Maya "is using the design [she rakes in the front yard] to organize feelings she could not otherwise order or express, just as Momma has used the song to organize her thoughts and feelings beyond the range of the children's taunts. She triumphs not only in spite of her restrictions, but because of them. It is because, as a Black woman, she must maintain the role of respect toward the white children that she discovers another vehicle for the true emotions" (108). Kinnamon, arguing that "Angelou's purpose is to portray cleanliness as a bonding ritual in black culture" (127), contrasts the importance of washing in the "powhitetrash" chapter with the scene in *Black Boy* in which Richard Wright tells about his grandmother's washing him.

9. See Bloom, who points to Mrs. Flowers as "a perceptive mother-substitute" (293). Sexual identity is central to the book's last two chapters, in which Angelou tells about Maya's concerns about her sexual identity and the birth of her son. For discussions of these last two chapters, see Smith (373-74), Buss (103-04), Schmidt (26-27), McPherson (53-55), Arensberg (290-91), Butterfield (213), Lionnet (135-36), Demetrakopoulos (198-99), and MacKethan (60).

10. By being herself, Mrs. Flowers made Maya proud of her racial background, "proud to be Negro," but the real lesson Maya needs to learn is double: by being herself, Maya herself can be "proud to be Negro," and by being "proud to be Negro," Maya can be herself. Thus the language of the phrase implies the link between being "proud to be Negro" and being oneself.

11. See MacKethan, who emphasizes "verbal humor as a survival strategy" in *Caged Bird*. Cudjoe, arguing that "speech and language became instruments of liberation in Afro-American thought," reads *Caged Bird* in the context of this important theme (10-11).

12. Examples of this abuse occur when Wright tells his grandmother to kiss his ass, when he nonchalantly answers his uncle's question about the time of day, or when a drunken white man bashes him in the face for forgetting to say "sir" (40-44, 149-53, 173-74).

13. Thanks to my colleague, Mark Richardson, for pointing out that in Sergei Eisenstein's *Potemkin* the sailors rebelled against their officers by smashing dishes and for implying that dish smashing as an act of rebellion may be a literary trope.

14. Angelou has spoken in at least two interviews about the importance of protest in her work (*"Zelo* Interviews Maya Angelou," 167; "The Maya Character," 198).

15. See, for example, Neubauer (118). Mary Jane Lupton also feels that in the dentist episode "the grandmother has been defeated and humiliated, her only reward a mere ten dollars in interest for a loan she had made to the dentist" (261).

16. On May 29, 1994, twenty-four years after *Caged Bird*'s initial publication, the paperback edition was in its sixty-seventh week on the *New York Times Book Review* list of paperback best sellers.

Works Cited

Angelou, Maya. "An Interview with Maya Angelou," with Carol E. Neubauer. *Massachusetts Review: A Quarterly of Literature, the Arts, and Public Affairs* 28 (1987): 286-92.

_____. *I Know Why the Caged Bird Sings*. (New York: Bantam, 1971).

_____. "Maya Angelou," with Claudia Tate. Elliot, 146-56.

_____. "Maya Angelou," with Greg Hitt. Elliot, 205-13.

_____. "The Maya Character," with Jackie Kay. Elliot, 194-200.

_____. "*Westways* Women: Life Is for Living," with Judith Rich. Elliot, 77-85.

_____. "*Zelo* Interviews Maya Angelou," with Russell Harris. Elliot, 165-72.

Arensberg, Liliane K. "Death as Metaphor of Self in *I Know Why the Caged Bird Sings*." *College Language Association Journal* 20 (1976): 273-91.

Bloom, Lynn Z. "Heritages: Dimensions of Mother-Daughter Relationships in Women's Autobiographies," in *The Lost Tradition: Mothers and Daughters in Literature*. Ed. Cathy N. Davidson and E. M. Broner (New York: Ungar, 1980), 291-303.

Braxton, Joanne M. "Ancestral Presence: The Outraged Mother Figure in Contemporary Afra-American Writing," in *Wild Women in the Whirlwind: Afra-American Culture and the Contemporary Literary Renaissance*. Ed. Joanne M. Braxton and Andrée Nicola McLaughlin (New Brunswick: Rutgers Univ. Press, 1990), 299-315.

Brooks, Cleanth. "Irony as a Principle of Structure." 1948; rev. 1951. In *Literary Opinion in America: Essays Illustrating the Status, Methods, and Problems of Criticism in the United States in the Twentieth Century*. Ed. Morton Dauwen Zabel. Rev. ed. (New York: Harper, 1951), 729-41.

Buss, Helen M. "Reading for the Doubled Discourse of American Women's Autobiography." *A/B: Auto/Biography Studies* 6 (1991): 95-108.

Butterfield, Stephen. *Black Autobiography in America* (Amherst: Univ. of Massachusetts Press, 1974).

Cudjoe, Selwyn R. "Maya Angelou and the Autobiographical Statement," in *Black Women Writers (1950-1980): A Critical Evaluation*. Ed. Mari Evans (Garden City: Doubleday-Anchor, 1984), 6-24.

Cullen, Countée. "Yet Do I Marvel," in *The Black Poets*. Ed. Dudley Randall (New York: Bantam, 1971), 100.

Demetrakopoulos, Stephanie A. "The Metaphysics of Matrilinearism in Women's Autobiography: Studies of Mead's *Blackberry Winter*, Hellman's *Pentimento*, Angelou's *I Know Why the Caged Bird Sings*, and Kingston's *The Woman Warrior*," in *Women's Autobiography: Essays in Criticism*. Ed. Estelle C. Jelinek (Bloomington: Indiana Univ. Press, 1980), 180-205.

Eagleton, Terry. *Literary Theory: An Introduction* (Minneapolis: Univ. of Minnesota Press, 1983).

Elliot, Jeffrey M., ed. *Conversations with Maya Angelou* (Jackson: Univ. Press of Mississippi, 1989).

Fish, Stanley. *Is There a Text in This Class? The Authority of Interpretive Communities* (Cambridge: Harvard Univ. Press, 1980).

Fox-Genovese, Elizabeth. "My Statue, My Self: Autobiographical Writings of Afro-American Women," in *The Private Self: Theory and Practice of Women's Autobiographical Writings*. Ed. Shari Benstock (Chapel Hill: Univ. of North Carolina Press, 1988), 63-89.

Froula, Christine. "The Daughter's Seduction: Sexual Violence and Literary History." *Signs: Journal of Women in Culture and Society* 11 (1986): 621-44.

Johnson, James Weldon. "O Black and Unknown Bards." *The Black Poets*. Ed. Dudley Randall (New York: Bantam, 1971), 42-43.

Kent, George E. "Maya Angelou's *I Know Why the Caged Bird Sings* and Black Autobiographical Tradition." *Kansas Quarterly* 7 (1975): 72-78.

Kinnamon, Keneth. "Call and Response: Intertextuality in Two Autobiographical Works by Richard Wright and Maya Angelou," in *Belief vs. Theory in Black American Literary Criticism*. Ed. Joe Weixlmann and Chester J. Fontenot (Greenwood: Penkevill, 1986), 121-34.

Lionnet, Françoise. *Autobiographical Voices: Race, Gender, Self-Portraiture* (Ithaca: Cornell Univ. Press, 1989).

Lupton, Mary Jane. "Singing the Black Mother: Maya Angelou and Autobiographical Continuity." *Black American Literature Forum* 24 (1990): 257-76.

MacKethan, Lucinda H. "Mother Wit: Humor in Afro-American Women's Autobiography." *Studies in American Humor* 4 (1985): 51-61.

McMurry, Myra K. "Role-Playing as Art in Maya Angelou's *Caged Bird*." *South Atlantic Bulletin* 41 (1976): 106-11.

McPherson, Dolly A. *Order Out of Chaos: The Autobiographical Works of Maya Angelou* (New York: Peter Lang, 1990).

Michaels, Walter Benn. *The Gold Standard and the Logic of Naturalism: American*

Literature at the Turn of *the Century* (Berkeley: Univ. of California Press, 1987).

Neubauer, Carol E. "Maya Angelou: Self and a Song of Freedom in the Southern Tradition," in *Southern Women Writers: The New Generation*. Ed. Tonette Bond Inge (Tuscaloosa: Univ. of Alabama Press, 1990), 114-42.

O'Neale, Sondra. "Reconstruction of the Composite Self: New Images of Black Women in Maya Angelou's Continuing Autobiography," in *Black Women Writers (1950-1980): A Critical Evaluation*. Ed. Mari Evans (Garden City: Doubleday-Anchor, 1984), 25-36.

Schmidt, Jan Zlotnik. "The Other: A Study of the Persona in Several Contemporary Women's Autobiographies." *The CEA Critic* 43, no. 1 (1980): 24-31.

Shklovsky, Victor. "Art as Technique," in *Russian Formalist Criticism: Four Essays*. Ed. Lee T. Lemon and Marion J. Reis (Lincoln: Univ. of Nebraska Press, 1965), 3-24.

Smith, Sidonie Ann. "The Song of a Caged Bird: Maya Angelou's Quest after Self-Acceptance." *Southern Humanities Review* 7 (1973): 365-75.

Tompkins, Jane P. *Sensational Designs: The Cultural Work of American Fiction, 1790-1860.* (New York: Oxford Univ. Press, 1985).

Wright, Richard. *Black Boy (American Hunger). Later Works: Black Boy (American Hunger); The Outsider* (New York: Library of America, 1991).

"What You Looking at Me For? I Didn't Come to Stay":
Displacement, Disruption, and Black Female Subjectivity in Maya Angelou's *I Know Why the Caged Bird Sings*_____

Yolanda M. Manora

> If growing up is painful for the Southern Black girl, being aware of her displacement is the rust on the razor that threatens the throat. It is an unnecessary insult.

The first volume of Maya Angelou's six-volume autobiography opens with the simple lines of a children's holiday speech.[1]

> What you looking at me for?
> I didn't come to stay . . .

Angelou uses the speech and the scene of the young Maya forgetting her lines during the Easter morning church service to immediately and artfully evoke a nostalgic image of the small Southern black community of which she was a part and about which she writes in *I Know Why the Caged Bird Sings*. These few words, however, along with the space in which they are uttered—the rite of passage space of a children's Easter program in a Southern black church—serve a more critical function, expressing Angelou's awareness of herself both as the subject of the autobiography, one who the reader will be "looking at" or reading, and as an "I" in the process of at once arriving and departing. These two lines foretell Angelou's autobiographical project: to write the story of the developing black female subject by sharing the tale of one Southern black girl's becoming.

As Angelou writes it, that story of subject formation is one fraught with tension between the subject in the process of becoming and those external forces that would define the possibilities of her being. Certainly, the opening scene can be reread as emblematic of that struggle:

the black girl child feels herself the object of the gaze, confronts and challenges those who are imposing the gaze, and asserts her intention to elude that gaze and disrupt the power of those who "look at her" to define her. Judith Butler's theory of the performative offers a language for the subject/social dynamic at work in the autobiography's opening speech-performance and throughout the text.

> The performative is not a singular act used by an already established subject, but one of the powerful and insidious ways in which subjects are called into social being from diffuse social quarters, inaugurated into sociality by a variety of diffuse and powerful interpolations. In this sense the social performative is a crucial part not only of subject formation, but of the ongoing political contestation and reformation of the subject as well. The performative is not only a ritual practice: it is one of the influential rituals by which subjects are formed and reformulated. (Butler 160)

The awareness of the imposition of such interpolations and the subsequent sense of displacement experienced by the developing black female subject are Angelou's points of departure. From the moment in the opening scene when the child Maya breaks free of the social performative space by forgetting the rest of her speech and fleeing the church, however, the text turns upon the girl's ongoing resistance of these interpolations and her negotiation of her own subjectivity. In a parallel fashion, within the text as a whole, Angelou the writer thwarts the performative space of genre, upsetting the individualist and intra-subjective yet allegorical imperatives of autobiography to craft a relational, intersubjective memoir. In the process, she reveals not only the displacement of her autobiographical subject but also the possibility of the relational to serve as a space for the disruption of the socially imposed narratives, Butler's interpolations, that create that displacement. In *Caged Bird*, Angelou creates a discursive space that subtly interrogates the social and political contestation and reformation of black female subjectivity, but which ultimately turns upon the cultural, cre-

---

ative, relational, and personal potential that emerges in the course of her becoming.

Interestingly enough, despite the early assertion of an emergent, even insurgent black female subjectivity, Angelou scholars have often taken as their point of departure the author's supposed reliance on and compliance with the norms of the genre as they have been established by white, male autobiographers. In her comprehensive work on Angelou's autobiographical oeuvre, *Order Out of Chaos*, Dolly McPherson begins her examination of the first volume by elaborating a theory of autobiography as genre.

> The subject of autobiographical writing is the self becoming conscious of itself in history. Hence, the main tasks of autobiography are to depict the individual in the circumstance of one's time, and to show to what extent the society stood in one's way and how the individual overcame it. (McPherson 2)

Having established a theoretical frame, one that situates the individual—an already formed and integrated, albeit preconscious self—at center, McPherson proceeds to read the opening lines as the encapsulation of the "pattern of mobility that characterized [Angelou's] formative years" (McPherson 18). Furthermore, McPherson locates the child's speech as the expression of a developing consciousness. The development of individual consciousness toward selfhood serves as McPherson's critical touchstone. According to McPherson's genre theory, the autobiographer's primary task is the definition and redefinition of self, and she takes as her critical project the exploration of the particular kind of self or subject that emerges in Angelou's autobiographies. Despite this seeming focus on the process of self-definition, however, McPherson has a particular kind of self in mind, however, the quintessential American Individual.

McPherson stresses at the outset of her study that Angelou writes an American autobiography. She identifies three of the themes in the work—community, family, and the individual—as distinctly American. McPherson, no doubt, intends this inclusion of Angelou in an American autobiographical canon to serve as a validation of the writer and her work. Ironically, the inclusion serves to validate the very hegemonic discourses that have historically excluded Angelou, inscribing her into limiting narratives of race, class, and gender, effectively crafting her displacement as a "Southern black girl." These discourses, turning upon ideologies of difference, consign Angelou to a space on the margins of, if not outside of, the social order. As that social order constructs and perpetuates narratives of community, family, and the individual, Angelou would likewise be excluded from those narrative spaces. Angelou's experiences of community, family, and individuality, then, are shaped by her experience of difference, so they cannot simply be designated "American" or written into or contained by the American autobiographical form, forged as they are in response to and outside of the narratives that characterize that genre. Instead, Angelou appropriates and adapts the autobiography to articulate a specific subjectivity, one that, despite exclusion, interpolation, and displacement, asserts itself within experiential and narrative spaces of its own crafting.

The opening lines, then, may be read as more than an instance of narrative craft(wo)manship, or even as a metaphor for patterns of physical mobility and the journey toward consciousness and self. Rather, with these lines, the autobiographical subject not only confronts and challenges the gaze—"What *you* looking at *me* for?"— through which the dominant culture seeks to objectify her, asserting her own subject position, but also suggests a subjectivity in the process of transformation: "*I* didn't come to stay." Taken together, these lines serve to articulate Angelou's critical project: the disruption of the narrative and social sites of her displacement and the crafting of a more socially liberating and psychically integrated discursive and experiential space for black female subjectivity.

McPherson's project of summarily considering Angelou's work as part of an American autobiographical discourse is especially curious when considered in light of her own assessment of the writer's work as "recreat[ing] [. . .] the dynamics of many young black girls' disillusionment and imprisonment in American society" (Mcpherson 25). Other scholars have also fallen into the paradox of studying Angelou as a distinctly African-American woman autobiographer, then simultaneously emphasizing and dismissing those particular social and political forces, specifically the interpolations based on race and gender, that shape Angelou's life and narrative. Françoise Lionnet effects an investigation into the "double voiced" nature of Angelou's text, her artful manipulation of language to tell a seemingly simple story to a white audience and, simultaneously, to signify something else to the black audience. Within her discussion, Lionnet focuses on the author's creation of herself as a literary picaresque heroine. Like McPherson's reading of Angelou's work as distinctly American, Lionnet uses the picaresque as paradigm, imposing a particularly European tradition, imbued with the ideological reification of the individual and his/her personal journey, upon Angelou's work.

Ostensibly interested in Angelou as a black autobiographer who practices in the "long tradition among oppressed peoples of understanding duplicitous uses of language for survival," Lionnet, for the most part, neglects the implications of the intersections of race and gender in the work. In the very act of exploring them—"Angelou's own narrative is a tragicomic tale of growing up Black and female in America"—she seems intent upon nullifying the specificity of the cultural forces that shape black female subjectivity—"She creates an allegory of the feminine condition which cuts across historical, social, and racial lines"(Lionnet 150).

Such an assertion should be read in light of what might be posited as Angelou's own statement of thematic concern in the opening pages of *Caged Bird*: "If growing up is painful for the Southern Black girl, being aware of her displacement is the rust on the razor that threatens the throat." Certainly with this passage, Angelou points to a project wherein she is specifically engaged in elaborating the formation of a particular subjectivity, one that is Southern, black, and female.

This is not to suggest that considering *Caged Bird* and the rest of Angelou's autobiography as an American story and searching for general, allegorical truths in it is a less-than-valuable scholarly project. Angelou's work must be read, however, within the context of the particular historical, social, and cultural experiences and narratives that shape the writer's life and serve as the discursive space in which, oftentimes, against which, the autobiographies are written. McPherson's reference to the autobiographical self becoming aware of itself in history is apt here. Angelou writes her life story with an acute awareness of her own historical situatedness in the cultural imagination as a person who is both black and female. This black woman, positioned at the interstices of race and gender, being non-white and non-male, becomes for the purposes of the hegemonic order, the Other of the Other. This positionality, along with the socioeconomic conditions that are its material manifestations, serves as the source of Angelou's displacement. It is this position out of which she seeks to write herself by disrupting the social and political to privilege the communal and relational in the formation of black female subjectivity.

Angelou's struggle toward a self-authored subjectivity takes place in the South of the 1930s and 1940s, but the black woman's battle with objectification and otherness is as old as her presence in this country. Paula Giddings explores the dialectic, established during slavery, which defined black women:

The Victorian "extended" family put the "moral" categories of women into sharp relief. The White wife was hoisted on a pedestal so high that she was beyond the sensual reach of her own husband. Black women were consigned to the other end of the scale, as mistresses, whores, or breeders. Thus in the nineteenth century, Black women's resistance to slavery took on an added dimension. [. . .] The focus of the struggle was no longer against the notion that they were less than human [. . .] but that they were different kinds of humans. (Giddings 43)

During this period, black women were consigned to a particular place in the social order, not only constructed in opposition to white women, but assigned roles that served to fix this binary. Once abolition "freed" them from the roles of "mistresses, whores, or breeders," the still dominant patriarchal order developed other means of keeping the white woman/black woman dichotomy in place, inscribing black women into equally denigrating and fragmenting narratives and stereotypes that turned upon their race and gender.

As black women have endured these historical realities and negotiated the narratives that have been socially and culturally imposed upon them, their relationships with each other, as mothers and daughters, as sisters, as friends, have often served as a source of strength and a space of resistance.[2] In Lionnet's study, however, she curiously asserts that Angelou, unlike Zora Neale Hurston, is not strongly connected to other women in a "network of friendly relationships," reading her instead as an individualistic heroine.[3] Emerging naturally out of analyses that Americanize and allegorize Angelou's story, such an assertion overlooks the critical and culturally specific communal ethos that makes Angelou's a distinctly African American autobiography and the relational dynamics that draw her unmistakably into the company of Hurston and other African American women writers who locate their relationships with other women as the spaces in which they are nurtured and allowed to grow. Angelou as the autobiographical subject does indeed come to a point of individuality, but it is a relational individualism, emerging only through a process of subject formation that is bound up in her connections with other women. Angelou's autobiography's communal and relational emphasis, along with the specificity of the subjectivity she centers, decenters the genre's individualistic and allegorical imperatives.

In the text, Maya, along with the critical female figures in her life, must negotiate the network of oppositional constructions of black female subjectivity which serve to define and limit the contours of their lives and Angelou's narrative. Sondra O'Neale is one early Angelou scholar whose scholarship centered upon the way race and gender intersect within culturally constructed, pejorative stereotypes of black women. In "Reconstruction of the Composite Self: New Images of Black Women in Maya Angelou's Continuing Autobiography," O'Neale examines the presence and significance of images of black women that take shape in Angelou's work. She credits Angelou with "remold[ing] perceptions" of black women, combating negative stereotypes that prevail in the cultural imagination.

> No Black women in the world of Angelou's books are losers. She is the third generation of brilliantly resourceful females, who conquered oppression's stereotypical maladies without conforming to its expectations of behavior. (O'Neale 26)

O'Neale's discussion of Angelou's depiction of black women in her life emphasizes the strength of those images, leading the critic to conclude that Angelou "effectively banishes several stereotypical myths about Black women," creating in the place of the dominant culture's myths "a new totality of archetypal black women: a composite self" (35).

While O'Neale's assertion that Angelou dismantles negative stereotypes is certainly upheld by the author's careful revelation of black women who give the lie to those images, the scholar's further point that Angelou creates a "new totality," an alternative "composite self," does not seem in keeping with the author's project of creating an expansive experiential and discursive space for black female subjectivity. Indeed, O'Neale's argument implies the exchange of a socially imposed stasis for another of one's own making. Just as social stereotypes objectify the black female subject, this new archetypal, composite self would impose a different manner of limitation on the black woman's becoming, establishing a fixed notion of what a black woman is and can become. Rather than a complacent composite, the black female subjectivity that Angelou forwards turns upon the potential for a resistant hybridity within black female subjectivity.

Angelou executes this project by establishing a complex tension between representation and disruption in her text. Her project moves beyond Lionnet's notion of "double voice" to evoke Mae Henderson's critical concept of internal heterogeneity.

> What is at once characteristic and suggestive about black women's writing is its interlocutory, or dialogic, character, reflecting not only a relationship with the "other(s)," but an internal dialogue with the plural aspects of self that constitute the matrix of black female subjectivity. (Henderson 118)

Just as Henderson locates the black female writer's "relationship with the 'other(s)'" as integral to the plurality of black female subjectivity, the dialogic nature of the black female subjectivity that emerges in *Caged Bird* begins with young Maya's relationship with the adult women in her life.

O'Neale offers an interestingly paradoxical take on the influence of these relationships on the child, diminishing the impact of the adult women in her life—"aside from will and determination [Angelou] could not extract dependable techniques from their experiences" (31)—yet asserting that Angelou's ultimate achievement is her development of a particular hybridized subjectivity through her emergence as a "Baxter-Henderson woman." Lionnet, on the other hand, holds firm to her positing of Angelou's mother, Vivian Baxter, as the critical figure in young Maya's development: "It is against [Vivian's] maternal persona and role model that Maya the narrator keeps measuring her accomplishments" (Lionnet 132).

Vivian Baxter certainly plays a crucial role in Maya's process of subject formation, but she is by no means the only black female figure that impacts the girl's development. Two other important female presences collaborate with Vivian to influence young Maya's becoming, Grandmother Annie Henderson and Mrs. Bertha Flowers. Together, these three women form a triad which serves as the critical matrix in which the child is nurtured and sustained during her journey through Southern black girlhood.

During the historical moment in which Maya is growing up, these women also seem to represent three images of black female identity which the young girl must negotiate in the course of her own subject formation. Angelou, the adult autobiographer, reveals these images and the identities they describe as constructs, however, disrupting them to collapse the dualistic portrayals of black women as embodied in the age-old images of the Matriarch and the Jezebel and the oppositional construction of black female identity and white female identity as embodied by the image of the Lady. Out of the rubble of dismantled images and identities, binaries and oppositional constructions, Angelou's autobiography opens up a discursive space of political resistance and personal potential arising from an organic, ever emerging, hybridized black female subjectivity.

As *Caged Bird* opens, Maya and her older brother Bailey, Jr., have been sent by train across country from California to Stamps, Arkansas to live with their paternal grandmother, Annie Henderson. Grandmother Henderson, or Momma, as the children call her, seems to typify a certain image of the black woman that, though superficially benign, has been wielded as a weapon against her by the dominant culture, the Matriarch. Angelou's depiction of Momma is suggestive of the Black Matriarch, the strong, independent woman who, out of necessity born of circumstance, serves as the head and the heart of her family. Indeed, Annie Henderson is an older Southern black woman, a pillar of her church and of her community, in which she runs the general store. Grounded in and strengthened by the religious tradition of the Black Church, she runs the store and her family with an ironclad resolve and authority. Angelou describes Momma in almost larger-than-life terms.

I saw only her power and strength. She was taller than any woman in my personal world, and her hands were so large they could span my head from ear to ear. Her voice was soft only because she chose to keep it so. In church, when she was called upon to sing, she seemed to pull out plugs from behind her jaws and the huge, almost rough sound would pour over the listeners and throb in the air. (38)

Despite its seemingly sympathetic, perhaps even validating, tone, the image of the matriarch has been used by the dominant culture, through the auspices or under the guise of sociology, to suggest the presence of a cultural pathology, an assault by black women upon black men andtheir manhood.[4] This view would have it that black women's independence, regardless of socioeconomic necessities, deprives black men of their rightful places as breadwinners and heads of family, thus stripping them of their masculinity. Moreover, according to this analysis, by assuming these supposedly masculine roles, black women relinquish their feminine identities and become lesser women. Rendered somehow androgynous and certainly asexual, the Black Matriarch becomes the embodiment of spiritual will, consigned to one-dimensional, thus limiting, narrative, communal, and experiential spaces.[5]

In opposition to the asexual construction of black female identity represented by the Matriarch, the dominant culture, more specifically the white patriarchy, created the image of the wanton Black Jezebel. This hypersexualized myth of black womanhood grew out of slavery as an explanation and rationale for slaveholders' sexual impositions upon and rape of enslaved black women. The abolition of slavery did not abolish this image from the national imaginary, however, as the dominant culture perpetuated a notion that without the moral authority imposed by that culture, black women's libidinous drives might well explode to the detriment of society. So for black women, the erotic, both the sensual and the sexual, must either be disowned, becoming a foreclosed aspect of their subjectivity, or owned and used against them, becoming a part of the unique confluence of race and gender oppression that marks their history in this country.

In *Caged Bird*, Vivian Baxter, Maya's mother, may be read in the context of this aspect of the black female erotic. Upon encountering her mother for the first time after a long separation, Maya is "assailed" by Vivian's beauty and knows immediately that she had sent Bailey, Jr., and herself away because "she was too beautiful to have children." Angelou paints Vivian in evocative, sensual terms in the novel—"to describe my mother would be to write about a hurricane in its perfect power. Or the climbing, falling colors of a rainbow"—and, in the process, places her in opposition to Momma—"her red lips (Momma said it was a sin to wear lipstick) split to show white teeth and her fresh butter color looked see-through clean" (49).

Vivian embodies sensuality not only through her physical beauty, however, but also through her lack of a certain quality of self-consciousness. Angelou best reveals this quality in a few lines describing the children's meetings with their mother in a St. Louis tavern:

At Louie's [. . .] while we sat on the stiff wooden booths, Mother would dance alone in front of us to music from the Seeburg. I loved her most at those times. She was like a pretty kite that floated just above my head. (54)

Vivian's life is one marked by a very different manner of independence from Momma's. She lives according to her own rules, redefining traditional views of maternity, eschewing conventionality, and, according to the times, violating accepted morality. She makes her living as a gameswoman in joints, working into the early hours of the morning and beyond, and lives with men to whom she is not married. The image of the Jezebel that Vivian's character suggests is explicitly negative (as opposed to the subtle denigration of the Matriarch), denying the black woman inscribed in it any subjectivity beyond her sexuality.

As the dominant culture consigns black women to the hypofeminine and hypersexualized images of the Matriarch and the Jezebel, respectively, it excludes them from other realms of female subjectivity, most notably those characterized by the "higher" virtues. Instead, they are constructed in opposition to this other image of womanhood and, in the process, in opposition to white women for whom this image, the idealized image of the Lady, is constructed and reserved. Giddings and other scholars have posited the black woman/white woman binary as a historically situated creation of the patriarchy through which women of African descent and women of European origin were cast into diametrically opposed spaces in the cultural (read: patriarchal) imagination, elaborating a continuum of womanhood, more specifically female sexuality, with the Black Matriarch (née Mammy) on the far right, the Black Jezebel on the far left, and the Lady at center, a decidedly white center.

Into this reserved space, Angelou writes Mrs. Bertha Flowers, "the *lady* who threw [her her] first life line" (77, emphasis added). After a trauma that leaves the young Maya psychically scarred and voluntarily mute, Mrs. Flowers is the one who begins to draw her out of her self-imposed silence.[6] For the young girl, Mrs. Flowers provides then and for the rest of her life "the measure of what a human being can be" and makes her "proud to be a Negro, just by being herself" (79). But Mrs. Flowers does not seem to embody "Negro-ness" as the dominant culture would define it. Indeed, Angelou says of her that "she was our side's answer to the richest *white woman* in town" and that "she acted just as refined as *whitefolks* in the movies and books" (78, 79, emphasis added).

Like Vivian, Mrs. Flowers, although more familiar, is not quite real to Maya; she reminds the child more of the women in the English novels she reads than of anybody in her material world, most notably her mother and grandmother. In contrast to the volatile and vivid Vivian, Mrs. Flowers transcends the sensual, having "the grace of control to appear warm in the coldest weather." More significantly, she is depicted as somehow removed from the rest of the black community; she does not belong to their Church and she is not, in the young Maya's approximation of things, "familiar with" anyone, as "no one would have thought of getting close enough to Mrs. Flowers to ruffle her dress . . . she didn't encourage familiarity" (78). The Lady, then, while valorized by the black community, is too aligned with whiteness to be a part of that community.

While Maya the child positions Mrs. Flowers outside of and somehow above the black community and draws Momma and Vivian as diametrically opposed figures, Angelou the autobiographer forwards an altogether different project. She takes quite a risk by portraying these three women in a manner that alludes to these culturally constructed images or interpolations; her project might be mistaken for an attempt merely to humanize these images, to somehow reappropriate and empower them. Such a gesture, however, would ultimately have only reiterated these interpolations and empowered the social and political forces that collude to create them, making Angelou complicit in black women's disempowerment and displacement. Instead of an ultimately negating attempt to redeem these images of black women, Angelou moves toward a critical transformation of black female subjectivity, disrupting the boundaries and collapsing the binaries that limit it to reveal a discursive hybridity within the text that, in turn, creates the promise and potential for a personal plurality in her life and the lives of other black women.

Angelou begins this project by (re)presenting the fragmented black female subject, dispossessed of her strength, sensuality, and intelligence through her cultural displacement into negative, stereotypic/mythic images. Rather than simply empowering these women, and, consequently, the images in which they are inscribed to offer a new composite, as O'Neale posits, Angelou frees the women from the images by collapsing the oppositional constructions and moving the disparate visions of womanhood toward convergence. This convergence is represented in two emblematic moments in the text.

My picture of Mother and Momma embracing on the train platform has been darkly retained. [. . .] The sounds they made had a rich harmony. Momma's deep, slow voice lay under my mother's rapid peeps and chirps like stones under rushing water. (171)

They talked and from the side of the building [. . .] I heard the soft-voiced Mrs. Flowers and the textured voice of my grandmother merging and melting. (79)

Angelou uses images of fluidity, of "rushing water" and "merging and melting" to suggest the way these women, so seemingly different, flow into each other. She elaborates this critical confluence beyond the symbolic, however. Within the text, there are other narrative moments when this convergence occurs. One such moment in relation to Mrs. Flowers and Momma occurs when the child, Maya, experiences a passionate hatred of Momma for "showing her ignorance" by addressing Mrs. Flowers as "Sister Flowers" and doing so in nonstandard English. The child Maya experiences only their difference, and it is only after many years, writes Angelou the autobiographer, that she realized that "they were as alike as sisters, separated only by formal education" (78). The blurring of black female images continues as Maya recognizes the beauty of each of the three women. Whereas her mother's beauty "assails" her immediately, and she appreciates Mrs. Flowers's beautiful warm color and graceful deportment, Maya only recognizes Momma's beauty in the aftermath of the traumatic, but pivotal incident when three white girls, in a deliberate show of racial privilege, arguably a part of their own inauguration into Southern, white sociality, expose their bare rear ends in the yard of Momma's store, already aware that they are impervious to any chastisement or reprimand by the older black woman because of the color of their skin. After the girls tire of their antics and attempted display of power, Maya's grandmother comes in and looks down on her, crying in her frustration and rage over the perceived humiliation of the girls' disrespectful behavior. "She looked until I looked up. Her face was a brown moon that shone on me. She was beautiful" (26). At that moment, Momma joins Vivian and Mrs. Flowers, becoming beautiful in Maya's eyes.

Perhaps the most effective area of convergence is the participation of all three women in mothering. The text contains a provocative sign for this multiplicity of mothers in Maya's imagination:

> I could cry anytime I wanted by picturing my mother (I didn't quite know what she looked like) lying in her coffin. [. . .] The face was brown, like a big O, and since I couldn't fill in the features I printed M O T H E R across the O. (43)

Although Maya only has one mother, "MOTHER" serves as a shifting signifier in the text, signifying all three of the adult women in Maya's life. This is not to say that Angelou's project is to establish or validate an image of the black woman as Mother; again, that would be just another socially sanctioned and reified interpolation. Rather, to destabilize the oppositional constructions, Angelou shows these disparate black women, Momma, Vivian, and Mrs. Flowers, all engaged in this critical relational dynamic. She is nurtured by all three women and each greatly influences her emerging subjectivity. Each bequeaths to her a particular legacy that helps the child make her way in the world and helps determine who she will be in the world. As the blank slate of the "O" is filled in by one then another woman, Angelou establishes mothering as a collaborative creative process; each woman engages the role of "MOTHER" in her own way, bringing her own inimitable colors and contours to the space, revealing mothering both as a potential form of resistance and a manner of artistry with the child Maya serving as the ultimate canvas. *Caged Bird* ends as Maya becomes a mother and an artist in her own right, learning from her mother, expressly Vivian, but really the hybridized mother of Momma, Vivian, and Mrs. Flowers, how to mother her own child.

It is most significant that the emblematic scenes of convergence reveal the voices of the women dissolving into one another. It is this coalescence that gives Maya her voice. Momma, Vivian, and Mrs. Flowers flow into each other and, in turn, into Maya. As Angelou, the autobiographer, frees the women in her text from the stasis of their assigned images, she writes her way out of her own displacement and into a new narrative of black female subjectivity.

Fluidity is finally the dominant image in Angelou's life and autobiography. The young Maya's physical mobility, her movement from California to Stamps to St. Louis to Stamps and finally, back to California, serves as a central metaphor for a psychic mobility. Ultimately, Maya must find her way out of the psychological and spiritual immobility of her displacement and find the means to awaken herself out of an "ugly black dream."

The girl-child, Maya, must ultimately discover that this dream is not her own; the dominant, patriarchal culture dreams, in Ntozake Shange's words, "a thing calt a colored girl" and inscribes her there, seeking to deny her the right to dream her own self. But Angelou writes her way out of their dream by developing in her life and text a space that defies definition. She opens up a narrative space that, in the end, allows her to not only escape her displacement but also to transcend the social interpolations used to displace her.

Critics, like McPherson and Lionnet, have often read Angelou's autobiography as the quintessential American story of the quest for self, celebrating Angelou's ability to "find her/Self" despite the social forces that would limit her. Such readings are based on the unexamined and so precarious precept that the person's emergence as an Individual is positive, liberating. Angelou's autobiography suggests that this mythic attainment is not so simple. As she negotiates the spaces to which she is consigned because she is Southern, black, and female, Angelou reveals the manner in which the black female subject, a distinctly communal and relational subject, is engaged in an ongoing series of negotiations with the social, cultural, and political interpolations of itself.

From its opening lines, *Caged Bird* reflects Angelou's awareness not only of her own displacement, but of the snare of becoming complacent with any one sense of herself, of becoming, then, complicit in her own containment. Angelou does not comply. Instead, by first establishing and then disrupting dominant images of the black female subject, she escapes stasis to become a subject in the perpetual process of forming and emerging. It is a dynamic subjectivity that emerges out of the young Maya's girlhood, setting the stage for the multidimensional nature of Angelou's adult years. *Caged Bird*, then, does not aspire toward or conclude with a sudden epiphany of identity. There is no final "I" or "Me" that is revealed and reveled in. But there is the process, the journey, not *toward* self, but *of* self. And so the question remains: "what you looking at me for?" The Maya at the end of the work has still not come to stay. She has escaped the gaze, transcended its displacement, and become "becoming." Like Angelou's continuing autobiography, she becomes a work in progress.

From *Women's Studies* 34, no. 5 (2005): 359-375. Copyright © 2005 by Taylor & Francis Ltd. Reprinted by permission of Taylor & Francis, Ltd, http://www.tandf.co.uk/journals.

Notes

1. Angelou subsequently published *Gather Together in My Name* (1974), *Singin' and Swingin' and Gettin' Merry Like Christmas* (1976), *The Heart of a Woman* (1981), *All God's Children Need Traveling Shoes* (1986), and *Wouldn't Take Nothing for My Journey Now* (1993).

2. Such relational dynamics have been critical for African-descended women in America. In *Ar'n't I a Woman?* Deborah Gray White describes the female slave networks in which enslaved women came together not only to achieve practical goals such as childcare, cooking, and craftwork, but also, in a slaveholding culture which denied them their basic humanity, to create a space in which they could affirm each other as women.

3. Lionnet's emphasis on the heroine as individual and McPherson's a priori notion of the American self both stem from the Western cultural ethos of individualism, arising itself from the enlightenment notion of the person as individual and the individual as the fundamental, indeed sacrosanct unit of society. By contrast, a communal ethos imbues traditional African cultures, and the self is perceived as, first and foremost, a communal being.

4. *The Negro Family: The Case for National Action*, issued in 1965 by Daniel Patrick Moynihan's office and generally referred to as the Moynihan Report, is the most notorious example of such studies.

5. The construction of the Black Matriarch and her androgynous asexuality might

be read as a curious corollary to the construction of the Black Mammy figure who is likewise deemed androgynous and asexual. But while the Mammy is rendered so within the context of her supposed servitude and servility to an Anglo family, the Matriarch is stripped of her gender identity and sexuality because of her strength in service to her own family.

6. Maya is raped by one of her mother's suitors and, when the man is kicked to death after she identifies him, the child stops speaking.

Works Cited

Angelou, Maya. *I Know Why the Caged Bird Sings*. New York: Bantam Books, 1971.

Butler, Judith. *Excitable Speech: A Politics of the Performative*. New York: Routledge, 1997.

Giddings, Paula. *When and Where I Enter. The Impact of Black Women on Race and Sex in America*. New York: William Morrow and Company, Inc., 1985.

Henderson, Mae. "Speaking in Tongues: Dialogics, Dialectics and the Black Woman Writer's Literary Tradition." In Ed. Henry Louis Gates Jr., *Reading Black, Reading Feminist: A Critical Anthology*. New York: Meridian, 1990.

Lionnet, Françoise. "Con Artists and Storytellers: Maya Angelou's Problematic Sense of Audience." In Ed. Françoise Lionnet, *Autobiographical Voices: Race, Gender, and Self-Portraiture*. Ithaca, NY: Cornell UP, 1989.

McPherson, Dolly A. *Order Out of Chaos: The Autobiographical Works of Maya Angelou*. New York: Peter Lang, 1990.

O'Neale, Sondra. "Reconstruction of the Composite Self: New Images of Black Women in Maya Angelou's Continuing Autobiography." In Ed. Mari Evans, *Black Women Writers 1950-1980*. Garden City, NY: Anchor-Doubleday, 1984.

White, Deborah Gray. *Ar'n't I a Woman?: Female Slaves in the Plantation South*. New York: Norton, 1985.

Role-Playing as Art in Maya Angelou's
*Caged Bird*_____

Myra K. McMurry

As a songwriter, journalist, playwright, poet, fiction and screen-writer, Maya Angelou is often asked how she escaped her past. How does one grow up, Black and female, in the rural South of the thirties and forties without being crippled or hardened? Her immediate response, "How the hell do you know I did escape?"[1] is subtly deceptive. The evidence of Angelou's creative accomplishments would indicate that she did escape; but a closer look reveals the human and artistic complexity of her awareness. For the first volume of her autobiography, *I Know Why the Caged Bird Sings*, is not an exorcism of or escape from the past, but a transmutation of that past. The almost novelistic clarity of *Caged Bird* results from the artistic tension between Angelou's recollected self and her authorial consciousness. Implicit in this dual awareness is the knowledge that events are significant not merely in themselves, but also because they have been transcended.

Angelou takes her title from Paul Laurence Dunbar's poem "Sympathy." Dunbar's caged bird sings from the frustration of imprisonment; its song is a prayer. Angelou's caged bird sings also from frustration, but in doing so, discovers that the song transforms the cage from a prison that denies selfhood to a vehicle for self-realization. The cage is a metaphor for roles which, because they have become institutionalized and static, do not facilitate interrelationship, but impose patterns of behavior which deny true identity.

In *Caged Bird* Angelou describes her efforts to adapt to the role of a young Black girl, the painfully humorous failures, and the gradual realization of how to transcend the restrictions. At a very early age, the child Angelou, Marguerite Johnson, is an intensely self-conscious child; she feels that her true self is obscured. The autobiography opens with an episode in which Marguerite must recite a poem beginning,

"What you looking at me for?" As she struggles for her lines in the Easter morning church service, she is conscious of her dual self, which is the constant subject of her fantasies. Beneath the ugly disguise—the lavender dress cut-down from a white woman's throwaway, the skinny legs, broad feet, nappy hair, and teeth with a space between—was the real Marguerite Johnson, a sweet little white girl with long blond hair, "everybody's dream of what was right with the world" (p. 1). She mixes elements of fairy tale and Easter story to imagine that a cruel fairy step-mother had changed her from her true self to her present condition. And she relishes the recognition scene in which people will say, "'Marguerite (sometimes it was "dear Marguerite"), forgive us, please, we didn't know who you were,' and [she] would answer generously, 'No, you couldn't have known. Of course I forgive you.'"[2] This introductory episode is emblematic of the child's perspective. She is in a cage which conceals and denies her true nature, and she is aware of her displacement. Someone whispers the forgotten lines and she completes the poem, which suggests transcendence:

> What you looking at me for?
> I didn't come to stay.
> I just come to tell you its Easter Day.

But for Marguerite there is no transcendence. After painful confinement in the humiliating situation, the pressure of her true self to escape takes on a physical urgency. She signals a request to go to the toilet and starts up the aisle. But one of the children trips her and her utmost control is then effective only as far as the front porch. In her view the choice was between wetting her pants or dying of a "busted head," for what was denied proper vent would surely back up to her head and cause an explosion and "the brains and spit and tongue and eyes would roll all over the place" (p. 3). The physical violence of the destruction imagined is the child's equivalent for the emotional violence of self-repression.

In Marguerite's world, rigid laws govern every aspect of a child's life: there are laws for addressing adults by proper title, laws for speaking and more for not speaking, laws about cleanliness and obedience, and about performance in school and behavior in church. Although she respects her brother Bailey for his ability to evade some laws, Marguerite is an obedient child. Her transgressions come, not of willful disobedience, but from loss of control in confrontations in which she is physically overpowered by a larger force.

Much of the story of growing up as Marguerite Johnson is the story of learning to control natural responses. Not to laugh at funny incidents in church, not to express impatience when the guest preacher says too long a blessing and ruins the dinner, not to show felt fear, are part of preparation for life in a repressive society.

Although much of Marguerite's repression is related to her being a child, the caged condition affects almost everyone in her world. The customers in her grandmother's store were trapped in the cotton fields; no amount of hope and work could get them out. Bailey, for all his clever manipulations, was "locked in the enigma . . . of inequality and hate" (p. 168). Her Uncle Willie's own body is his cage. Marguerite observes with the sensitivity of the adult Angelou looking back that he "must have tired of being crippled, as prisoners tire of penitentiary bars and the guilty tire of blame." When Marguerite catches Uncle Willie pretending not to be crippled before some out-of-town visitors, she finds the common condition of being caged and the desire to escape ground for sympathy. "I understood and felt closer to him in that moment than ever before or since" (p. 11).

Even the indomitable grandmother, Annie Henderson, rises each morning with the consciousness of a caged animal. She prays, "Guide my feet this day along the straight and narrow, and help me to put a bridle on my tongue" (p. 5). But it is from her that Marguerite begins to learn how to survive in the cage. Angelou recalls a particular incident that happened when she was about ten years old in which she began to realize her grandmother's triumph. Momma, as Marguerite calls her, has come onto the porch to admire a design that Marguerite had raked in the yard. At the approach of some troublesome "powhitetrash" children, Momma sends Marguerite inside where she cowers behind the screen door. Momma stands solidly on the porch humming a hymn. The impudent children tease, mimic, and insult the older, respectable woman who, by any measure that Marguerite can think of, is their superior. As Marguerite watches and suffers humiliation for her grandmother, she wants to scream at the girls and throw lye on them, but she realizes that she is "as clearly imprisoned behind the scene as the actors outside are confined to their roles" (p. 25). Throughout the performance, Momma stands humming so softly that Marguerite knows she is humming only because her apron strings vibrate. After the children leave, Momma comes inside and Marguerite sees that she is beautiful; her face is radiant. As Momma hums "Glory, glory, hallelujah, when I lay my burden down," Marguerite realizes that whatever the contest had been, Momma had won. Marguerite goes back to her raking and makes a huge heart design with little hearts inside growing smaller toward the center, and draws an arrow piercing through all the hearts to the smallest one. Then she brings Momma to see. In essence she is using the design to organize feelings she could not otherwise order or express, just as Momma has used the song to organize her thoughts and feelings beyond the range of the children's taunts. She triumphs not only in spite of her restrictions, but because of them. It is because, as a Black woman, she must maintain the role of respect toward the white children that she discovers another vehicle for her true emotions. She has used her cage creatively to transcend it.

The same principle works for a group as well as for an individual. What Maya Angelou had understood intuitively or subconsciously as a ten-year-old comes to the level of conscious realization after her eighth-grade graduation. Marguerite's graduation ceremony begins in an aura of magic, but just after the national anthem and the pledge of allegiance, the point at which they normally would have sung the song they considered to be the Negro national anthem, the principal nervously signals the students to be seated. Then he introduces as commencement speaker a white politician who is on his way to another engagement and must speak out of order so that he can leave. His speech and the suppression of feeling his mere presence entails are humiliating reminders to the students of the restrictive white world in which they live. He talks of plans for an artist to teach at Central High, the white school, and of new microscopes and equipment for the Chemistry labs at Central. For Lafayette County Training School he promises the "only colored paved playing field in that part of Arkansas" and some equipment for the home economics building and the workshop. The implications of his talk are crushing to the graduates. For Marguerite the occasion is ruined; she remembers that

> Graduation, the hush-hush magic time of frills and gifts and congratulations and diplomas, was finished for me before my name was called. The accomplishment was nothing. The meticulous maps, drawn in three colors of ink, learning and spelling decasyllabic words, memorizing the whole of *The Rape of Lucrece*—it was for nothing. Donleavy had exposed us.
>
> We were maids and farmers, handymen and washerwomen, and anything higher that we aspired to was farcical and presumptuous. (p. 152)

The white politician rushes off to his next engagement, leaving a gloom over the ceremony. One student recites "Invictus"—"I am the master of my fate, I am the captain of my soul"—but now it is a farce. As Henry Reed, the valedictorian, gives his address, Marguerite wonders that he could go on. But at the end, Henry turns to the graduates and begins to sing the song omitted earlier, the Negro national anthem. The students, parents and visitors respond to the familiar song—their own song, and as they sing, "We have come over a way that with tears has been watered,/ We have come, treading our path through the blood of the slaughtered," the separate, isolated individuals become a community with a common soul:

We were on top again. As always again. We survived. The depths had been icy and dark, but now a bright sun spoke to our souls. I was no longer simply a member of the proud graduating class of 1940; I was a proud member of the wonderful, beautiful Negro race. (p. 156)

Maya Angelou abstracts from this incident that "we [the Negro race] survive in exact relationship to the dedication of our poets (include preachers, musicians and blues singers)" (p. 156). Art organizes consciousness; it brings people together with a sense of shared experience, and a sympathy of feeling. It provides a focal point that gives unified structure to emotional response. In this sense even a prizefighter becomes an artist, as when people gather at the store to listen to the radio broadcast of a Joe Louis fight. Joe Louis becomes symbolic of their repressed selves; his victory, limited and defined by the boxing ring, is nonetheless a spiritual victory for all Blacks. Like Marguerite's finally triumphant graduation, it is a victory, the significance of which largely depends on the sense of limitation overcome. Louis is simultaneously an oppressed man and "the strongest man in the world," and the full import of his achievement in winning the heavyweight championship lies in the context of the restrictions he overcame.

The same role that may be destructive to selfhood can, when played creatively, be transformed to a role that enhances self. The artist is able to do what the con men friends of Daddy Clidell do. They find a mark, someone who has obvious prejudices, and use these prejudices against him. Similarly the artist uses the bitter reality of his experience to produce a vehicle for essential human values. The artist achieves the same victory as the hero of the Black American ghettos, whom Maya Angelou describes as "that man who is offered only the crumbs from his country's table but by ingenuity and courage is able to take for himself a Lucullan feast" (p. 190). The artist also achieves a victory over reality; he too is able to take crumbs and "by ingenuity and courage" make a feast.

When Maya Angelou speaks of "survival with style" and attributes survival to the work of artists, she is talking about a function of art similar to that described by Ralph Ellison. Speaking of his own early discovery of the role of art, he calls it "a mode of humanizing reality and of evoking a feeling of being at home in the world. It is something which the artist shares with the group," and he describes how he and his friends yearned "to make any-and-everything of quality Negro-American; to appropriate it, possess it, re-create it in our own group and individual images. . . . [We] recognized and were proud of our group's own style wherever we discerned it—in jazzmen and prize fighters, ballplayers and tap dancers; in gesture, inflection, intonation, timbre and phrasing. Indeed, in all those nuances of expression and attitude which reveal a culture. We did not fully understand the cost of that style but we recognized within it an affirmation of life beyond all question of our difficulties as Negroes."[3]

Such an affirmation of life, a humanizing of reality, is Maya Angelou's answer to the question of how a Black girl can grow up in a repressive system without being maimed by it. Art protects the human values of compassion, love, and innocence, and makes the freedom for the self-realization necessary for real survival. Her answer, like Ellison's, skirts the reformer's question: is "the cost of that style" too high? In this sense she and Ellison are religious writers rather than social ones, for their ultimate concern is self-transcendence. It is unlikely that either would deny the practical value of the past twenty years' progress toward attainment of Negroes' full citizenship in America. But ultimately, as artists, their concern is with the humanity which must survive, and even assimilate into its own creative potential, such restrictions as these writers have encountered. For if this humanity cannot survive restriction, then it will itself become assimilated to the roles imposed upon it.

From *South Atlantic Bulletin* 41, no. 2 (May 1976): 106-111. Copyright © 1976 by South Atlantic Modern Language Association. Reprinted by permission of South Atlantic Modern Language Association.

Role-Playing as Art

Notes

1. Quoted in an interview by Sheila Weller, "Work in Progress/Maya Angelou," *Intellectual Digest*, June, 1973.

2. Maya Angelou, *I Know Why the Caged Bird Sings* (New York: Bantam Books, 1971), p. 2. Hereafter page numbers will be cited in the text. (*Editor's note*: The second volume of the autobiography, *Gather Together in My Name* [New York: Random House, 1974], was not available until after this essay was completed and submitted for publication.)

3. Ralph Ellison, *Shadow and Act* (New York: Random House, 1964), p. xvii.

Singin' de Blues, Writing Black Female Survival in *I Know Why the Caged Bird Sings*_____

Cherron A. Barnwell

> The blues is an impulse to keep the painful details and episodes of a brutal experience alive in one's aching consciousness, to finger its jagged grain, and to transcend it, not by the consolation of philosophy but by squeezing from it a near-tragic, near-comic lyricism. As a form, the blues is an autobiographical chronicle of personal catastrophe expressed lyrically.
>
> —Ralph Ellison

When the Modern Library paid tribute to her life writing with its publication of her six-volume autobiographical series in a handsome one-volume edition titled *The Collected Autobiographies of Maya Angelou* (2004), Dr. Angelou's place in America's literary and cultural traditions was reaffirmed. Angelou's autobiographies are monumental memoirs of inspiration, celebrating life and encouraging survival. Dr. Angelou launched her canon of life writing with the 1970 publication *I Know Why the Caged Bird Sings*. A coming-of-age story, fashioned after the slave narrative, recalls the experience of a Southern black girl, in the throes of an imprisoning and chaotic socialization, growing up in segregated Stamps, Arkansas, during the 1930s, and ends with her becoming a teenaged single mother frightened but determined to face the world and fulfill her duty of motherhood. It is the foundational text in her six-volume autobiographical series, which introduces to the black autobiographical genre a powerfully candid, bordering-the-absurd, style of writing about true-life black woman's tragedy, trauma, and survival. The style Angelou brings to black autobiography is aptly described by George Kent in his essay titled "Maya Angelou's *I Know Why the Caged Bird Sings* and Black Autobiographical Tradition": *Caged Bird*'s place within the black autobiographical tradition is cemented for "its use [of] forms that exploit the full measure of imagination necessary to acknowledge both beauty and absurdity" (20).

Many of us, having read Angelou's *Caged Bird*, find it no surprise that her work would be accorded the prominence of *American* (meaning, white mainstream) literary status. Critics have steadfastly granted it attention. They praise her autobiographies for the universal sense of self that emanates from them, claiming as does Harold Bloom that "[. . .] [T]he secret of Angelou's enormous appeal to American readers, whether white or black [. . . is] her remarkable literary voice[, which] speaks to something in the universal American 'little me within the big me'" (1). And, while readings of the Americanness of Angelou's *Caged Bird* are valid, and the institutional accolades accorded her autobiographies appreciated, for this writer, the greatness of *Caged Bird* is rooted in its blackness. It is Angelou's drawing of that which is beautifully universal in black culture that propels her into canonization.

Caged Bird has been examined over and anon for what it owes to other elements in the African American cultural tradition, such as Negro spirituals, the blues, black vernacular, and of course black poetry. Sidonie Smith, in a 1973 essay titled "The Song of a Caged Bird: Maya Angelou's Quest after Self-Acceptance," acknowledges that *Caged Bird* is indebted to "the earliest form of black autobiography, the slave narrative, which traced the flight of the slave northward from slavery into full humanity" (qtd. in Bloom 5); Joanne Braxton in *Black Women Writing Autobiography: A Tradition Within A Tradition* (1999) finds traditional black American women's autobiographical themes in *Caged Bird*, themes such as "the importance of family and the nurturing and rearing of one's children, as well as the quest for self-sufficiency, self-reliance, personal dignity, and self-definition" (127); regarding black vernacular and traditional linguistic influences, in "Con Artists and Storytellers: Maya Angelou's Problematic Sense of Audience," Françoise Lionnet finds that in "gesturing toward the black community," *Caged Bird* uses a duplicitous language of survival traditionally understood by oppressed peoples (143). My celebration of *Caged Bird*'s distinct black forms, then, is a revival of sorts, a project that aligns me with these precursory readings of *Caged Bird*.

Of the African American cultural elements present in the text, the blues is most influential in *Caged Bird*. The blues shapes its form and content, and in using the blues aesthetic, Angelou meets the challenge of writing autobiography as literature. Descending from the Negro spiritual, the blues is a music native to America, having its genesis in the African American culture; it is expressive of blackness encountering that which is commonly called American. Amiri Baraka's classic text *Blues People: Negro Music in White America* (1963) articulates this understanding of the blues. "[B]lues could not exist if the African captives had not become American captives" (17), asserts Baraka. Moreover, the blues is valued for both its music and meaning. Its polyphonic rhythms, loud and brass timbres accent the history of black America's uprooting encounters and cultural ransacking. The whoops and hollers scream out the pain of being the nation's exploited laborers who have been denied the right to possess even the vestiges of ransacked ancestral cultures. To ascertain a textual sign system of Angelou's blues aesthetic in the literariness of her autobiography, a semiotic examination of *Caged Bird*'s prefatory opening and specifically chapter 23, is helpful.

Houston A. Baker Jr.'s *Blues, Ideology, and Afro-American Literature: A Vernacular Theory* (1984), supports theoretical readings of black writing that use "readily discernible Afro-American expressive cultural referents" (89). For Baker, the African American literary critic, who is "versed in the vernacular and unconstrained by traditional historical determinants, may well be able to discover blues inscriptions and liberating rhythms" (115). Blues forms in *Caged Bird*, then, are its liberating rhythms, re-inscribing (or replacing) Angelou's socialized sense of placelessness with American literary prominence. A semiotic analysis makes evident the traits of *Caged Bird* that anticipate blues forms as the aesthetic in Angelou's other autobiographies.

It is necessary to note here that the blues functions as an autobiographical act. At the heart of the blues are individualizing features comparable to those in autobiography. Baraka offers an explanation:

"Though certain techniques and verses came to be standardized among blues singers, the singing itself remained as arbitrary and personal as the shout. [. . .] The music remained that personal because it began with the performers themselves, and not with formalized notions of how it was to be performed" (Baraka, 67). Through the formal techniques of the blues, Angelou enters into an inner-retrospective meditation on her life experiences and depicts the self that obtains from such meditation. This self-understanding is in an image of a blues priestess endowed with self-healing, life-affirming powers.

As Sidonie Smith states about any good autobiography, the opening defines its narrative strategies. *Caged Bird* consists of a prefatory opening, and 36 episodic chapters that chronicle the life of a southern black girl growing up in the 1930s, aware of her feelings of displacement and a debilitating socialization. Right away in its prefatory opening the work sings the blues. It is young Maya's blues. She is at an Easter Sunday recital, standing before the children's section of the Colored Methodist Episcopal Church in Stamps, Arkansas, trying to remember the lines of a children's poem. On this dreaded Easter Sunday, young Maya wears a "cut-down from a white woman's once-was-purple throwaway" dress, a dress she imagined as beautiful, and hoped would transport her out of her blues reality and turn her into "one of the sweet little white girls who were everybody's dream of what was right with the world" (2). But, young Maya's lavender-taffeta, ruffled-hem dress failed her. Even the Easter's early morning sun betrayed her, showing her dress to be plain ugly and her to be a "too-big Negro girl, with nappy black hair, broad feet and a space between her teeth that would hold a number-two pencil" (3). So, young Maya, "painfully aware of her displacement" (4) had a blues to sing: "What you looking at me for?/ I didn't come to stay [. . .]/ What you looking at me for?/ I didn't come to stay [. . .]/ Ijustcometotellyouit'sEasterDay" (1). Angelou thrusts us right into this blues by the way the lines from the poem are actually quoted. Those of us who recognize the poem as a blues form might even hum the quoted lines as a blues tune while reading it. The first two lines are the same, quoted in intervals between autodiegetic narrative; the third line, consisting of nine words, is quoted but with all nine words slurred together. All three quoted lines together form closely a "classic" blues of 12-bars, 3-lines, AAB structure with the third line, B structure, ensuring that we read it as a blues in its capturing syntactically the style Baraka calls "'blueing' the notes." He explains this as "sliding and slurring effects in Afro-American music, the basic 'aberrant' quality of a blues scale" (25). The quoted lines from song or poetry patterned into blues forms are textual signs in Angelou's blues aesthetic.

Because the three lines are set in quotation marks as direct speech, they evoke with immediacy Angelou's present-writing situation and thereby signal the new intended meaning(s) and function she gives them. In quotation marks, the poem signals not merely a present speech act but rather a present act of expression—a present blues, if you will. The word "you" in the line "What you looking at me for," along with the immediacy of the quotation marks, connects *Caged Bird* to its readers, marking what Baker calls "an invitation to energizing intersubjectivity" (5). Thus, the quoted lines are inviting in the same ways the blues invites its audience to share in the experiencing of it. The children at the Colored Methodist Episcopal Church had no choice but to look at young Maya, identify her, and complete her sense of self when she declared "What *you* looking at me for" (emphasis added). Recited in *Caged Bird*, however, the same line calls to present-writing Angelou's black readership (who themselves have sat in the children's section of their black churches) to "look" at young Maya's childhood experience in the black church and recall their own, thereby asking them to identify with her. They are encouraged to sing their blues. Thus, the blues function as an autobiographical act and allows *Caged Bird* to exhibit what Joanne Braxton observes about black women's autobiography: "Black women's autobiography is [. . .] the occasion for viewing the individual in relation to those others w/whom she shares emotional, philosophical, and spiritual affinities, as well as political realities" (9). As such, *Caged Bird*'s opening produces an intersubjectivity that is black, female, and in relation to the black community.[1]

Furthermore, the inviting qualities the blues forms give to Angelou's autobiographical act require readers to complete present-writing Angelou's sense of self just as the children of the Colored Methodist Episcopal Church did; and after readers identify with Maya's childhood experience, they become attuned to their own childhood experience and the sense of self that obtains. Baker explains,

> The blues singer's signatory coda is always *atopic*, placeless: "If anybody ask you who sang this song / Tell 'em X done been here and gone." The signature is a space already "X"(ed), a trace of the already "gone"—the fissure rejoined. Nevertheless, the "you" (audience) addressed is always free to invoke the X(ed) spot in the body's absence. (5)

So, while the "you" in the line "What you looking at me for" immediately addresses black readers who are thus encouraged to identify with young Maya's childhood experience(s), the "I" in the line "I didn't come to stay" encourages readers to invoke self-understanding and understanding of what Angelou is (or should be) in the transient "I" space. Readers are made ever cognizant of the present-writing Angelou attempting to recapture her childhood experience(s) as already changed—for young Maya has grown up—as readers superimpose our understanding of the experience onto present-writing Angelou's self-understanding. Black experience is universalized, but not as a constant. It is understood as a changing same, which the prefatory opening predicts will be dramatized inside the covers of *Caged Bird*.

As a way to begin the autobiography, then, the quoted line from a children's poem, "I didn't come to stay," signals that movement and placelessness will be a motif throughout *Caged Bird*. It is a transience that marks the transformative and thus transforming nature of the blues, or what Baker describes as "a phylogenetic recapitulation of experience" (5). Therefore, Angelou's self-representation will be transforming as well as transformative; as phylogenetic as a blues song.[2]

The remainder of the autobiography's opening sings Angelou's blues of black survival as rendered in the embarrassing moment when she runs out of the church urinating. After she recited her poem, she suddenly had to go to the bathroom, barely able to hold back her urine. She found herself caught in a quandary, for if she did not urinate "it would probably run right back up to [her] head and [her] poor head would burst like a dropped watermelon, and all the brains and spit and tongue and eyes would roll all over the place" (3-4). Urinating freely as she ran home, young Maya experienced the joy of release and relief "not only from being liberated from the silly church but from the knowledge that [she] wouldn't die from a busted head" (4). Of this humorously ironic past experience, Angelou sings a hysterically releasing blues. There is sadness and humor. There is defiance, symbolized in "urinating," towards her feelings of humiliation and displacement. Baker's further description of the blues applies here: Angelou's blues of embarrassment is ironic self-accusation, which "seamlessly fades into humorous acknowledgement of duplicity's always duplicitous triumph" (4). *Caged Bird*'s opening, therefore, forecasts the ways in which past experience will be made into episodic anecdotes that teach survival of a blues reality: life-lessons are found in ordinary, everyday experiences of black life; and, like every blues song, the condition can be transcended. It can be survived.

Following the prefatory opening, the narrative proceeds to the episode of three-years-young Maya along with her one-year older brother, Bailey, traveling alone on a train ride from Long Beach, California, to Stamps, Arkansas, to stay with their Grandmother Henderson. Angelou's earliest memory of feeling abandoned and displaced is captured. She states that she doesn't remember the trip, but she remembers that "Negro passengers, who always traveled with loaded lunch boxes, felt sorry for 'the poor little *motherless* darlings' and plied [her and her brother] with cold fried chicken and potato salad" (5, emphasis added).

These feelings were not solely her own. Angelou ensures us in this first episode that she shared these feelings with many black children growing up during the depression and the great black migration: "Years later I discovered that the United States had been crossed thousands of times by frightened Black children traveling alone to their newly affluent parents in Northern cities, or back to grandmothers in Southern towns when the urban North reneged on its economic promises" (5-6). In retelling young Maya's migration South, Angelou gains understanding of the experience as a traumatizing social condition of all black Americans in the 1930s. The child's migration is retold as a symbolic act recalling social displacement in the African American historical experience. The experience is a blues. It is an experience that imparts self-understanding to the present-writing Angelou because she treats the experience as transformative. While the motif of movement is influenced by the slave narrative, the blues form treats movement as transforming. Angelou's phylogenetic recapitulation of young Maya's migration South and signals the change to be dramatized in her coming-of-age autobiography.

Each chapter of the autobiography contains an episode of displacement and trauma, which ends in a further understanding of self, usually how the self overcomes the trauma. Stories of the retired white sheriff's warning Grandmother Henderson of the Klan's random, lynch-law escapades, which led to the night crippled Uncle Willie hid in a bin beneath layers of potatoes and onions; of grandmother Henderson's maintaining her dignity before the "powhitetrash" children's insults and mocking gestures, shape the body of *Caged Bird* into episodic anecdotes of survival and transcendence of a blues reality. Of course, the most drastic episode is Angelou's sexual molestation and rape by her mother's boyfriend Mr. Freeman. The segments detailing her vow to live in silence and thus remain mute for several years after learning of Mr. Freeman's death; her "life-line" friendship with Mrs. Flowers who gave her the gift of self-love and voice; the violent fight with her father's pretentious "white-airs" girlfriend; and driving her father's car and getting herself back to town because a drunk father couldn't, all touch upon issues of displacement, self-doubt, self-hatred, and resilience, thus survival, in the face of adversity. Of the 36 chapters, chapter 23, Graduation of 1940, demonstrates most apparently the semiotics of Angelou's blues aesthetic at work.

Chapter 23 recounts twelve-year-old Maya's graduation from Lafayette County Training School. Angelou remembers this was an exciting day for the whole Stamps black community, especially the youth:

> The children in Stamps trembled visibly with anticipation. Some adults were excited too, but to be certain the whole young population had come down with graduation epidemic. Large classes were graduating from both the grammar school and the high school. Even those who were years removed from their own day of glorious release were anxious to help with preparations as a kind of dry run. [. . .] Even teachers were respectful of the now quiet and aging seniors, and tended to speak to them, if not as equals, as beings only slightly lower than themselves.

Just days before graduation, young Maya took possession of a new happiness; she took to "smiling more often [so that her] jaws hurt from the unaccustomed activity," Angelou recollects (172). On the day of graduation, she believed that her youthful prayers had been answered. She recounts:

> I gave myself up to the gentle warmth and thanked God that no matter what evil I had done in my life He had allowed me to live to see this day. Somewhere in my fatalism I had expected to die, accidentally, and never have the chance to walk up the stairs in the auditorium and gracefully receive my hard-earned diploma. Out of God's merciful bosom I had won reprieve. (175)

The haunting fatalism foreshadows *Caged Bird*'s thematic expectations resulting from the semiotic of episodic anecdote, as the story takes a turn for the worse and a blues develops. The sunshine day of

Graduation 1940 turns into clouds of ugliness the when guest speaker, the white Donleavy, delivered the customary, racist speech he reserved for southern black schools' graduating ceremonies. It was laden with half-hearted inspirations representative of a larger, mainstream society's low expectations of black people. Donleavy's spirit-killing speech was successful: "Constrained by hard-learned manners [she] couldn't look behind [her], but to [her] left and right the proud graduating class of 1940 had dropped their heads" (179), recalls Angelou. The speech conjured up again her feelings of displacement and the collective consciousness of Stamps' black community: "It was awful to be Negro and have no control over my life. It was brutal to be young and already trained to sit quietly and listen to charges brought against my color with no chance of defense. We should all be dead" (180).

After Donleavy's spirit-killing speech, valedictorian Henry Reed delivers his address to Graduation Class 1940 as planned. Angelou recalls that Reed's address possessed the promise of great fortune for the black graduates in spite of Donleavy's statement to the contrary. Little Henry Reed had the mind and wherewithal to restore black pride and self-determination in his fellow graduates. The epitome of self-determination, he stated in his address, "I am the master of my fate, I am the captain of my soul" (181), and he turned to his audience and began to sing the Negro National Anthem, "Lift Ev'ry Voice and Sing." The graduating class joined him; the audience joined them. Everyone joined in song and sermon, overcoming their feelings of displacement. Through the healing forces of the Negro National Anthem, faith, pride, and self-determination were restored. Young Maya was proud again not only to be a member of the Graduation Class 1940, but also of the "wonderful, beautiful Negro race" (184).

Quotations from the Negro National Anthem are patterned into a blues form as the lines, interspersed with autodiegetic narrative, take the shape of a blues, this one closer to what Baraka describes as primitive blues, a musical form which precedes classic blues, succeeds the work song, and issues directly from the spiritual. Like the classic blues, primitive blues reflects the social and cultural problems plaguing African American life; however, a new self-determination is part of this experience, and the primitive blues sings of it as a changing sense of being, asserts Baraka:

> There was a definite change of direction in the primitive blues. The metaphysical Jordan of life after death was beginning to be replaced by the more pragmatic Jordan of the American master: the Jordan of what the ex-slave could see vaguely as self-determination. [. . .] [T]he American Negro wanted some degree of self-determination where he was living. [. . .] The Negro began to feel a desire to be more in this country, America, than chattel. (64-65)

The lines quoted from the anthem sing of African American historical determination:

> "Lift ev'ry voice and sing
> Till earth and heaven ring
> Ring with the harmonies of Liberty [. . .]
> Stony the road we trod
> Bitter the chast'ning rod
> Felt in the days when hope unborn had died;
> Yet with a steady beat,
> Have not our weary feet
> Come to the place for which our fathers sighed?" (182-183)

These lines are reflective of the primitive blues form as they celebrate social transcendence rather than spiritual or religious transcendence.

Because the anthem is a transformative song, quoting the passages that best capture this, Angelou reconstitutes the experience of displacement and all its complexity into a blues matrix composed of converging negative and positive feelings. Within the covers of *Caged Bird*, the anthem is understood as a song of survival, by the use of blues strategies, making concrete the transient experience of displacement conjoined by the healing properties of song.

Indeed, *Caged Bird*'s blackness rings with the harmonies of liberties, beckoning its black readers socialized by the Negro National Anthem to join present-writing Angelou in song. At the end of chapter 23, the apostrophe to black poets and blues singers best illustrates the chronotopic collapse of narrative and thus the difficulty of distinguishing young Maya from writerly Angelou:

> Oh, Black known and unknown poets, how often have your auctioned pains sustained us? Who will compute the lonely nights made less lonely by your songs [. . .] less tragic by your tales? If we were a people much given to revealing secrets, we might raise monuments and sacrifice to the memories of our poets, but slavery cured us of that weakness. It may be enough, however, to have it said that we survive in exact relationship to the dedication of our poets (include preachers, musicians and blues singers). (184)

At this juncture, *Caged Bird*, once again, is self-reflexive, calling attention to its blues form. Inasmuch as Angelou's apostrophized survival is "in exact relationship to the dedication of our poets, preachers, and blues singers" so too is the work's. *Caged Bird*'s textures and themes intersect and interanimate to unfold a self-conscious autobiographical act, producing an intersubjective Angelou who is well aware of the cultural referents that shape her.

Knowing the Maya Angelou that is a poet whose auctioned pains have sustained many, *Caged Bird*'s readers see how the apostrophe summons an understanding of Angelou. It functions as an inviting energizing intersubjectivity: Angelou's autobiographical act. Through the apostrophe, she is cast in the image of a Black poet/blues priestess, who, as Baker describes: "[L]ustily transform[s] experiences of durative landscape [. . .] into the energies of rhythmic song. Like [a] translator of written texts, [the blues priestess, Angelou . . .] offer[s] interpretations of the experiencing of experience" (7). The result is an intersubjective Angelou, who is created (or rather completed by her readers) as she creates. Furthermore, the life-sustaining powers of the quoted spiritual infuse *Caged Bird*, shaping graduation 1940 into an episodic anecdote of survival and transcendence of a blues reality. Maya and her classmates survived their momentary blues reality of socialized displacement chanted to them in Donleavy's speech. In the moment of retelling the phylogenetic experience of socialized displacement, Angelou transforms into a blues priestess whose auctioned pains sustain us, her readers.

Because chapter 23's first line of the apostrophe, alone, signifies on James Weldon Johnson's poem titled "Black and Unknown Bards," in the way *Caged Bird*'s title signifies upon Paul Laurence Dunbar's "Sympathy," *Caged Bird* does more than sing young Maya's blues. Signifyin' upon Dunbar's and Johnson's poetry and music, respectively, Angelou makes her autobiography resonate with these renowned African American creators' praiseworthy stylistics. While joining this canon on the one hand, on the other, her six-volume autobiographical series, indeed makes Dr. Angelou a canon unto herself. *Caged Bird* lays the foundation for this canon, using a life writing blues aesthetic, which can be traced in the other volumes. Because readers know Dr. Angelou has written five more autobiographies after this initial one, because they know the self undergoes five more transformations, they know her blues aesthetic proves successful.

In *Gather Together in My Name* (1993), for example, the semiotics of Angelou's blues aesthetic allows her to dramatize again her life as a story about surviving displacement with pride and dignity, and to do so in the image of black poet/blues priestess. *Gather* recounts teenaged, single-mother Maya's struggle to find her niche in life while raising her son alone. Particularly in chapter 16 of *Gather*, episodic anecdote of survival and transcendence of a blues reality shapes the chapter and foregrounds Angelou's self-understanding. Chapter 16 recounts an instance at the Dew Drop Café, when a male-friend/suitor, L. C., rescues single-mother Maya from a drunken humiliation planned surreptitiously by people she thought were her friends. Angelou remembers the episode with the force, energy, and complexity of the blues so that her readers can partake in the experiencing of her blues reality:

> Well, I ain't got no
> special reason here.
> No, I ain't got no
> special reason here.
> I'm going leave
> 'cause I don't feel welcome here. (67)

Quotations of song or poetry patterned into blues form are used again here as they were in *Caged Bird*, making *Gather* sing her blues in its present writing situation. The lyrics foreshadow the outcome of the Dew Drop Café episode. Once Maya finds out from L. C. that she was the butt of her "friends'" joke, the "unwelcomeness" or feelings of displacement *Gather* sings about is actualized. The blues captures Angelou's understanding of the experience as another one that shapes her into a blues priestess who sings about surviving life's cruel and humiliating moments with pride and dignity.

Angelou's third autobiography, *Singin' and Swingin' and Gettin' Merry Like Christmas* (1976), modifies her textual sign system of a blues aesthetic by reinforcing self-signifying as a practice. *Singin'* continues with the life-story of finding her artistic niche in pursuing a show business career as dancer, singer, performer. When in chapter 8, the Garden of Allah episode, she recounts how three white women, who pressured the owner of the Garden of Allah to put Maya on notice, approach her with their phony well-wishes, *Singin'* signifies on the episode in *Caged Bird* when Momma Henderson remained dignified and withstood the "powhitetrash" girls' disrespectful jeers. Here, self-signifying constructs Angelou's autobiographical series into a canon that must be read in its entirety.

It is in autobiography number four, *The Heart of a Woman* (1981), that the semiotics of Angelou's blues aesthetic addresses the issue of gender and thus takes on a feminized structure. In *Heart* Maya is now thirty years old and her son, Guy, is fourteen years old; she has acquired some show-business fame, and is involved in the Civil Rights struggle as one of Dr. Martin Luther King's coordinators. It is no wonder for the reader who appreciates Angelou's blues aesthetic that Angelou opens *The Heart of a Woman* showcasing Billie Holiday. Though Billie might be thought of more as a jazz than blues singer, through evoking her presence, Angelou clearly assumes the self-image of a female blues singer whose stature equals Lady Day's.

To the semiotics of Angelou's blues aesthetic is added self-signifying, which allows the transformative nature of the blues to modify Angelou's blues priestess self-image in *All God's Children Need Traveling Shoes* (1986). Angelou attributes the survival of the black community to the African American intellectual community, as well as the black poet, preacher, musician, blues singer. *All God's Children* recounts Angelou's recovering her independence and spiritual solitude after giving too much of herself in a failed marriage to an African revolutionary. Specifically in the episode describing the protest march she and her fellow "Revolutionist Returnees" arranged in Ghana to coincide with Dr. King's famous August 1963 March on Washington at 7:00 a.m., Angelou remembers W. E. B. Du Bois' death. People broke out into song. Angelou quotes from the song, explaining her understanding of the moment. Her explanation is self-referential:

We were singing for Dr. Du Bois' spirit, for the invaluable contributions he made, for his shining intellect and his courage. To many of us he was the first American Negro intellectual. We knew about Jack Johnson and Jesse Owens and Joe Louis. We were proud of Louis Armstrong and Marian Anderson and Roland Hayes. We memorized the verses of James Weldon Johnson, Langston Hughes, Paul Laurence Dunbar and Countee Cullen, but they were athletes, musicians, and poets, and White folks thought all those talents came naturally to Negroes. So, while we survived because of those contributors and their contributions, the powerful White world didn't stand in awe of them. Sadly, we also tended to take those brilliances for granted. But W. E. B. Du Bois and of course Paul Robeson were different, held on a higher or at least on a different plateau than the others.

There is no mistaking the apparent echo this passage has to the apostrophe in *Caged Bird*. Signifyin' on her first volume, Angelou modifies her understanding of self. No longer is it only the black poets, preachers, musicians, and blues singers whom she commemorates for their life-sustaining forces. Now, she commemorates the AfricanAmerican intellectual, represented by W. E. B. Du Bois and Paul Robeson, for their contributions to the survival of the black community. The self-referential nature of this passage endows Angelou with the voice of the African American intellectual. As blues priestess, now, she sings with the shining intellect and courage possessed by Du Bois and Robeson.

In her final autobiography, *A Song Flung Up to Heaven*, Angelou makes it clear through the self-reflexive elements and a consciousness of the writing process, that her six autobiographies are to be treated as a series. In the closing description of James Baldwin's encouraging her to write, *A Song* explains Angelou's purpose for writing poetry. As such, *A Song* reinforces the self-image Angelou creates in her other five autobiographies, the image of blues priestess contributing to the survival of the black community. The African American community has sustained itself, as Angelou quotes Baldwin, because

We put surviving into our poems and into our songs. We put it into our folk tales. We danced surviving in Congo Square in New Orleans and put it in our pots when we cooked pinto beans. We wore surviving on our backs when we clothed ourselves in the colors of the rainbow. We were pulled down so low we could hardly lift our eyes, so we knew, if we wanted to survive, we had better lift our own spirits. (197)

Autobiography, for Angelou, serves the same purpose: to teach survival and invoke the sense of transcendence of blues reality. It lifts her spirit and her autobiography lifts ours.

In using the blues in a textual sign system, Angelou patterns her six-volume autobiographical series into a canon of life-sustaining songs which situate her firmly in the black literary and cultural canon of black survival. Her autobiographies present her in the image of blues priestess who auctions her pains for the survival of her community. Her songs echo those of the black poet, preacher, musician, blues singer, African American intellectual. Alone Angelou's body of life writing has its own unique significance as inspirational literature that is monumental. And, so, to the list of contributors of black survival commemorated in *Caged Bird* and again in *All God's Children Need Traveling Shoes* should be added the black autobiographer. For using the autobiographical occasion to share cultural, historical, socio-political, and spiritual affinities, which upon inner-retrospection impart self-understanding, Angelou ensures the longevity of a significant genre as well as the survival of a monumental black humanity.

From *The Langston Hughes Review* 19 (Spring 2005): 48-60. Copyright © 2005 by the Langston Hughes Society. Reprinted by permission of the Langston Hughes Society.

Notes

1. In its prefatory opening there is a pact formed with those of us who read *Caged Bird* for its blues blackness. Angelou and her readers agree to share in her autobiographical enterprise because any dramatization of a blues reality must be inviting and energizing.

2. Movement as motif in *Caged Bird* has usually been attributed to the slave narrative's influence. And, yes, the slave narrative does offer *Caged Bird* a theme of movement, of "enslavement from which the black self must escape" (Bloom 5); but, here in the quoted lines patterned in blues form, the movement motif, as influenced by the blues forms, signals an autobiographical act whereby Angelou is granted an intersubjectivity, which is at once transient and shared.

Works Cited

Angelou, Maya. *All God's Children Need Traveling Shoes*. New York: Vintage, 1991.

_____. *Gather Together in My Name*. New York: Bantam, 1993.

_____. *The Heart of a Woman*. New York: Random House, 1981.

_____. *I Know Why the Caged Bird Sings*. 1970. New York: Bantam, 1997.

_____. *Singin' and Swingin' and Gettin' Merry Like Christmas*. New York: Bantam, 1976.

_____. *A Song Flung Up to Heaven*. New York: Bantam, 2003.

Baker, Houston A., Jr. *Blues, Ideology, and Afro-American Literature: A Vernacular Theory*. Chicago: University of Chicago Press, 1984.

Baraka, Amiri [LeRoi Jones]. *Blues People: Negro Music in White America*. New York: Perennial, 1963.

Bloom, Harold, ed. *Maya Angelou*. Philadelphia: Chelsea House, 1999.

Braxton, Joanne M., ed. *Maya Angelou's I Know Why the Caged Bird Sings: A Casebook*. New York: Oxford University Press, 1999.

Brooks, Tilford. "The Blues." *America's Black Musical Heritage*. Englewood Cliffs, NJ: Prentice-Hall, 1984. 51-60.

Ellison, Ralph. "Richard Wright's Blues." *Shadow And Act*. New York: Vintage, 1972. 77-94.

Megna-Wallace, Joanne. *Understanding I Know Why the Caged Bird Sings: A Student Casebook to Issues, Sources, and Historical Documents*. Westport, CT: Greenwood, 1998.

A Discursive Trifecta:
Community, Education, and Language in
*I Know Why the Caged Bird Sings*_____

Clarence Nero

Maya Angelou's writing transcends race, gender, class, and culture. There have been few writers—living or dead—who have commanded the written word with such vigor and definitive purpose. She has lived every noun, verb, adjective, and adverb on her pages, and the body of work has a literary aesthetic of its own that is inextricably linked to the African American tradition of storytelling. Dr. Angelou's writing is on the level of discursiveness, which the *American Heritage Dictionary* describes as "a verbal expression in speech and writing." In taking a closer look at *I Know Why the Caged Bird Sings* (1970) we find community, education, and language working as a "discursive trifecta" to bring dignity, hope, and pride to a black community "fragmented by Diaspora" (Folks 1).

Caged Bird was the first in a series of autobiographical portraits of the life and history of a phenomenal woman with a strong sense of community and pride. Dr. Angelou's life has been a testimony to the strength and tenacity of the human spirit to rise in the face of adversity. She grew up during an era of much racial tension and oppression. She was dirt poor and shuffled between the homes of her birth mother in California and grandmother in Stamps, Arkansas. She was raped and left mute for years, but from all the tragedies and despair, Angelou survived this harsh reality through the "triumphant spirit of her community's endurance" (Eller 3). The community's involvement in establishing the young Marguerite's (Maya Angelou's) identity is noteworthy because it contributes to a discursive trifecta that shows the importance of communal affirmation in maintaining the African American community.

George Gutman notes in his book *The Black Family in Slavery and Freedom, 1750-1925* (1976) that community has always been necessary for the survival of black culture formed out of slavery:

Developing Afro-American behavior patterns were reinforced by the development of Afro-American slave institutions that took their shape within the parameters of the masters' monopoly of power, but separate from the masters' institutions, and the emergence of such communities defined the moment when Africans can be described as Afro-Americans. (4)

The behavior pattern that "was reinforced by the slaves" is the emergence of a black folk tradition—expressed through songs and religious hymns—and separate from that of the dominant culture (4). In fact, these songs of inspiration provided a means for blacks to resolve their "conflict of white perceptions and actions" (Eller 3).

Consequently, in looking at Angelou's *Caged Bird* there exists a thematic unity of subtle racial resistance along with the establishment of pride and identity mainly conveyed through the medium of songs and music (Walker 3). In chapter 18, with poignant detail Angelou recalls words that moved her at a church revival: "Bye and Bye, when the morning come/ when all the saints of God's are gathering home/ we will tell the story of how we overcome and we'll understand it better bye and bye" (129). What made this revival enriching and memorable for Angelou was its bringing together a community of blacks from all religious backgrounds. Angelou writes in *Caged Bird*:

> Everyone attended the revival meetings. Members of the hoity-toity Mount Zion Baptist Church mingled with the intellectual members of The African Methodist Episcopal and African Methodist Episcopal Zion, and the plain working people of the Christian Methodist Episcopal. These gatherings provided the one time in the year when all of those good village people associated with the followers of the Church of God in Christ. (123-24)

Many other relevant examples illustrate the importance of community in developing Marguerite's identity; for instance, Angelou's Grandmother Henderson ran a small country store in Stamps where she was the backbone of the community. When hard times befell anyone, they turned to her for assistance. Grandmother Henderson was indeed strong and supportive. Angelou highlights her firm religious beliefs as significant in dealing with overt oppression and racial hostility. In fact, Chapter 5 illuminates religious hymns as a discursive device in fighting racism "with a dignified course of silent endurance" (McPherson 33).

The scene with the "powhitetrash" girls (32), who corner Grandmother Henderson in her own front yard, throwing insults and racial slander, was included to show the power of faith, which has always been at the heart and fabric of the black community. While the "powhitetrash" girls taunt and tease, Grandmother Henderson responds by humming a quiet hymn: "Glory, glory, hallelujah, when I lay my burden down" (33). Angelou notes that there was a contest between the girls and her grandmother, a contest that Grandmother Henderson wins (33). As a black woman, Grandmother Henderson must "perform" respect towards the children, who should be showing her genuine respect, but she uses the vehicle of song as a mechanism to triumph over her restrictions and limitations (McMurry 3). Elizabeth Fox-Genovese notes in her essay "Myth and History: Discourse of Origins in Zora Neale Hurston and Maya Angelou" that there has always been this singing tradition in the black community: "Black communities developed their own vibrant life, black women raised up black girls in the way that they should go. Singing in the face of danger, singing to thwart the stings of insolence, singing to celebrate their Lord, singing to testify to a better future, and singing with the life blood of their people" (222). Even though Grandmother Henderson could not overtly display her dislike towards the "powhitetrash" girls, she taught Angelou how to stand in the midst of adversity and how to calm the spirit in the face of ignorance. The most significant display of communal affirmation and the power of song as a force comes with the graduation scene in *Caged Bird*, a scene often referenced by scholars in discussions of the "subtle racial resistance" intertwined throughout the novels' themes (Walker 7). Moreover, the graduation scene valorizes education, language, and community as a discursive trifecta in elevating an oppressed and deprived people to a level of worthiness and respect.

Slave masters understood that "knowledge is power," and through communication access to the world is gained. They therefore denied slaves the right to available forms of education. The canon of black literature responded by making education an important symbol affirming the black identity and demonstrating black intelligence and ability to survive within American culture. This symbolism stretches across a broad spectrum of literary aesthetics ranging from poetry to fiction and including African American autobiographies. In *Caged Bird*, Angelou's recollection of her eighth-grade graduation bears heavily upon this discussion of education as an important discursive element.

We must remember that this graduation was taking place during a time of much racial tension in America, when Jim Crow laws and the notion of separate but equal were still a reality for African American citizens. Regardless of this fact, however, Angelou recalls how proud she was of her achievement and how important graduation was to the entire community:

> Parents who could not afford it had ordered new shoes and ready-made clothes for themselves from Sears Roebuck or Montgomery Ward. They also engaged the best seamstresses to make the floating graduating dresses and to cut down secondhand pants which would be pressed to a military slickness for the important event. [. . .] oh, it was important, all right. (171)

Unknown to Angelou and the community, the graduation was about to take an unexpected turn when an uninvited guest, Mr. Edward Donleavy, took the podium. A racist politician, Donleavy quickly reminds Marguerite and the other graduates of their limited possibilities despite the achievement of a formal education: "Donleavy had exposed us. We were maids and farmers, handymen, and washerwomen, and anything higher that we aspired to was farcical and presumptuous"

(180). This incident was immediately followed by Henry Reed's valedictory address. He leads the students, parents, and visitors in a rendition of James Weldon Johnson's "Lift Ev'ry Voice and Sing," which bonded "the community with a common soul" (Walker 4): "We have come over a way that with tears has been watered/ We have come, treading our path through the blood of the slaughtered." This act of employing song to avert racism makes the graduation a scene of communal resistance (Walker 8). Having seen the profound impact that song had in bringing together the black community, Angelou developed a deep respect for literacy and song at an early age: "Oh, Black known and unknown poets, how often have your auctioned pains sustained us? It may be enough, however, to have it said that we survive in exact relationship to the dedication of our poets" (184). Angelou and the graduates were proud of their achievement because they used words and songs as a communal affirmation to produce a positive outcome in the face of prejudice.

This awareness of the power of language and education occurs in an earlier section of the book as well. With Mrs. Flowers's chapter, Angelou harnesses a greater respect for literature and the power that words (language) have in transforming a reality of hopeless shame to one of empowerment. It was under Mrs. Flowers's guidance that formal education became Angelou's salvation. Mrs. Flowers taught Angelou to embrace the spoken and written word and not allow language to be a stumbling block in her development:

Bear in mind that language is man's way of communicating with his fellow man and it is language alone that separates him from the lower animals. [. . .] Words mean more than what is set down on paper. It takes that human voice to infuse them with the shades of deeper meaning. (82)

Mrs. Flowers became the catalyst that gave Angelou the courage to transcend her muteness and begin speaking once again, an illustration of language and education as a discursive medium establishing identity and worthiness. Mrs. Flowers's speech and their shared reading made Angelou appreciative of literature and proud of her heritage: "I was liked, and what a difference it made. I was respected [. . .] for just being Marguerite Johnson. [. . . S]he made me proud to be Negro, just by being herself" (79, 85). Through poetic verse, education (which was mostly self-taught through reading), and a long-standing appreciation of black history, Angelou freed herself from the cage of her own imperfections, insecurities, and doubts of self-loathing to find authentic inner peace.

Angelou has used that knowledge to craft a banner of hope for all humanity, for the underprivileged, the broken, the educated, the homeless, the rich. Her legacy stretches from urban streets to the continent to Africa. Her history is America's history.

Works Cited

Eller, Edward. "An Overview of *I Know Why the Caged Bird Sings*." *Exploring Novels*. New York: Gale, 1998.

Folks, Jeffrey J. "Communal Responsibility in Ernest J. Gaines's *A Lesson Before Dying*." *Mississippi Quarterly* 52 (1999): 259-272.

Genovese, Elizabeth. "Myth and History: Discourse of Origins in Zora Neale Hurston and Maya Angelou." *Black American Literature Forum* 24.2 (1999): 221-235.

Gutman, Herbert George. *The Black Family in Slavery and Freedom, 1750-1925*. New York: Pantheon Books, 1976.

McMurry, Myra. "Role-Playing as Art in Maya Angelou's *Caged Bird*." *South Atlantic Bulletin* 2 (1976): 106-11.

McPherson, Dolly A. *Order Out of Chaos: The Autobiographical Works of Maya Angelou*. New York: Peter Lang, 1990.

Walker, Pierre A. "Racial Protest, Identity, Words, and Form in Maya Angelou's *I Know Why the Caged Bird Sings*." *College Literature* 22.3 (1995): 91-121.

Critical Insights

Maya Angelou's *Caged Bird* as Trauma Narrative

Since the publication of the first volume of her serial autobiography in 1970, Maya Angelou has frequently spoken out about the profound effects of childhood sexual trauma and her lifelong struggle to heal the shattered self through autobiographical acts of narrative reformulation. Angelou feels righteously indignant that American society refuses to imagine the powerful impact of traumatic assault on the psychological integrity of the Black female subject. News reports of rape and childhood sexual abuse are so prevalent in today's culture that their heinous perpetration seems to have fallen into the amorphous political space of "no woman's land," between the fissures of class and racial consciousness.[1]

In *I Know Why the Caged Bird Sings* (hereafter cited as *CB*), Angelou re-creates her child-self in the persona of Marguerite Johnson (her birth name). She reclaims the horror of childhood sexual abuse from statistical anonymity through a poignant autobiographical account of the traumatic impact of physical violation on an eight-year-old victim, a young girl stunned and confused by a brutal sexual initiation and by the adult emotional betrayal that it signifies. Separated from her mother at the age of three, Marguerite Johnson felt haunted by the specter of parental absence. It is little wonder that Maya/Ritie developed the naïve conviction that she existed as a racial changeling. Fed on celluloid fantasies of Shirley Temple beauty, the ingenuous child dissociated her subject position and personality from what she considered a dark, ungainly body with sludge-colored skin and nappy hair. Lost in Eurocentric fairy-tale fantasy, she harbored extravagant dreams of physical transformation and believed that, beneath an African American persona or mask, there resided a slim, cream-skinned, blue-eyed, blond-haired sylph—"one of the sweet little white girls who were everybody's dream of what was right with the world" (*CB*

Caged Bird as Trauma Narrative   **243**

1). Only no one knew the secret of her identity—not even God: "Wouldn't they be surprised when one day I woke out of my black ugly dream?" (*CB* 2).

Angelou's infantile version of Freud's family romance gave startling proof of the subaltern syndrome of "internalized inferiority" diagnosed by Frantz Fanon in *Black Skin, White Masks* (1967). Interviewed by the journalist Bill Moyers, the adult Angelou explains: "I thought [...] maybe I'm really a white girl. And what's going to happen is I am going to wake up. I am going to have long blond hair and everybody is going to just go around loving me. [...] It's tragic" (*Conversations* 26). "How much of this is the pretense of self-rejection," asks Audre Lorde, "how much the programmed hate that we were fed to keep ourselves a part, apart?" (*Zami* 58). In response to the false self-system constructed for African Americans by southern white culture, Angelou declares: "I decided many years ago to invent myself. I had obviously been invented by someone else—by a whole society—and I didn't like their invention" (*Conversations* 88).

In Angelou's *Caged Bird*, negritude and femininity make contradictory, irreconcilable demands on Ritie's sense of personal identity. The color of her skin, the kinkiness of her hair, and the fullness of her lips all contribute to socially engendered feelings of physical inadequacy bordering on self-hatred. During the 1930's, the American social ideal of white female beauty was touted in newspapers and in ladies' magazines and, most powerfully, in romantic cinematic representations. In the South at mid-century, there was little consciousness of the kind of African American pride that grew out of the Civil Rights movement of the 1960's. To be young, gifted, and Black in Stamps, Arkansas, meant, quite simply, to be lonely and to be doubly marginal—twice removed from the dominant power group and handicapped by a burden of racial and gender stereotypes. "The Black female," Angelou insists, "is assaulted in her tender years by all those common forces of nature at the same time that she is caught in the tripartite crossfire of masculine prejudice, white illogical hate and Black lack of power" (*CB* 3).

The dominant tone of Ritie's narrative, modulated by wry humor and pervasive vitality, is one of shattering isolation: "If growing up is painful for the Southern Black girl, being aware of her displacement is the rust of the razor that threatens the throat" (*CB* 3). From early childhood, Marguerite feels uncomfortable with the societal role of specular object assigned her by Anglo-America's racial constructions. She finds herself at the center of an alienating *regard*, a psychological location that makes her perpetually the object of another's critical gaze. As Mae Henderson observes, the "complex situatedness of the black woman as not only the 'Other' of the Same, but also the 'other' of the other(s) implies [. . .] a relationship of difference and identification with the 'other(s)'" (18). "What distinguishes black women's writing, then, is the privileging (rather than repressing) of 'the other in ourselves'" (19).

Maya/Ritie's perpetual struggle throughout *Caged Bird* is for acceptance, recognition, valorization, caring, and *love*. As a young Black girl, she desperately craves something more and different—a return to the welcoming arms of a fantasmatic (m)other figure, that sanctuary from which she feels painfully exiled. A mature Angelou nostalgically recalls, "my mother had left me when I was three and I saw her only once between the ages of three and thirteen" (*Conversations* 39). And so the resourceful Ritie must set out, from earliest childhood, to reinvent a matrifocal heritage by developing respect for the strength and beneficence of her paternal grandmother—a stalwart, patient, long suffering matriarch imaginatively invested with Amazonian Powers. In the tradition of Afra-American autobiography, Maya fashions an iconic figure identified by Joanne Braxton as the "outraged mother" who "sacrifices and improvises for the survival of flesh and spirit. [. . .] Implied in all her actions and fueling her heroic ones is outrage at the abuse of her people and her person" (1-2).

Angelou's early years were dominated by the pain of mother-absence, a source of bereavement that made her "so highly sensitive as to be paranoid" (*Conversations* 60). A loving Momma Henderson set about the task of socializing her granddaughter in the strict disciplinarian code of Black fundamentalist religion and time-tested principles of African American survival in the deep South. Cleanliness was godly, impudence impugned. Silence seemed a sensible tactic to confound the inscrutable white "ghosts," whose spectral lives of conspicuous consumption defined the parameters of African American indigence. "Momma intended to teach Bailey and me to use the paths of life that she and her generation [. . .] found to be safe ones" (*CB* 39), Ritie explains. And yet, paradoxically, this heroic grandmother continually triumphs over white racism through wise-woman strategies of faith, patience, self-respect, dogged persistence, enduring courage, and a tenacious adherence to principles of social justice. Through cunning silences and wicked locutions, she not only endures, but prevails in the face of outrageous bigotry. Her quiet, unassuming victory over the abominable dentist Dr. Lincoln proves morally superior to, and more pragmatic than, the hyperbolic "Captain Marvel" scenarios her granddaughter conjures by dint of a vivid and fanciful imagination.

Bundled up and sent south by train at the age of three, Marguerite felt, along with her brother Bailey, a beleaguered sense of emotional abandonment. How could her parents laugh and eat oranges in a paradise called "sunny California" while their children suffered the disciplinarian wrath of Uncle Willie, a crippled avuncular pedagogue teaching mathematics by the coal-stove method, and a loving but cantankerous grandmother whose religious sensibilities savagely bristled at the utterance of an innocent phrase like "by the way"? No, Ritie concludes, her real mother had to be dead, laid in a beautiful white coffin and forever embalmed in the sweet sadness of mortality: "I could cry anytime I wanted by picturing my mother (I didn't quite know what she looked like) lying in her coffin. [. . .] The face was brown, like a big O, and since I couldn't fill in the features I printed M O T H E R across the O, and tears would fall down my cheeks like warm milk" (*CB* 43).

Since Maya/Ritie luxuriates in the possibility of entertaining nurturant maternal images at will, she feels stunned by the unexpected delivery of parental Christmas presents—a children's tea-set and a white, blue-eyed doll with "yellow hair painted on her head" (*CB* 43). Both gifts silently mock the poverty-stricken and astonished siblings who greet these offerings with wonder and incredulity. How could such affectionate parents have abandoned their progeny? Of what terrible sins were the children guilty, to be so cruelly punished? Marguerite and Bailey, in an act of consummate fury, angrily disembowel their white-skinned doll, whose blond hair mimics the Shirley Temple tresses that earlier entranced an infantile Ritie. The bewildered siblings cherish their tea-set, however, as a memento of the mother of their dreams, a figure to be worshipped and longed for but forever enshrined in the inaccessible world of the imaginary.

When Ritie and Bailey are finally delivered to "Mother Dear" in St. Louis by their inscrutable father (an apparently high-class gentleman, "the first cynic I had met," and reputedly the proprietor of "a castle out in California" [*CB* 45]), they both feel awestruck and seduced by the idealized figure of Vivian Baxter, who appears out of a mirage in the guise of an unapproachable Venus, light-skinned and lovely but too gorgeously erotic to function in the mundane role of maternal caregiver. Adoring and mute, Ritie proclaims: "To describe my mother would be to write about a hurricane in its perfect power. [. . .] My mother's beauty literally assailed me. [. . .] I knew immediately why she had sent me away. She was too beautiful to have children" (*CB* 49-50). Watching Bailey swept away by filial passion and intensely enamored of his long-lost mother/lover, Ritie becomes convinced that she herself must be an orphan, an abandoned waif adopted by the family to serve as an amusing companion for her gifted sibling. Vivian and Bailey, she tells us, "both had physical beauty and personality, so I figured it figured" (*CB* 50). Like a ghost or goddess, this newfound mother seems too beautiful to be nurturant, too remote and evanescent to offer her daughter the satisfactions of emotional attachment. And reunion with the long-lost female parent exacts a high price indeed, as Vivian's live-in boyfriend begins to express his jealous insecurities by sexually molesting his lover's daughter.[2]

Ritie's own uncanny experiences in St. Louis border on the unspeakable. Childhood sexual abuse takes the form of molestation, then rape, by her mother's frustrated and demented boyfriend, Mr. Freeman, whose confusing attentions initially mimic paternal expressions of physical affection. "From the way he was holding me," thinks the innocent girl, "I knew he'd never let me go or let anything bad ever happen to me" (*CB* 61). But when Mr. Freeman admonishes her not to "tell anybody what we did," lest he be forced to "kill Bailey" (*CB* 62), the benevolent father figure turns out to be a demonic predator enacting a torturous nightmare. "The child trapped in an abusive environment," explains Judith Herman, "must find a way to preserve a sense of trust in people who are untrustworthy, safety in a situation that is unsafe, control in a situation of helplessness. Unable to care for or protect herself, she must compensate for the failure of adult care and protection with the only means at her disposal, an immature system of psychological defenses" (102).[3]

Angelou's adult narrative voice recounts the experience of rape in a controlled style that is taut, laconic, and deliberately restrained by biblical allusion. She articulates the trauma in carefully modulated testimonial tones that compensate psychologically for the horror of the child's excruciating pain: "The act of rape on an eight-year-old body is a matter of the needle giving because the camel can't. The child gives, because the body can, and the mind of the violator cannot" (*CB* 65). Through the helpless, vulnerable body of his lover's daughter, Mr. Freeman exacts both sexual satisfaction and pathological vengeance. Marguerite, the stunned rape victim, is so severely traumatized that she tries to keep the abuse a secret even from herself, since the only "means she has at her disposal are frank denial [. . .] and a legion of dissociative reactions" (Herman 102). As Janet Liebman Jacobs observes,

> In this retelling of the rape, Angelou reconstructs the child self who simultaneously experiences the suffering of the victim while responding to the remorse of the victimizer. Immediately after the assault, the perpetrator is

[. . .] asking that she, the abused child, understand that he did not mean to hurt her. [. . .] In that moment of awareness, the physical and emotional boundary violations converge as the child feels both her pain and the pain of the abuser. Empathy is thus engendered under conditions of sexual violence. (62)

Accusing herself of tacit complicity, a traumatized Marguerite retreats into the silence of post-traumatic dysphoria. "What he did to me, and what I allowed, must have been very bad if already God let me hurt so much" (*CB* 68), she reasons. "Participation in forbidden sexual activity," Judith Herman tells us, "confirms the abused child's sense of badness. Any gratification that the child is able to glean from the exploitative situation becomes proof in her mind that she instigated and bears full responsibility for the abuse" (104). By uttering the unspeakable in court, and by denying that she initially took pleasure in Mr. Freeman's embraces, Marguerite believes that it was she who condemned her assailant to death. The young girl is bereft of language to articulate the double pain of rape and emotional betrayal. "I had in fact liked his holding me," she confesses (*CB* 65). And because she responded warmly to those brief moments of physical intimacy, Ritie fully expects to be punished as a biblical harlot. Reproducing infantile tones of shock and bereavement, the adult narrator recalls, "How I despised the man for making me lie. Old, mean nasty thing. Old, black, nasty thing" (*CB* 71). Ritie's only guide to the mysterious terrain of adult sexuality is the New Testament, a tract that would, she believes, condemn her to be stoned to death as an adulterous sinner.[4]

Sexual assault robs the prepubescent child of both dignity and language. She spoke, and a man was killed. Like Shakespeare's Iago, she determines never more to speak a word: "I had to stop talking. [. . .] I could talk to Bailey, but to no one else." "I knew that [. . .] if I talked to anyone else that person might die too. Just my breath, carrying my words out, might poison people and they'd curl up and die" (*CB* 73). Survivors of childhood sexual trauma, Herman explains, "face the task of grieving not only for what was lost but also for what was never theirs to lose. The childhood that was stolen from them is irreplaceable. They must mourn the loss of the foundation of basic trust" (193).

Brutally traumatized by rape and emotional betrayal, Maya responds by constructing a wall of protective silence around her imperilled ego. She exhibits the classic symptoms of post-traumatic stress disorder, delineated in the fourth edition of the American Psychological Association's *Diagnostic and Statistical Manual of Mental Disorders* as "recurrent and intrusive recollections of the [traumatic] event [. . .] or recurrent distressing dreams"; "[d]iminished responsiveness to the external world, referred to as 'psychic numbing' or 'emotional anesthesia'"; and a "markedly reduced ability to feel emotions especially those associated with intimacy, tenderness, and sexuality" (424-425). Other effects of severe psychological trauma include "self-destructive and impulsive behavior; dissociative symptoms; somatic complaints; feelings of ineffectiveness, shame, despair, or hopelessness; . . . hostility; [and] social withdrawal" (425). As Judith Herman tells us, traumatic events "shatter the construction of the self that is formed and sustained in relation to others" and "cast the victim into a state of existential crisis" (51).

As an adult, Maya Angelou would later identify bitterness as a spiritual cancer that feeds upon its angry host: "It doesn't do a damned thing to the object of bitterness. Retention and exclusivity and isolation and distance do nothing to anyone but the person who set them up" (*Conversations* 174). The explicit purpose of Angelou's autobiographical project is defined in terms of self-conscious narrative recovery in the genre of *testimonio*.[5] As Daniel Schacter and Bessel Van der Kolk have shown, traumatic memories, obtrusive and haunting, are imprinted on the amygdala of the brain in the mode of infantile recollections that constitute an incoherent "prenarrative" that does not progress or develop in time but remains stereotyped, repetitious, and devoid of emotional content. These persistent iconic and visual images intrude on consciousness in the form of relentless traumatic flashbacks and terrible, repetitive nightmares. In the healing autobiographical project, the narrator plays both analyst and analysand in a discursive drama of scriptotherapy. According to Judith Herman, the organized narrative reformulation of traumatic experience can virtually restructure the mind's obsessive-compulsive processing of embedded personal scripts.

In the act of narrative articulation, the trauma story becomes a public, potentially communal testimony that sets the stage for psychic reintegration. It is the very process of rehearsing and emotionally reenacting a tale of survival and triumph that gives meaning to an otherwise meaningless experience of victimization and effects both psychological catharsis and reintegration into a sympathetic discourse community (Henke, *Shattered Subjects* xv-xix). In the words of Janice Haaken, the articulation of ineffable pain "anoints the survivor with an heroic status—as the bearer of unspeakable truths" (1083). In *Caged Bird*, Angelou successfully reconstructs the experience of incest trauma in the form of a coherent testimony, even as she heroically struggles to overcome obsessive-compulsive flashbacks by compassionately imagining the pathology of her perpetrator and "trying to understand how really sick and alone that man was." There has "not been a day since the rape 50 years ago," she confesses, "during which I have not thought of it" (*Conversations* 175).

When the young Marguerite Johnson, taciturn and traumatized, is sent back to Stamps, Arkansas, and remitted to the sympathetic care of Momma Henderson, she inhabits a private cage of self-imposed silence until released by the skilled and patient tutelage of her mentor Bertha Flowers. Angelou recalls that "from the time I was 7½ until I was almost 13, I didn't talk. I was persuaded to talk by a woman who knew I loved and memorized poetry" (*Conversations* 142). Because post-traumatic recovery must necessarily entail the "empowerment of the survivor and the creation of new connections," it is understandable that contact with a single "caring, comforting person maybe a lifeline. [. . .] The reward of mourning is realized as the survivor sheds her stigmatized [. . .] identity" (Herman 133, 194).

When Marguerite slowly begins to regain hard-won mastery over speech and writing, her filial relationship with Bertha Flowers opens doors and worlds that stretch far beyond the limits of a small southern town in rural Arkansas. After Shakespeare and Dickens win Maya's intellectual commitment, she finds herself able to identify with a vast panorama of history that liberates her mind and fires her curious imagination. It is through literature, moreover, that she begins to discover a repressed African American heritage. When young Black children at a grammar school graduation are humiliated by a patronizing oration reminding them of white society's circumscribed expectations for their collective future, the poetry of James Weldon Johnson consolidates their energies into a sense of racial solidarity that inaugurates the first stirrings of political rebellion.

Ritie's adolescent rites of passage are acted out in relative seclusion. Searching for the freedom of personal expression, she must, as a Black woman, prove her competence in meeting a complex set of emotional challenges. Her narrative becomes a picaresque series of adventures, sometimes comic and sometimes dangerous and bizarre. In the slums of Los Angeles, she survives in a community of homeless, vagabond children who sleep in abandoned cars. On a pleasure trip across the border to Mexico, she rescues her inebriate father and learns spontaneously to drive an automobile. Through sheer persistence and stubbornness, she becomes the first Black ticket-collector on the San Francisco cable cars, and this socially inconsequential challenge to the unwritten color bar has, for her, the force of a momentous personal victory. If discrimination can be overcome by the patient self-assertion of a lone, determined teenager, what might racial solidarity and communal Black struggle for empowerment be able to achieve in combating entrenched American racism? Ritie feels that she has, by her own small step toward equality, taken a giant leap toward the cultural liberation of oppressed peoples everywhere.

I Know Why the Caged Bird Sings is not James Joyce's *Portrait of the Artist*; nor does it claim to be. Many of Marguerite's battles, like those of Stephen Dedalus, have to do with adolescent sexual crises and the need for the young adult to construct a firm sense of gender identity from a curious army of bewildering possibilities. When Joyce's sixteen-year-old protagonist visits the red-light district of Dublin, he can luxuriate in furtive sexual acts, then atone for his transgression through the auspices of a kindly father-confessor. Angelou's alter-ego, in contrast, must face the painful ambiguities of female sexuality, physiologically interior and hidden from consciousness by a society that defines femininity through Freudian images of genital castration. Without the benefit of sex education, Ritie becomes panic-stricken at the sight of her own developing labia and comically confuses genital maturation with hermaphroditism. If, as Luce Irigaray suggests, society regards feminine sexuality as a "nothing-to-see," a hole or vessel to be filled by the phallus, then the maturing female has no positive model to explain her blossoming genitalia.

Baffled and panic-stricken, a teenaged Ritie feels compelled to engineer her own sexual researches, with the cooperation of an attractive young man willing to help choreograph her ritual defloration. In planning her sexual encounter with this neighborhood stud, Marguerite seems oblivious of the fact that such casual experimentation might well involve an obsessive-compulsive repetition of earlier trauma. Most survivors of childhood sexual abuse continue, through adulthood, to "feel unsafe in their bodies" (Herman 160). Ritie's astonishingly naive rhetoric, mimicking the ingenuousness of adolescence, might also mask the etiology of psychosomatic vulnerability, a syndrome that gives way to masochistic revictimization. In the wake of post-traumatic stress disorder, the rape victim continues to suffer from such low self-esteem that she unwittingly reduces her body to a specular object, an "other" from which she feels coolly detached, as she watches this sexual tableau from the safe location of post-traumatic disavowal. Angelou's teenaged self resembles those survivors of childhood abuse who, in the face of continued vulnerability, "choose actively to engage their fears" (Herman 197).[6]

Taking a gutsy initiative that startles even herself, Marguerite brashly invites an adolescent acquaintance to "have sexual intercourse" with her. Her detached tone of voice replicates the premeditated objectivity of a scientific experiment. Still suffering from symptoms of traumatic dysphoria, Ritie feels entirely removed from emotional affect and cannot cathect with the personal dimensions of sexual expression. When the boy she propositions eagerly complies, Marguerite at first feels delighted by her successful initiation into heterosexuality, then becomes anxiety-ridden over an unexpected pregnancy. In her own mind, she has taken control of an awkward and ungainly adolescent body through a bold act of wily seduction. But the audacious project to validate her feminine gender identity might also be interpreted in terms of obsessive-compulsive repetition, with Ritie desperately struggling to seize the initiative and to assume mastery over sexual confusion. Asserting her dubious sense of womanhood, she inadvertently reenacts the earlier trauma of childhood molestation. The results of Ritie's carefully choreographed "second defloration" are reassuring but life-transforming. "I had had help in the child's conception" the beleaguered teenager observes, "but no one could deny that I had had an immaculate pregnancy" (*CB* 245).

Luckily, Marguerite Johnson is *not* Hester Prynne, and no scarlet letter awaits her. African American communities have traditionally been more compassionate in matters of sexual fallibility than their white puritanical counterparts. Ritie's pregnancy is cause for temporary alarm, but no one in her immediate family interprets it as irreparable tragedy. After all, her lapse results in the birth of a beautiful, healthy baby. And Ritie finally attains through her infant son much of the emotional warmth and affection she has always craved. She has collaborated in the creation of a child whose presence reinforces something she instinctively feels: that Black is beautiful, or potentially so; and that she is worthy of a dignified place in a society of caring adults. As her mother affectionately assures her, "If you're for the right thing, then you do it without thinking" (*CB* 246).

The end of *I Know Why the Caged Bird Sings* is comic and triumphant. Unlike Joyce's Stephen Dedalus, who defines his manhood in proud opposition to family, church, and state, Marguerite Johnson realizes her womanhood by symbolic reintegration into the African American community that supports her. Her victory suggests an implicit triumph over the white bourgeoisie, whose values have been flagrantly subverted. Angelou writes in the tradition of African American authors who, according to Valerie Smith, "in their manipulation of received literary conventions [. . .] engage with and challenge the dominant ideology" (*Self-Discovery* 2). The final tableau of Ritie and her son offers a revolutionary paradigm of the Black anti-Madonna. As Joanne Braxton reminds us, the Black female autobiographer, unlike the solitary male hero, "uses language—sass, invective, impertinence, and ritual invocation—to defend herself physically and psychologically" (205-206).

At the conclusion of the first volume of her autobiography, Maya Angelou/Marguerite Johnson has stopped serving white masters and, in the process, has become mistress of herself. In stunning metamorphosis, a proud Maya emerges from the cocoon enveloping a younger, trembling Ritie. Killing the celluloid specter of Shirley Temple, she gives birth not only to a healthy manchild but to a revitalized sense of herself as an African American woman spiritually empowered and psychologically liberated from the debilitating effects of childhood sexual abuse.[7] As Janet Jacobs declares, in "a very real sense, the birth of a child for the adolescent mother who has been victimized symbolizes the rebirth of the child self who can now be embraced and nurtured" (164).

Quoting from one of her poems, "Harlem Hopscotch," Angelou concludes her conversation with Bill Moyers by asserting a cryptic parable of narrative recovery: "the game is down. They think you lost and I think you've won" (*Conversations* 27). "If I have a monument in this world, it is my son," she proudly proclaims. "He is a joy, a sheer delight. A good human being who belongs to himself. [. . .] It's so thrilling to be here on this tiny blob of spit and sand, reading our own mean-ing into the stars" (*Conversations* 203). It is precisely the act of scriptotherapy, the candid and heroic autobiographical articulation of haunting trauma, that allows Angelou to read meaning into her own life-story and to reconstruct an enabling, communal testimonio from the shards of childhood tragedy.[8]

From *The Langston Hughes Review* 19 (Spring 2005): 22-35. Copyright © 2005 by the Langston Hughes Society. Reprinted by permission of the Langston Hughes Society.

Notes

1. Janice Haaken notes: "While the voices of women of color in the survivors' movement are few, incest and sexual abuse are powerful themes in literary explora-tions of women's lives. [. . .] Black women writers [. . .] are more apt to place private enactments of violence within a broader dehumanizing context" (1072). Throughout this essay, I follow Maya Angelou's practice of using the uppercase *B* when referring to Black culture.

2. Because Mr. Freeman is clearly a father surrogate for young Ritie, his sexual abuse falls into the category of "incest trauma." Karin Meiselman notes that the perpe-trator of incest, either a father or a father surrogate, often lacks "a secure sense of his masculine identity" and attempts "to compensate for his feelings of inadequacy" through the perpetration of sexual abuse on a powerless victim (91-92). He compen-sates for his own literal or metaphorical impotence by attacking a helpless child in a grotesque instance of displacement. In certain kinds of abusive betrayals of children, Jennifer Freyd reminds us, "escape is not an option" (10). And Alice Miller observes in *Thou Shalt Not Be Aware* that infantile or childish "helplessness awakens a feeling of power in insecure adults" (6).

3. "On one level of imagination," hypothesizes Hortense Spillers, "incest simply cannot occur and never does. Under the auspices of denial, incest becomes the measure of an absolute negativity, the paradigm of the outright assertion *against*—the resound-ing no! But on the level of the symbolic, [. . .] incest translates into the unsayable which is all the more sayable by very virtue of one's muteness before it" (128).

4. Incest survivors, Alice Miller explains, "have a stake in keeping secret or cover-ing up what has happened to them or in blaming themselves for it" (*Thou Shalt Not Be Aware* 7). Jennifer Freyd believes that secrecy itself constitutes a "secondary trauma" for the victim of sexual abuse (77-78). Sondra O'Neale writes that, at this point in *Caged Bird*, "the tenuous psyche of a gangly, sensitive, withdrawn child is traumati-cally jarred by rape, a treacherous act from which neither the reader nor the protagonist has recovered by the book's end. All else is cathartic: [. . .] even her absurdly unlucky

pregnancy at the end does not assuage the reader's anticipatory wonder: isn't the act of rape by a trusted adult so assaultive upon an eight-year-old's life that it leaves a wound which can never be healed?" (32). Judith Herman reiterates the tragic dimensions of abuse, as a "profound sense of inner badness becomes the core around which the abused child's identity is formed, and it persists into adult life" (*Trauma* 105).

5. As John Beverley explains, the genre of *testimonio* "constitutes an affirmation of the individual self in a collective mode," whereby the narrator "speaks for, or in the name of, a community or group, approximating in this way the symbolic function of epic hero," and evoking "an absent polyphony of voices, other possible lives and experiences" (95-97). Throughout her autobiographical project, Angelou articulates the plight of an entire generation of African American women, as well as of those who have suffered the unspeakable wound of childhood sexual abuse.

6. Jennifer Freyd notes that incest survivors "commonly suffer damage to their ability to enjoy their sexuality. Their sexual behavior may be either excessively restricted or excessively promiscuous" (9172-9173). A number of survivors interviewed in Louise Armstrong's *Kiss Daddy Goodnight* testify to persistent anger and insecurity, masochism, and self-destructive practices, including the impulsive choice of inappropriate sexual partners.

7. As O'Neale remarks, the "process of her autobiography is not a singular statement of individual egotism but an exultant explorative revelation that she is because her life is an inextricable part of the misunderstood reality of who Black people and Black women truly are" (26). Selwyn Cudjoe goes on to explain that the "Afro-American autobiographical statement emerges as a *public* rather than a *private* gesture," as "*me-ism* gives way to *our-ism* and superficial concerns about the *individual subject* usually give way to the *collective subjection* of the group" (10). In Angelou's case, who could have guessed that this talented single mother, defiant and unbowed, would one day read her poetry before millions of Americans at the 1993 presidential inauguration of Bill Clinton? For reasons of space and compression, I have limited my discussion to the inaugural volume of Angelou's multi-volume autobiography which continues to elaborate a similar chorus: "Black people and Black women do not just endure, they triumph with a will of collective consciousness that Western experience cannot extinguish" (O'Neale 28).

8. Cheryl Wall notes: "Although *I Know Why the Caged Bird Sings*, the first volume of Maya Angelou's popular series of memoirs, partook more in th[e] mood of righteous anger and triumphant struggle, its dramatic center [. . .] was the rape of a girl. In a society ordered by hierarchies of power based on race, class, and gender, no one is more powerless, hence more vulnerable, than a poor black girl. [. . .] Necessarily, the fierce young female characters who are survivors rather than victims are trenchant social critics" (3). Moving from issues of social ideology to linguistic dialogue, Mae Henderson suggests that contemporary Black women's writing amalgamates Mikhail Bakhtin's notion of heteroglossia with African American religious practices of glossolalia to produce a unique combination of "testimony" and "testifying": "It is this notion of discursive difference and identity underlying the simultaneity of discourse which typically characterizes black women's writing. Through the multiple voices that enun-

ciate her complex subjectivity, the black woman writer not only speaks familiarity in the discourse of other(s), but as Other she is in contestorial dialogue with the hegemonic dominant and subdominant or 'ambiguously (non)hegemonic' discourses" (20).

Works Cited

American Psychiatric Association. *Diagnostic and Statistical Manual of Mental Health Disorders*. 4th ed., rev. Washington DC: American Psychiatric Association, 1994.

Angelou, Maya. *All God's Children Need Traveling Shoes*. New York: Random House, 1986.

_____. *Conversations with Maya Angelou*. Ed. Jeffrey M. Elliot. Jackson: University Press of Mississippi, 1989.

_____. *Gather Together in My Name*. New York: Random House, 1974.

_____. *The Heart of a Woman*. New York: Random House, 1980.

_____. *I Know Why the Caged Bird Sings*. New York: Random House, 1970.

_____. *Singin' and Swingin' and Gettin' Merry Like Christmas*. New York: Random House, 1976.

Arensberg, Liliane K. "Death as Metaphor of Self." In Braxton, 111-127.

Armstrong, Louise. *Kiss Daddy Goodnight: A Speak-Out on Incest*. 1978; rpt. New York: Pocket Books, 1979.

Beverley, John. "The Margin at the Center: On *Testimonio* (Testimonial Narrative)." In Smith and Watson, *De/Colonizing the Subject*, 91-114.

Braxton, Joanne M. *Black Women Writing Autobiography: A Tradition Within a Tradition*. Philadelphia: Temple University Press, 1989.

_____, ed. *I Know Why the Caged Bird Sings: A Casebook*. Oxford: Oxford University Press, 1999.

Brodzki, Bella, and Celeste Schenck, eds. *Life/Lines: Theorizing Women's Autobiography*. Ithaca: Cornell University Press, 1988.

Butterfield, Stephen. *Black Autobiography in America*. Amherst: University of Massachusetts Press, 1974.

Christian, Barbara. *Black Feminist Criticism: Perspectives on Black Women Writers*. New York: Pergamon, 1985.

Cudjoe, Selwyn R. "Maya Angelou and the Autobiographical Statement." In Evans, 6-24.

Evans, Mari, ed. *Black Women Writers (1950-1980)*. London: Pluto Press, 1985.

Fanon, Frantz. *Black Skin, White Masks*. 1952. New York: Grove, 1967.

Freyd, Jennifer. *Betrayal Trauma: The Logic of Forgetting Childhood Abuse*. Cambridge: Harvard University Press, 1996.

Gilbert, Susan. "Paths to Escape." In Braxton, 99-110.

Haaken, Janice. "The Recovery of Memory, Fantasy, and Desire: Feminist Approaches to Sexual Abuse and Psychic Trauma." *Signs* 21.4 (1996): 1069-1094.

Henderson, Mae Gwendolyn. "Speaking in Tongues: Dialogics, Dialectics, and the Black Woman Writer's Literary Tradition." In Wall, 16-37.

Henke, Suzette A. *Shattered Subjects: Trauma and Testimony in Women's Life-Writing.* New York: St. Martin's/Palgrave, 1998/2000.

Herman, Judith Lewis. *Trauma and Recovery.* New York: Harper Collins, 1991.

Irigaray, Luce. *This Sex Which Is Not One.* Trans. Catherine Porter and Carolyn Burke. Ithaca: Cornell University Press, 1985.

_____. *Speculum of the Other Woman.* Trans. Gillian C. Gill. Ithaca: Cornell University Press, 1985.

Jacobs, Janet Liebman. *Victimized Daughters: Incest and the Development of the Female Self.* New York: Routledge, 1994.

Lorde, Audre. *Zami: A New Spelling of My Name.* Freedom, CA: The Crossing Press, 1982.

Lupton, Mary Jane. "Singing the Black Mother: Maya Angelou and Autobiographical Continuity." In Evans, 129-148.

McPherson, Dolly A. *Order Out of Chaos: The Autobiographical Works of Maya Angelou.* London: Virago, 1991.

Meiselman, Karin C. *Incest: A Psychological Study of Causes and Effects With Treatment Recommendations.* London: Jossey-Bass Ltd, 1978.

Miller, Alice. *Breaking Down the Wall of Silence: The Liberating Experience of Facing Painful Truth.* Trans. Simon Worrall. 1990; rpt. New York: Dutton, 1991.

_____. *The Drama of the Gifted Child.* Trans. Ruth Ward. 1979; rpt. New York: Harper Basic Books, 1990.

_____. *Thou Shalt Not Be Aware: Society's Betrayal of the Child.* Trans. Hildegarde and Hunter Hannum. 1981; rpt. New York: New American Library, 1986.

Moore, Opal. "Learning to Live: When the Bird Breaks from the Cage." In Braxton, 49-58.

O'Neale, Sondra. "Reconstruction of the Composite Self: New images of Black Women in Maya Angelou's Continuing Autobiography." In Evans, 25-36.

Personal Narratives Group, ed. *Interpreting Women's Lives: Feminist Theory and Personal Narratives.* Bloomington: Indiana University Press, 1989.

Pryse, Marjorie, and Hortense J. Spillers, eds. *Conjuring: Black Women and Literary Tradition.* Bloomington: Indiana University Press, 1985.

Schacter, Daniel L. *Searching for Memory: The Brain, the Mind, and the Past.* New York: Basic Books, 1996.

Smith, Sidonie. "The Song of a Caged Bird: Maya Angelou's Quest After Self-Acceptance." *Southern Humanities Review* 7 (1973): 368-375.

Smith, Sidonie, and Julia Watson, eds. *Decolonizing the Subject: The Politics of Gender in Women's Autobiography.* Minneapolis: University of Minnesota Press, 1992.

Smith, Valerie. "Black Feminist Theory and the Representation of the 'Other.'" In Wall, 38-57.

_____. *Self-Discovery and Authority in African-American Narratives.* Cambridge: Harvard University Press, 1987.

Sommer, Doris. "Not Just a Personal Story: Women's Testimonies and the Plural Self." In Brodzki and Schenck, 107-130.

Spillers, Hortense. "The Permanent Obliquity of an In(pha)llibly Straight: In the Time of the Daughters and the Fathers." In Wall, 127-149.

Tate, Claudia, ed. *Black Women Writers at Work*. New York: Continuum, 1983.

Van der Kolk, Bessel A. "The Body Keeps Score: Approaches to the Psychobiology of Posttraumatic Stress Disorder." In Van der Kolk et al. *Traumatic Stress: The Effects of Overwhelming Experience on Mind, Body, and Society*. New York: Guilford, 1996. 214-241.

Vermillion, Mary. "Reembodying the Self." In Braxton, 59-76.

Wall, Cheryl A., ed. *Changing Our Words: Essays on Criticism, Theory, and Writing by Black Women*. New Brunswick, NJ: Rutgers University Press, 1989.

Willis, Susan. *Specifying: Black Women Writing the American Experience*. Madison: University of Wisconsin Press, 1987.

RESOURCES

Chronology of Maya Angelou's Life _____

1928	Maya Angelou is born in St. Louis, Missouri, to Bailey and Vivian Baxter Johnson. Her parents name her Marguerite Annie Johnson.
1931	Angelou's parents divorce and she and her brother, Bailey, Jr., are sent to Stamps, Arkansas, to live with their grandmother.
1935	Angelou returns to St. Louis with Bailey to live with their mother.
1936	Angelou is raped by her mother's boyfriend, Mr. Freeman. The man is found dead soon after Angelou tells her brother about the incident, and, blaming herself for his death, she falls mute for five years.
1937	Angelou returns to Stamps with Bailey.
1940	Angelou graduates from Lafayette County Training School at the top of her eighth-grade class. She moves with Bailey to San Francisco to live with their mother.
1945	Angelou graduates from high school, becomes San Francisco's first black female streetcar conductor, and gives birth to a son, Clyde.
1950	Angelou marries Tosh Angelos, a Greek sailor.
1953	Angelou's marriage to Angelos ends. She wins a dance scholarship and begins her dance career at the Purple Onion.
1954-1955	Angelou tours internationally with a production of George Gershwin's *Porgy and Bess*.
1957	Angelou moves to New York and becomes involved in the Harlem Writers Guild.
1959-1960	At the request of Martin Luther King, Jr., Angelou becomes the northern coordinator for the Southern Christian Leadership Conference.

1960	Angelou stars in an Off-Broadway production of Jean Genet's *The Blacks*; works with Godfrey Cambridge to write and produce *Cabaret for Freedom*, in which she also performs; and meets Vusumzi Make, a South African freedom fighter.
1961	Angelou travels with Make to Africa and becomes associate editor at the *Arab Observer* in Cairo, Egypt.
1963-1966	Angelou's relationship with Make ends. She works at the University of Ghana as assistant administrator of the School of Music and Drama and also becomes a contributor to the Ghanaian Broadcasting Company and the *Ghanaian Times*.
1966	Angelou takes a position as a lecturer at the University of California, Los Angeles. She appears in Jean Anouilh's *Medea*.
1970	*I Know Why the Caged Bird Sings* is published on January 12 (with a copyright date of 1969); it is nominated for a National Book Award.
1971	*Just Give Me a Cool Drink of Water 'fore I Diiie* is published and nominated for a Pulitzer Prize.
1972	Angelou becomes the first African American woman to have a screenplay produced with *Georgia, Georgia*.
1973	Angelou debuts on Broadway in *Look Away* and is nominated for a Tony Award. She marries Paul du Feu.
1974	*Gather Together in My Name* is published. Angelou is named distinguished visiting professor at Wake Forest University.
1975	*Oh Pray My Wings Are Gonna Fit Me Well* is published. President Gerald Ford appoints Angelou to the American Revolution Bicentennial Council, and she is named a member of the National Commission on the Observance of International Women's Year.
1976	*Singin' and Swingin' and Gettin' Merry Like Christmas* is published.
1977	Angelou appears in the television miniseries *Roots*.
1978	*And I Still Rise* is published.

1980	Angelou's marriage to du Feu ends in divorce.
1981	*The Heart of a Woman* is published. Wake Forest University appoints Angelou lifetime Reynolds Professor of American Studies.
1983	*Shaker, Why Don't You Sing?* is published. *Ladies' Home Journal* names Angelou to its list of the "Top 100 Most Influential Women."
1986	*All God's Children Need Traveling Shoes* is published.
1987	*Now Sheba Sings the Song* is published.
1990	*I Shall Not Be Moved* is published.
1993	*Wouldn't Take Nothing for My Journey Now* is published. Angelou writes "On the Pulse of Morning" and reads the poem at President Bill Clinton's inauguration ceremony.
1994	*The Complete Collected Poems of Maya Angelou* is published.
1995	*A Brave and Startling Truth* is published. Angelou costars in the film *How to Make an American Quilt*.
2000	President Clinton presents Angelou with the Presidential Medal of Arts.
2002	*A Song Flung Up to Heaven* is published, and Angelou's audio recording of the book wins a Grammy Award for best spoken-word performance. Angelou wins the Ethnic Multicultural Media Awards' Lifetime Achievement Award.
2004	*Hallelujah! The Welcome Table: A Lifetime of Memories with Recipes* and four children's books in the Maya's World series are published.
2005	*Amazing Peace: A Christmas Poem* is published.
2006	*Mother: A Cradle to Hold Me* and *Celebrations: Rituals of Peace and Prayer* are published.
2008	*Letter to My Daughter* is published.

Works by Maya Angelou _____

Nonfiction
I Know Why the Caged Bird Sings, 1970
Gather Together in My Name, 1974
Singin' and Swingin' and Gettin' Merry Like Christmas, 1976
The Heart of a Woman, 1981
All God's Children Need Traveling Shoes, 1986
Wouldn't Take Nothing for My Journey Now, 1993
Even the Stars Look Lonesome, 1997
A Song Flung Up to Heaven, 2002
Hallelujah! The Welcome Table: A Lifetime of Memories with Recipes, 2004
Letter to My Daughter, 2008

Poetry
Just Give Me a Cool Drink of Water 'fore I Diiie, 1971
Oh Pray My Wings Are Gonna Fit Me Well, 1975
And Still I Rise, 1978
Shaker, Why Don't You Sing?, 1983
Poems: Maya Angelou, 1986
Now Sheba Sings the Song, 1987
I Shall Not Be Moved, 1990
On the Pulse of Morning, 1993
The Complete Collected Poems of Maya Angelou, 1994
Phenomenal Woman: Four Poems Celebrating Women, 1994
A Brave and Startling Truth, 1995
Amazing Peace: A Christmas Poem, 2005
Mother: A Cradle to Hold Me, 2006
Celebrations: Rituals of Peace and Prayer, 2006

Drama
Cabaret for Freedom, produced 1960 (musical; with Godfrey Cambridge)
The Least of These, produced 1966
Encounters, produced 1973
Ajax, produced 1974 (adaptation of Sophocles' play)
And Still I Rise, produced 1976
King, produced 1990 (musical; lyrics with Alistair Beaton, book by Lonne Elder III; music by Richard Blackford)

Screenplays

Georgia, Georgia, 1972
All Day Long, 1974

Teleplays

Black, Blues, Black, 1968 (ten episodes)
The Inheritors, 1976
The Legacy, 1976
I Know Why the Caged Bird Sings, 1979 (with Leonora Thuna and Ralph B. Woolsey)
Sister, Sister, 1982
Brewster Place, 1990

Short Fiction

"Steady Going Up," 1972
"The Reunion," 1983

Children's Literature

Mrs. Flowers: A Moment of Friendship, 1986 (illustrated by Etienne Delessert)
Life Doesn't Frighten Me, 1993 (poetry; illustrated by Jean-Michel Basquiat)
Soul Looks Back in Wonder, 1993
My Painted House, My Friendly Chicken, and Me, 1994
Kofi and His Magic, 1996
Angelina of Italy, 2004
Izak of Lapland, 2004
Mikale of Hawaii, 2004
Renie Marie of France, 2004

Bibliography

Blackburn, Regina. "In Search of the Black Female Self: African-American Women's Autobiographies and Ethnicity." *Women's Autobiography: Essays in Criticism.* Ed. Estelle C. Jelinek. Bloomington: Indiana University Press, 1980. 133-48.

Bloom, Harold, ed. *Bloom's Guides: "I Know Why the Caged Bird Sings."* Philadelphia: Chelsea House, 2004.

_____. *Bloom's Major Poets: Maya Angelou.* Philadelphia: Chelsea House, 2001.

_____. *Bloom's Modern Critical Interpretations: Maya Angelou's "I Know Why the Caged Bird Sings."* Philadelphia: Chelsea House, 1998.

Braxton, Joanne M., ed. *Maya Angelou's "I Know Why the Caged Bird Sings": A Casebook.* New York: Oxford University Press, 1999.

_____. "A Song of Transcendence: Maya Angelou." *Black Women Writing Autobiography: A Tradition Within a Tradition.* Philadelphia: Temple University Press, 1989. 181-202.

Butterfield, Stephen. "Autobiographies of Black Women: Ida Wells, Maya Angelou, Anne Moody." In *Black Autobiography in America.* Amherst: University of Massachusetts Press, 1974. 201-17.

Cudjoe, Selwyn R. "Maya Angelou: The Autobiographical Statement Updated." In *Reading Black, Reading Feminist: A Critical Anthology.* Ed. Henry Louis Gates, Jr. New York: Meridian, 1990. 272-306.

Elliot, Jeffrey M., ed. *Conversations with Maya Angelou.* Jackson: University Press of Mississippi, 1989.

Fox-Genovese, Elizabeth. "Myth and History: Discourse of Origins in Zora Neale Hurston and Maya Angelou." *Black American Literature Forum* 24.2 (Summer 1990): 221-36.

Froula, Christine. "The Daughter's Seduction: Sexual Violence and Literary History." *Signs: Journal of Women in Culture and Society* 11.4 (Summer 1986): 621-44.

Gilbert, Susan. "Maya Angelou's *I Know Why the Caged Bird Sings:* Paths to Escape." *Mount Olive Review* 1.1 (Spring 1987): 39-50.

Hagen, Lyman B. *Heart of a Woman, Mind of a Writer, and Soul of a Poet: A Critical Analysis of the Writings of Maya Angelou.* Lanham, MD: University Press of America, 1997.

Hord, Fred Lee. "Someplace to Be a Black Girl." *Reconstructing Memory: Black Literary Criticism.* Chicago: Third World Press, 1991. 75-85.

Johnson, Claudia D. *Racism in Maya Angelou's "I Know Why the Caged Bird Sings."* Detroit: Greenhaven Press, 2008.

Kent, George E. "Maya Angelou's *I Know Why the Caged Bird Sings* and Black Autobiographical Tradition." *Kansas Quarterly* 7.3 (Summer 1975): 72-80.

Kinnamon, Keneth. "Call and Response: Intertextuality in Two Autobiographical Works by Richard Wright and Maya Angelou." *Belief Versus Theory in Black American Literary Criticism.* Ed. Joe Weixlmann and Chester J. Fontenot. Greenwood, FL: Penkevill, 1986. 121-34.

Lionnet, Françoise. "Con Artists and Storytellers: Maya Angelou's Problematic Sense of Audience." *Autobiographical Voices: Race, Gender, Self-Portraiture.* Ithaca, NY: Cornell University Press, 1989. 130-66.

Lupton, Mary Jane. *Maya Angelou: A Critical Companion.* Westport, CT: Greenwood Press, 1998.

_____. "Singing the Black Mother: Maya Angelou and Autobiographical Continuity." *Black American Literature Forum* 24.2 (Summer 1990): 257-76.

Mcpherson, Dolly A. *Order Out of Chaos: The Autobiographical Works of Maya Angelou.* New York: Peter Lang, 1990.

Megna-Wallace, Joanne. *Understanding "I Know Why the Caged Bird Sings": A Student Casebook to Issues, Sources, and Historical Documents.* Westport, CT: Greenwood Press, 1998.

Neubauer, Carol E. "Maya Angelou: Self and a Song of Freedom in the Southern Tradition." *Southern Women Writers: The New Generation.* Ed. Tonette Bond Inge. Tuscaloosa: University of Alabama Press, 1990. 114-42.

O'Neale, Sondra. "Reconstruction of the Composite Self: New Images of Black Women in Maya Angelou's Continuing Autobiography." In *Black Women Writers (1950-1980).* Ed. Mari Evans. Garden City, NY: Doubleday, 1984. 25-36.

Saunders, James Robert. "Breaking Out of the Cage: The Autobiographical Writings of Maya Angelou." *Hollins Critic* 28.4 (Oct. 1991): 1-11.

Smith, Sidonie Ann. "The Song of a Caged Bird: Maya Angelou's Quest for Self-Acceptance." *Southern Humanities Review* 7.4 (Fall 1973): 365-74.

Tangum, Marion M., and Marjorie Smelstor. "Hurston's and Angelou's Visual Art: The Distancing Vision and the Beckoning Gaze." *Southern Literary Journal* 31.1 (Fall 1998): 80-97.

Wisker, Gina. "Identity and Selfhood: The Fictionalised Autobiography—Maya Angelou." *Post-colonial and African American Women's Writing: A Critical Introduction.* Houndmills, Basingstoke, Hampshire: Palgrave Macmillan, 2000. 49-52.

CRITICAL INSIGHTS

About the Editor_____

Mildred R. Mickle is Assistant Professor of English and English Coordinator at Penn State Greater Allegheny. She has published essays on Octavia E. Butler's works in the *Xavier Review*; *The Oxford Companion to African American Literature*, edited by William L. Andrews, Frances Smith Foster, and Trudier Harris (1997); and *New Essays on the African American Novel*, edited by Lovalerie King and Linda Selzer (2008). She published an essay on award-winning poet Lillian Allen in *Beyond the Canebrakes: West Indian Women Writers in Canada*, edited by Emily Allen Williams (2008). She also published an interview with Jaki Shelton Green, winner of the 2003 North Carolina Award in Literature, in *Obsidian III: Literature in the African Diaspora*. She has essays on Octavia E. Butler's works forthcoming in *Contemporary African American Fiction (1970-present)*, edited by Dana A. Williams, and *Strange Matings: Remembering Octavia E. Butler and Her Impact on Science Fiction and Feminism*, edited by Rebecca Holden and Nisi Shawl. She is currently at work on an essay on Percival Everett's collection of poems *re: f(gesture)* and on two volumes of her own poetry.

About *The Paris Review*_____

The Paris Review is America's preeminent literary quarterly, dedicated to discovering and publishing the best new voices in fiction, nonfiction, and poetry. The magazine was founded in Paris in 1953 by the young American writers Peter Matthiessen and Doc Humes, and edited there and in New York for its first fifty years by George Plimpton. Over the decades, the *Review* has introduced readers to the earliest writings of Jack Kerouac, Philip Roth, T. C. Boyle, V. S. Naipaul, Ha Jin, Jay McInerney, and Mona Simpson, and published numerous now classic works, including Roth's *Goodbye, Columbus*, Donald Barthelme's *Alice*, Jim Carroll's *Basketball Diaries*, and selections from Samuel Beckett's *Molloy* (his first publication in English). The first chapter of Jeffrey Eugenides's *The Virgin Suicides* appeared in the *Review*'s pages, as well as stories by Edward P. Jones, Rick Moody, David Foster Wallace, Denis Johnson, Jim Shepard, Jim Crace, Lorrie Moore, Jeanette Winterson, and Ann Patchett.

The Paris Review's renowned Writers at Work series of interviews, whose early installments include legendary conversations with E. M. Forster, William Faulkner, and Ernest Hemingway, is one of the landmarks of world literature. The interviews received a George Polk Award and were nominated for a Pulitzer Prize. Among the more than three hundred interviewees are Robert Frost, Marianne Moore, W. H. Auden, Elizabeth Bishop, Susan Sontag, and Toni Morrison. Recent issues feature conversations with Salman Rushdie, Joan Didion, Stephen King, Norman Mailer, Kazuo Ishiguro, and Umberto Eco. (A complete list of the interviews is available at www .theparisreview.org.) In November 2008, Picador will publish the third of a four-volume series of anthologies of *Paris Review* interviews. The first two volumes have received acclaim. *The New York Times* called the Writers at Work series "the most remarkable and extensive interviewing project we possess."

The Paris Review is edited by Philip Gourevitch, who was named to the post in 2005, following the death of George Plimpton two years earlier. Under Gourevitch's leadership, the magazine's international distribution has expanded, paid subscriptions have risen 150 percent, and newsstand distribution has doubled. A new editorial team has published fiction by Andre Aciman, Damon Galgut, Mohsin Hamid, Gish Jen, Richard Price, Said Sayrafiezadeh, and Alistair Morgan. Poetry editors Charles Simic, Meghan O'Rourke, and Dan Chiasson have selected works by Billy Collins, Jesse Ball, Mary Jo Bang, Sharon Olds, and Mary Karr. Writing published in the magazine has been anthologized in *Best American Short Stories* (2006, 2007, and 2008), *Best American Poetry*, *Best Creative Non-Fiction*, the Pushcart Prize anthology, and *O. Henry Prize Stories*.

The magazine presents two annual awards. The Hadada Award for lifelong contribution to literature has recently been given to William Styron, Joan Didion, Norman Mailer, and Peter Matthiessen in 2008. The Plimpton Prize for Fiction, given to a new voice in fiction brought to national attention in the pages of *The Paris Review*, was presented in 2007 to Benjamin Percy and to Jesse Ball in 2008.

The Paris Review won the 2007 National Magazine Award in photojournalism, and the *Los Angeles Times* recently called *The Paris Review* "an American treasure with true international reach."

Since 1999 *The Paris Review* has been published by The Paris Review Foundation, Inc., a not-for-profit 501(c)(3) organization.

The Paris Review is available in digital form to libraries worldwide in selected academic databases exclusively from EBSCO Publishing. Libraries can contact EBSCO at 1-800-653-2726 for details. For more information on *The Paris Review* or to subscribe, please visit: www.theparisreview.org.

Contributors

Mildred R. Mickle is Assistant Professor of English and English Coordinator at Penn State Greater Allegheny. She is the author of several essays on Octavia E. Butler's works and has published essays on Lillian Allen and an interview with Jaki Shelton Green.

Judith Barton Williamson was professor of English at Sauk Valley Community College in Dixon, Illinois, until her retirement in 2004.

Christopher Cox is a senior editor at *The Paris Review*. He has written for *Bookforum* and *Words Without Borders*. He is currently working on an Art of Fiction interview with Annie Proulx.

Amy Sickels is an M.F.A. graduate of Pennsylvania State University. Her fiction and essays have appeared or are forthcoming in *DoubleTake, Passages North, Bayou, The Madison Review, LIT, Natural Bridge*, and *The Greensboro Review*.

Pamela Loos has researched or written numerous books of literary criticism. Some of her recent publications include *A Reader's Guide to Amy Tan's* The Joy Luck Club (2008) and *A Reader's Guide to Lorraine Hansberry's* A Raisin in the Sun (2008).

Neil Heims is a writer and teacher living in Paris. His books include *Reading the Diary of Anne Frank* (2005), *Allen Ginsberg* (2005), and *J. R. R. Tolkien* (2004). He has also contributed numerous articles for literary publications, including essays on William Blake, John Milton, William Shakespeare, and Arthur Miller.

Robert C. Evans earned his Ph.D. from Princeton University in 1984. In 1982 he began teaching at Auburn University Montgomery, where he has been named Distinguished Research Professor, Distinguished Teaching Professor, and University Alumni Professor. External awards he has received include fellowships from the ACLS, the APS, the NEH, and the Folger, Huntington, and Newberry libraries. He is the author or editor of more than twenty books and of numerous essays, including recent work on twentieth-century American writers.

Liliane K. Arensberg is a former Professor of English at Emory University. Her work has appeared in the *College Language Association Journal* and *American Notes & Queries*.

Martin A. Danahay is Professor of English at Brock University. His publications include the books *Gender at Work in Victorian Culture: Literature, Art and Masculinity* (2005) and *A Community of One: Masculine Autobiography and Autonomy in Nineteenth Century Britain* (1993) and articles in *Victorian Literature and Culture*. He is the editor of the Broadview Press editions of H. G. Wells's *The War of the Worlds* (2003) and Robert Louis Stevenson's *The Strange Case of Dr. Jekyll and Mr. Hyde* (1999).

Mary Vermillion is Associate Professor of English at Mount Mercy College. Her scholarly publications include articles on Samuel Richardson and postfeminism, and her creative publications include two mystery novels, *Death by Discount* and *Murder by Mascot*.

Lyman B. Hagen is Professor Emeritus of English at Arkansas State University. He is the author of *Heart of a Woman, Mind of a Writer, and Soul of a Poet: A Critical Analysis of the Writings of Maya Angelou* (1997).

Pierre A. Walker is Professor of English at Salem State College. He is the author of *Reading Henry James in French Cultural Contexts* (1995), editor of *Henry James on Culture: Collected Essays on Politics and the American Social Scene* (2004), and coeditor of *The Complete Letters of Henry James* (2006-2009).

Yolanda M. Manora is Assistant Professor of English at the University of Alabama. Her articles have appeared in *Women's Studies*, *Southern Studies*, and *Reconstruction: Studies in Contemporary Culture*. She is currently at work on a book titled *Mamas? Maybe: The Dialectics of Modernity and Maternity in the Works of the Harlem Renaissance*.

Myra K. McMurry earned her Ph.D. in English from Emory University. Her dissertation was titled "Self and World: The Problem of Proportion in the Novels of George Meredith." Her work has been published in *South Atlantic Bulletin* and she has taught at Valdosta State University.

Cherron A. Barnwell earned her Ph.D. in English from Howard University in 2002, where she wrote her dissertation on African American women's autobiographies. She has taught at Hunter College and Stony Brook University. Her work has appeared in *The Langston Hughes Review*.

Clarence Nero is a novelist from New Orleans. His novels include *Cheekie: A Child Out of the Desire* (1998), *Three Sides to Every Story* (2006), and *Too Much of a Good Thing Ain't Bad* (2009). He earned a B.S. from Howard University and received his M.F.A. in creative writing from Louisiana State University.

Suzette A. Henke is Thruston B. Morton, Sr., Professor of English and Chair of Literary Studies at the University of Louisville. She is the author of *Shattered Subjects: Trauma and Testimony in Women's Life-Writing* (2000) and *James Joyce and the Politics of Desire* (1990) and coauthor of *Virginia Woolf and Trauma: Embodied Texts* (2007).

Acknowledgments_____

"Maya Angelou" by Judith Barton Williamson. From *Dictionary of World Biography: The 20th Century*. Copyright © 1999 by Salem Press, Inc. Reprinted with permission of Salem Press.

"The *Paris Review* Perspective" by Christopher Cox. Copyright © 2010 by Christopher Cox. Special appreciation goes to Christopher Cox and Nathaniel Rich, editors for *The Paris Review*.

"Death as Metaphor of Self in *I Know Why the Caged Bird Sings*" by Liliane K. Arensberg. From *College Language Association Journal* 20, no. 2 (December 1976). Copyright © 1976 by College Language Association. Reprinted by permission of College Language Association.

"Breaking the Silence: Symbolic Violence and the Teaching of Contemporary 'Ethnic' Autobiography" by Martin A. Danahay. From *College Literature* 18, no. 3 (1991). Copyright © 1991 by *College Literature*. Reprinted by permission of *College Literature*.

"Reembodying the Self: Representations of Rape in *Incidents in the Life of a Slave Girl* and *I Know Why the Caged Bird Sings*" by Mary Vermillion. From *Biography: An Interdisciplinary Quarterly* 15, no. 3 (Summer 1992). Copyright © 1992 by the Biographical Research Center. Reprinted by permission of the Biographical Research Center, University of Hawaii at Manoa.

"*I Know Why the Caged Bird Sings:* 'Childhood Revisited'" by Lyman B. Hagen. From *Heart of a Woman, Mind of a Writer, and Soul of a Poet: A Critical Analysis of the Writings of Maya Angelou*, 54-73. Copyright © 1997 by University Press of America. Reprinted by permission of University Press of America.

"Racial Protest, Identity, Words, and Form" by Pierre A. Walker. From *College Literature* 22, no. 3 (October 1995). Copyright © 1995 by *College Literature*. Reprinted by permission of *College Literature*.

"'What You Looking at Me For? I Didn't Come to Stay': Displacement, Disruption, and Black Female Subjectivity in Maya Angelou's *I Know Why the Caged Bird Sings*" by Yolanda M. Manora. From *Women's Studies* 34, no. 5 (2005). Copyright © 2005 by Taylor & Francis, Ltd. Reprinted by permission of Taylor & Francis, Ltd, http://www.tandf.co.uk/journals.

"Role-Playing as Art in Maya Angelou's *Caged Bird*" by Myra K. McMurry. From *South Atlantic Bulletin* 41, no. 2 (May 1976). Copyright © 1976 by South Atlantic Modern Language Association. Reprinted by permission of South Atlantic Modern Language Association.

"Singin' de Blues, Writing Black Female Survival in *I Know Why the Caged Bird Sings*" by Cherron A. Barnwell. From *The Langston Hughes Review* 19 (Spring 2005). Copyright © 2005 by the Langston Hughes Society. Reprinted by permission of the Langston Hughes Society.

Index

Abandonment, 93, 225, 246
Affirmative action, 121
African American women;
  autobiographies, 6, 38, 130, 186, 196,
  220, 223, 255; body images, 131,
  136, 139, 142, 206; identity, 201;
  poets, 4; and slavery, 130, 134, 197,
  202; stereotypes, 42, 130, 133, 137,
  143, 145, 162, 198-199, 244; as
  storytellers, 31
African Americans; adaptability, 185;
  autobiographies, 21, 24, 31, 88, 91,
  107, 128, 154, 165, 176, 198, 219,
  240, 245, 257; communities, 52, 62,
  237-238; cultural traditions, 38, 44,
  220, 238; identity, 58; literary
  tradition, 168, 182, 231; poetry, 7,
  168, 184; slave narratives, 23, 33;
  stereotypes, 158, 164; teachers, 69
African Review, 28
Aggression, 94
All God's Children Need Traveling Shoes
  (Angelou), 233
Andrews, William L., 132, 134
Angelou, Maya; acting career, 10;
  awards and honors, 10; on bitterness,
  250; blues priestess self-image, 222,
  230, 233, 235; cable car job, 14, 44,
  59, 169, 175, 181, 183, 252; in
  California, 59, 76, 85, 101, 151, 158;
  childhood, 9; compared to Baldwin,
  53, 62, 65; compared to Hurston, 44,
  198; compared to Jacobs, 42, 130;
  compared to Magona, 47; compared
  to Wright, 24, 40; education, 9, 69; in
  Egypt, 28; eighth-grade graduation,
  58, 214, 240; in Ghana, 9, 28; humor
  and wit, 88, 100, 140, 153, 188; in St.
  Louis, 247; influences, 4, 87, 97, 100,

141; motherhood, 104, 137, 142, 164,
  255; poetry, 4, 184; at presidential
  inauguration, 10, 151; role models
  for, 29, 77, 163, 200; in St. Louis, 59,
  71, 155; as social activist, 5, 19, 27;
  and somatophobia, 136, 144; on
  writing, 22, 27, 30, 167, 234; writing
  style, 150, 154, 223-224
Anger, 57, 93, 171, 182, 257
Arab Observer, 28
Arensberg, Liliane K., 37, 74, 158
Armstrong, Louise, 257
Art and artists, 216
Autobiographical writing, 21, 23, 26, 31,
  44, 109, 152, 154, 167, 169, 194, 219

Baker, Houston A., Jr., 221, 223, 225,
  230
Bakhtin, Mikhail, 111, 121, 126
Baldwin, James, 13, 20, 25, 27, 53, 57,
  61, 63, 65, 151, 187, 234
Baraka, Amiri, 20, 221, 223, 228
Barnwell, Cherron A., 48
Baxter, Vivian, 9, 45, 94, 96, 104, 138,
  143, 158, 163, 200, 202, 207, 247
Beauty standards, 3, 8, 22, 29, 56, 138,
  140, 175, 206, 243
Beyond Ethnicity (Sollors), 109
Bildungsroman tradition, 40, 66, 149,
  170
"Black and Unknown Bards" (Johnson),
  231
Black Arts movement, 7, 20, 27
Black Boy (Wright), 22, 24, 40, 176,
  188
*Black Family in Slavery and Freedom,
  1750-1925, The* (Gutman), 237
Black Jezebel, 201-202, 204
Black Matriarch, 201-202, 204, 209

Rabesa, José, 109
Race; and oppression, 52, 55, 170, 173, 178, 180, 183; and stereotyping, 42, 133, 137, 143, 158, 162, 164, 199, 244
Racism, 6, 22, 26, 28, 53, 119, 138, 147, 153, 168, 173, 183, 186, 239
Rape, 32, 36, 42, 59, 85, 96, 100, 128, 131, 137, 146, 155, 164, 169, 187, 210, 226, 243, 248, 253, 256-257; aftermath for Angelou, 15, 40, 94, 112, 116, 138, 141, 174, 250; and slavery, 6, 202
Rape of Lucrece, The (Shakespeare), 128, 141
Rebirth, 37, 90, 104, 255
Reed, Henry, 75, 182, 215, 228, 241
Religion, 95, 135, 162, 246
Repression, 37, 47, 93, 118, 126, 212, 217
Resistance to oppression, 106, 170-171, 174, 178, 182, 184
Revenge, 75, 95, 118, 185, 248
Richardson, Samuel, 145
Roach, Abbey Lincoln, 149
Robeson, Paul, 234
Rodriguez, Richard, 106, 108, 117, 119-122
Rowson, Susanna, 131
Rubenstein, Roberta, 109

Sands, Mr. (*Incidents in the Life of a Slave Girl*), 131, 133, 136, 143
Schacter, Daniel, 250
Schmidt, Jan Zlotnik, 188
Schools, 66-67, 71, 73, 76
Schultz, Elizabeth, 154
Seduction, 128, 131, 135, 146, 254
Segregation, 28, 52, 173
Self-actualization, 36, 47
Self-confidence, 36, 71, 79, 174

Self-consciousness, 36, 56, 203, 211, 250
Self-definition, 194, 197
Self-determination, 155, 228
Self-hatred, 38, 56, 92, 98, 175, 244
Self-image, 93, 103, 140, 144-145, 233-234
Self-realization, 211, 217
Self-understanding, 222, 224, 226, 231
Self-worth, 77
Sensational Designs (Tompkins), 170
Sentimental novels, 131, 135
Sexual abuse, 5, 33, 40, 226, 243, 248-249, 253-257
Sexuality, 42, 89, 130, 133, 204, 253
Shakespeare, William, 128, 131, 141, 145, 148
She's Gotta Have It (Lee), 130
Silence, 15, 59, 96, 121, 138, 140, 249, 251; breaking of, 108, 112, 117, 120, 124-125, 204
Singin' and Swingin' and Gettin' Merry Like Christmas (Angelou), 232
Slave narratives, 23, 26, 33, 41
Slavery, 4, 6, 134, 168, 237
Smelstor, Marjorie, 44
Smith, Sidonie Ann, 25, 33, 35, 117, 147, 220, 222
Smith, Valerie, 135
Social class system, 107, 116, 122, 137
Socialization, 107, 115
Sollors, Werner, 109
Somatophobia, 128, 131, 133, 135-136, 144, 147
Song Flung Up to Heaven, A (Angelou), 234
Southern Christian Leadership Conference, 9, 27
Speech patterns, 40
Spelman, Elizabeth, 128
Spillers, Hortense, 256